The New Witches

The New Witches
Critical Essays on 21st Century Television Portrayals

Edited by AARON K.H. HO

McFarland & Company, Inc., Publishers
Jefferson, North Carolina

This book has undergone peer review.

LIBRARY OF CONGRESS CATALOGUING-IN-PUBLICATION DATA

Names: Ho, Aaron K.H., editor.
Title: The new witches : critical essays on 21st century television portrayals / edited by Aaron K.H. Ho.
Description: Jefferson, North Carolina : McFarland & Company, Inc., Publishers, 2021 | Includes bibliographical references and index.
Identifiers: LCCN 2021019769 |
ISBN 9781476679150 (paperback acid free paper) ∞
ISBN 9781476642888 (ebook)
Subjects: LCSH: Witches on television. | Television programs—United States—History—21st century. | Television programs—Great Britain—History—21st century. | Feminism. | BISAC: PERFORMING ARTS / Television / Genres / Science Fiction, Fantasy & Horror
Classification: LCC PN1992.8.W58 N49 2021 | DDC 791.45/677—dc23
LC record available at https://lccn.loc.gov/2021019769

BRITISH LIBRARY CATALOGUING DATA ARE AVAILABLE

ISBN (print) 978-1-4766-7915-0
ISBN (ebook) 978-1-4766-4288-8

© 2021 Aaron K.H. Ho. All rights reserved

No part of this book may be reproduced or transmitted in any form or by any means, electronic or mechanical, including photocopying or recording, or by any information storage and retrieval system, without permission in writing from the publisher.

Front cover image © Shutterstock / Ironika

Printed in the United States of America

McFarland & Company, Inc., Publishers
Box 611, Jefferson, North Carolina 28640
www.mcfarlandpub.com

To Melissa He

Acknowledgments

Layla Milholen at McFarland has been wonderful to work with and I appreciate her guidance on this book greatly. I learned much from the contributors with their wide-ranging expertise. It has been a thrilling ride and I could ask for no better company.

Table of Contents

Acknowledgments   vi

Introduction—"That's how I like my witches": The New Witches on 21st-Century Television
    AARON K.H. HO   1

Intersectional Politics and History: Race, the #MeToo Movement and the Witch

"This is a reckoning": Intersectional Feminism and the #MeToo Movement in *Charmed*
    KATHERINE J. LEHMAN   10

From Witchcraft Activism to Witch Hunt Sentiments: The Changing Political Landscape in *American Horror Story*
    JOHANNA BRAUN   28

Re-Remembering the Past: Hauntological Feminist Memories of Salem in *Chilling Adventures of Sabrina*
    BRYDIE KOSMINA   41

Good Witch, Bad Witch: Identities and Ethics

Declawing the Jungle Cat: Caging Feminine Power on the CW's *The Secret Circle*
    CHARITY A. FOWLER   56

The Witches of the West and the Boundaries of Goodness
    LINDSEY MANTOAN   73

"When witches don't fight, we burn!" Monstrosity and Violence in *American Horror Story: Coven*
    EMILY BRICK   87

viii   Table of Contents

The Witchy Body: Sexualities and Disabilities

Condensing the Palate: Queer Representation and
Heteronormativity in *Charmed*
  SAMUEL NAIMI 100

Queerness and Historical Sadomasochism in *Salem*
  TANNER ALAN SEBASTIAN 111

Teenage Furies: The Rape-Revenge Genre in *American Horror Story: Coven*
  CHRISTINE R. PAYSON 126

Witches with Disabilities on 21st-Century Television Programs
  AARON K.H. HO 139

Disembodiment of the Witch: Ecofeminism, Digital Humanities and Beyond Blood

The Literal and the Metaphorical: Othered Voices in *Salem*
  FERNANDO GABRIEL PAGNONI BERNS 158

"The world never did help a smart girl": Disembodied Digitalization, the Open Access Library and BuzzFeed in *The Magicians*
  NATALIE R. SHEPPARD 172

Beyond Blood: The Negotiation of Biological and Chosen Families in *Chilling Adventures of Sabrina*
  ALISSA BURGER 187

Appendix: 21st-Century Television and Streaming Programs with Witches 203

About the Contributors 205

Index 207

Introduction

"That's how I like my witches": The New Witches on 21st-Century Television

Aaron K.H. Ho

SABRINA: I want freedom and power.
PRUDENCE: He will never give you that. The Dark Lord. The thought of you, of any of us, having both terrifies him.
SABRINA: Why is that?
PRUDENCE: He's a man, isn't he?
—1x2 "The Dark Baptism"

Rewatching *Chilling Adventures of Sabrina* (2018–2020) for the third time, I am still awestruck at the scene above, not because Sabrina and the Weird Sisters have banded together in solidarity to combine their powers to humiliate four entitled, misogynistic, transphobic jocks, magically trapping their manhood in birdcages; not because the artful scene blends a triumphant tone with humor, disquiet, and foreboding; not because the scene is empowering to viewers, especially women and minorities, who have been bullied before; not because the scene offers the satisfaction of revenge on the misbehaved boys; and not because they pass the Bechdel test of two powerful young women not talking about heterosexual romance but instead they are exchanging information and sharing knowledge. The scene's power comes from all those elements, but the most striking of all, to me, is the almost 16-year-old Sabrina's cocksure proclamation of desiring both power and freedom in the coming-of-age series. It is rare to see on the small screen a confident and ambitious woman, and rarer still to witness a *girl* with the same qualities. In this sense, Sabrina isn't the common fictional teenager. Most fictional teenagers—from Harry Potter to Spiderman—doubt their abilities, reject at some point their powers, and question and second-guess their actions; Sabrina revels in power. Even though Sabrina has a half witch, half human lineage, which may infer that her powers may be lesser than that of a full witch, she has little self-doubt. Although she can be rebellious and headstrong, she is mostly unwavering, unlike other fictional teenagers. She forges on despite obstacles and concocts elaborate plans to resolve sticky situations. Sabrina comes fully formed and possesses a strong sense of self-identity: assertive, loyal, ambitious, intelligent. At the beginning of and throughout the series, she announces her name when she meets a foe, implying that she knows who she is right from the start. In other words, the teenage girl behaves with the derring-do and prerogative of a heterosexual white male adult television character.

This 21st-century Sabrina deviates from the phenotype of the late 20th-century witch, or as Dorothy in a famous witch narrative puts it, "Toto, I've a feeling we're not in Kansas anymore." Compare Sabrina to famous witches on late 20th-century television: Buffy's sidekick, Willow (Alyson Hannigan), from *Buffy the Vampire Slayer* (1997–2003), begins as a shy, diffident 16-year-old girl. Although she eventually becomes so powerful that she turns out to be the sixth season's villain (around the time when her lesbian partner dies, wearing out the stereotypes of lesbians not able to have happy endings and of lesbians being evil), her character vacillates between good witch and bad witch, in contrast to Sabrina's complex characterization of refusing to be labeled. Sabrina's immediate televisual predecessor came from the feel-good sitcom *Sabrina the Teenage Witch* (1996–2003). Sabrina (Melissa Joan Hart) begins her 16th birthday by discovering that she is a witch and has to learn the ropes while juggling high school. When her aunts inform her about her witch heritage, she does not believe them until her father (a man!) tells her so. Unlike the Netflix version, this Sabrina is a good-natured, loveable, bumbling girl-next-door trying to find her identity, guided by her aunts; all three of them, blonde white heterosexual domestic women who are shown in their kitchen most times. The first spell Sabrina learns is to turn an orange into an apple, but she keeps fumbling the spell and turning oranges into pineapples. "At the very least, you will always be able to garnish a ham steak," her aunt jokes (1x1 "Pilot"). Then they use the pineapples to bake cakes. One of the first things Sabrina learns that magic cannot do is: "You also can't get rid of cellulite!" (1x1). In school, Sabrina and Libby fight over a boy they both like. The series implies that even as witches, Sabrina and her aunts cannot escape traditional values of femininity and domesticity. The three sister-witches of *Charmed* (1998–2006) follow a strict moral code, use their magic for good, are forbidden to use it to benefit themselves, and have to work together to banish demons. On the other hand, Netflix's Sabrina's source of power comes from evil, Satan, and she uses magic individually to benefit herself, her family, and her friends.

Netflix's *Sabrina* deviates from these popular late 20th-century television programs featuring white mostly heterosexual middle-class women who, despite their powerful witchcraft, demonstrate idiosyncrasies of traditional feminine traits that are appealing to heterosexual men: They are domestic, beautiful, shy, good-natured, and svelte. No matter how powerful they are, they are portrayed to be vulnerable and needed to be superintended by men, usually a patriarch figure: Hart's Sabrina by her father; Willow by Buffy's Watcher, Rupert Giles (Anthony Stewart Head), and eventually saved from her villainous ways by Xander (Nicholas Brendon), not Buffy (Sarah Michelle Gellar); the Charmed sisters by their whitelighter, Leo Wyatt (Brian Krause), who, naturally, marries one of them. In the vein of Joan Riviere's famous article, "Womanliness as Masquerade," in which she argues that successful women are deferential to men in order to downplay success, witches on late 20th-century programs behave as such. Seen in this perspective, the witches reify the concept of second-wave feminism which focuses on white heterosexual middle-class women's success as a collective. In contrast, Netflix's *Sabrina* could be said to represent third-wave feminism as the series casts actors of different ethnicities, ages, genders, and sexualities. This is not to say that *Sabrina* is the first ever television series to present a third-wave feminist perspective; Others have done so by incorporating diversity in their programs. The diversity is a concerted effort of a prevailing cultural change, which started in the 2010s with advocacy from different minority groups and the rise of international streaming services wooing a global crowd desiring representation onscreen. However, using witches on television as a focus could potentially demonstrate cultural change.

After the end of *Charmed* in 2006, witches appeared mostly on children's programs or as secondary characters in vampire or supernatural shows. It wasn't until 2013 and 2014 when *American Horror Story: Coven* and *Salem*, respectively, gained high viewership that witches began to pop up everywhere on television (although, personally, I like and would recommend readers watch *Eastwick* [2009], based on the John Updike novel). Perhaps the peak occurred in 2018 when seven new television series on witches, including the immensely popular *Sabrina*, the *Charmed* reboot, *American Horror Story: Apocalypse* (which saw the return of the witches from *Coven*), and the British program, *A Discovery of Witches*, were released; all seven series are renewed. In 2019, six more original series were aired. The renewed interest in witches in the late 2010s is the focus of this collection of essays.

This volume stands on its own although readers who desire to find out about the history of witches on television may consult Heather Greene's excellent *Bell, Book and Camera: A Critical History of Witches in American*

Film and Television (McFarland, 2018), which traces the history of witches in media from 1896 to 2016. While there is some overlap in this volume, our focus is mainly on programs in the latter half of 2010s. Furthermore, Greene's book offers breadth on the theme and our volume, depth; she surveys how technical and social issues affect the narratives of witches over time whereas our focus on late 2010s television allows us to delve into many different themes.

This volume does not presume that all late 2010s witch television programs are progressive or present third-wave feminism. For instance, *Good Witch* (2015–present), screened by the Hallmark channel, is a conservative though very appealing, addictive, attractive narrative about a good witch, Cassie Nightingale (Catherine Bell), in a small fictional town full of heterosexual white people. Although she runs a bed and breakfast for out-of-town travelers, her guests are also mostly heterosexual white people. When Cassie does receive a non-white guest, Daphne Randall (played by Carolyne Maraghi, of Egyptian descent), she turns out to be the major villain of the series and perhaps the entire run of the show, almost uprooting the source of Cassie's magical powers (3x1 "A Budding Romance"). In most episodes, Cassie wields her power to assist her partner, Dr. Sam Radford (James Denton), secretly at most times, like a good supportive helpmate, but, unlike Netflix's Sabrina, the modest Cassie does not acknowledge and desire any credit. Against the common misconception that televisual witches are transgressive, we employ a critical lens of assuming nothing during our analyses of the programs. As such, in this collection of essays, we point out the latent hegemony affected by current social norms in putative audacious programs despite their good intentions.

The first section of this collection, "Intersectional Politics and History: Race, the #MeToo Movement and the Witch," documents the rise of witches on television in the mid–2010s after the character of the witch is marginalized for just short of a decade. In the wake of the #MeToo movement, both Katherine J. Lehman and Johanna Braun connect the proliferation of programs on witches to the Magical Activism movement where more and more disenfranchised Americans turn to witchcraft to ameliorate the vagaries of their lives during Donald Trump's presidency. As *Newsweek* has reported, from 8,000 witches in the U.S. in 1990, there are now 1.5 million practicing witches, exceeding the number of Presbyterians by 100,000 (Fearnow 2018). With the increase of media representations on witches, Lehman and Braun also point out that the rebooted version of *Charmed* (2018–present) and *American Horror Story* (2011–present), respectively, propound a third-wave feminist viewpoint involving a diversity of sexualities and races, perhaps in reference to the disenfranchised Americans who joined the Magical Activism movement. This diversity, however, is treated differently in *Charmed* and *AHS*. Braun notes how *AHS: Coven* (2013) and *AHS: Apocalypse* (2018) reflect the changing cultural attitudes of the times for the #MeToo movement that started in 2006 but only gained traction in 2017. Lehman, on the other hand, observes that despite *Charmed*'s good intention to broaden representation of minorities onscreen, the series does not escape racial, gender, and queer stereotypes, undermining its own message of diversity and acceptance. While Lehman and Braun perceive the connection between current affairs and the series on witches, Brydie Kosmina's essay, in the same section, differs by arguing how Netflix's *Sabrina* revises collective memory of the historical trials of Salem, through Derrida's theory of hauntology, to tender its third-wave feminist perspective in light of the current sociopolitical situation. For Kosmina, she sees *Sabrina* partake in a conversation on the historical suffering of women and the series represents a fantasy for women's revenge. In essence, all three essays in the first section engage with actual events—past, current, and future—and provide an exordium before we zoom into specific topics.

The next section, "Good Witch, Bad Witch: Identities and Ethics," focuses on the representations of witches, and by extension, the representations of women. Charity A. Fowler's essay discusses the breakdown of good and evil: she compares *The Secret Circle* trilogy (1992) by novelist L.J. Smith, who also wrote *The Vampire Diaries* (1991), and its eponymous television adaptation (2011), and laments the simplification and reduction of identities into good and bad in the series from the complex, powerful female characters in the novels. Viewed in this light, the television program is a regression from the novels: postfeminism to second-wave. The ur-story of the American witch, *The Wonderful Wizard of Oz* by L. Frank Baum, sends a girl on the cusp of womanhood down a yellow brick road, having two women she can model after: the Wicked Witch of the West or Glinda the Good Witch, a mass murderer or a gentle, tiara-wearing, but unambitious and one-dimensional woman allowing the Wizard to rule over Oz despite her powers and the fact that the wizard is a charlatan. However, Lindsey Mantoan, through an examination of film and television productions, contends that contemporary adaptations of *The Wizard of Oz* have blurred the lines between good and evil, aligned with third-wave feminist principles. The implication of moral ambiguity mirrors personal and national identities as Mantoan investigates the patriarchal oppression of women in *Emerald City* (2017)—though one witch happens to be a female-to-male transgender person, not female—and female friendship in the children's animation series, *Lost in Oz* (2015–2018). Emily Brick, too, observes the collapse of good and evil in her essay on *American Horror Story: Coven*, claiming that the series reimagines the American society where women are in power and "femininity is the structuring norm." In this matriarchal society, Brick continues to argue, the Monstrous-Feminine, exemplified by the figure of the witch, becomes complicated when imbricated with violence, motherhood, and sadism.

The third and fourth sections of the collection revolve around issues of embodiment and disembodiment, respectively. The third section, "The Witchy Body: Sexualities and Disabilities," begins with Samuel Naimi's essay on *Charmed*, which uses Suzanna Walters' theory of assimilation to argue that the series erases queer identity and oppression by heteronormalizing the lesbian couple's relationship, much like queer voters' critique of Pete Buttigieg's brand of homosexuality. ("The Queer Opposition to Pete Buttigieg, Explained," by *New Yorker*'s Masha Gessen provides a nice complement, explaining how heteronormalizing queer relationships denies the legitimacy of queer oppression and suffering, demonstrating that the ideological hegemony in *Charmed* has roots in reality.) In the essay on *Salem* (2014–2017), Tanner Alan Sebastian writes about the female, often queer, body as a battleground for patriarchal control and how women can be seen to seize patriarchal power through performative acts of sadomasochism. Christine R. Payson's essay juxtaposes the rape-revenge trope in *Coven*, a fantasy of female empowerment, against other well-known productions and concludes that the series is a call for action to bring women together and fight against sexual violence. All four essays in this section are concerned with the body, but while the three aforementioned essays discuss sexualities of women, my essay surveys *Sabrina, Coven, Apocalypse,* and *The Magicians* (2015–2020) and argues that although these series are known for their bold transgressions in gender and sexual matters, they try but sometimes fail to do justice to representations of disabilities. Granted that male witches with disabilities are emasculated, female witches with disabilities become more empowered, allowing audiences to imagine that disabled lives offer a different kind of value to society.

In the fourth section, "Disembodiment of the Witch: Ecofeminism, Digital Humanities and Beyond Blood," Fernando Gabriel Pagnoni Berns intersects linguistics and ecofeminism to study *Salem* and proves convincingly that the series combines the power of nature and women to contest patriarchy. Like Pagnoni Berns, Natalie R. Sheppard's essay, ad rem to our digital age, engages with digital humanities in her reading of *The Magicians*, whereby female witches counter established organizations (coded as masculine spaces) by digitalizing, disseminating, and sharing knowledge through online spaces. Pagnoni Berns, Sheppard, and Alissa Burger, who rounds out the collection, all see beyond the body, as Burger notes the formation of families in *Sabrina*, sometimes bound by blood, others by choice, all somewhat queer, subverting the traditional family structure. This representation of families not only reflects the current state of the American family but is also indicative of the values and social fabric that hold the country together. Burger's essay, rooted in contemporary cultural imagination on familial units that constitute America, brings the collection full circle from where we begin in the first section with current affairs in the U.S.

When I was collecting essays for this volume, I deliberately left out the Red Witch in *Game of Thrones* (2011–2019) because, while the HBO series holds great cultural significance, essays on the Red Witch are ubiquitous. What I envision for this collection is a coven of diverse, original, sharp discourses on various themes on the trending phenomenon of witches on television, suited for laypersons, readers, witches, feminists, men, the disenfranchised, queers, undergraduates, researchers, and professors alike, in hopes that these essays could elucidate the world we live in. As Hermione Granger would say: "Lumos!"

References

Fearnow, Benjamin. 2018. "Number of Witches Rises Dramatically Across U.S. as Millennials Reject Christianity." *Newsweek,* Nov 18. Accessed on Feb 13, 2020. https://www.newsweek.com/witchcraft-wiccans-mysticism-astrology-witches-millennials-pagans-religion-1221019?fbclid=IwAR0qJQU1_gLxfmm1r5f3ydU8u5le76--P2-2fD-eNNR_vaAZwKOXRzuOJTI.

Gessen, Masha. 2020. "The Queer Opposition to Pete Buttigieg, Explained," *New Yorker,* Feb 12. Accessed Feb 13, 2020. https://www.newyorker.com/news/our-columnists/the-queer-opposition-to-pete-buttigieg-explained.

Greene, Heather. 2018. *Bell, Book and Camera: A Critical History of Witches in American Film and Television.* Jefferson, NC: McFarland.

Riviere, Joan. 1929. "Womanliness as Masquerade." *Journal of Psychoanalysis* 10: 303–13.

Intersectional Politics and History
Race, the #MeToo Movement and the Witch

"This is a reckoning"

Intersectional Feminism and the #MeToo Movement in Charmed

Katherine J. Lehman

In 2016, The CW announced plans to reboot its iconic series *Charmed* (1998–2006). Much like the original series, the reboot would center on three sisters who discover they are witches and combine their powers to fight nefarious demons. However, the "fierce, funny, and feminist" reboot would be set in the 1970s, and "really tie the women's liberation movement to witchcraft" (Kilkenny 2018). Those plans changed, however, with the election of President Donald Trump. According to a head writer, "All the issues that we were talking about in the '70s seemed so relevant and so timely, we just felt like we had to talk about it now" (Kilkenny 2018). The new *Charmed* (2018–present) takes place in a contemporary university town, with an ethnically diverse group of witches at the forefront of #MeToo activism. As executive producer Jennie Snyder Urman explained, the widespread movement against sexual assault and harassment "felt like a bubbling up of something that had been needing to come up for a long time, like an earthquake. It was impossible not to include that in a story about three powerful women" (Kilkenny 2018).

The series has faced a fair amount of backlash from fans and creators of the original series. On Twitter, Holly Marie Combs claimed that she and her co-stars were the sole owners of *Charmed* and mocked the idea that the original series wasn't feminist (Jones 2018). Viewers have seized upon the series' shortcomings—uneven acting, rushed pacing—as evidence that it is a poor imitation of the long-running original. In contrast, I argue that the new series is a worthy endeavor for its exploration of racial and sexual diversity and its direct engagement with feminist politics. While the crop-topped witches in the original *Charmed* did tackle key issues such as work-life balance, theirs was a fashionable "lifestyle feminism" that prioritized individual achievement over collective change (Sanders 2007). Placing a trio of black and Latina women at the forefront of the new *Charmed* not only broadens the terrain of representation but encourages viewers to rethink the cultural basis of witchcraft and magic itself. Despite its progressive politics, however, *Charmed*'s reboot relies on media tropes that reinforce racial stereotypes, erase queer lives, and undermine protagonists' power.

Magical Activism

Charmed was already associated with the #MeToo movement prior to the reboot's release, given the public activism of original stars Alyssa Milano and Rose McGowan. McGowan's crusade against the predatory Harvey Weinstein has been documented in her memoir and the reality series *Citizen Rose* (2018). Milano, an outspoken women's rights advocate, is often credited with reinvigorating the #MeToo movement on Twitter in late 2017. She was a visible spectator at the nomination hearings of Supreme Court justice Brett Kavanaugh, which centered on the sexual assault allegations brought against him. In a meme circulated afterward, a bespectacled Milano fixes her gaze on Kavanaugh as if to curse him. "I've never wished so hard that Alyssa Milano was a real witch," the caption reads (Millard 2018).

Charmed's reboot also coincides with the rise of feminist organizations connecting magical practice and political activism. In Brooklyn, a metaphysical bookstore twice hosted public rituals to hex "rapists" including Kavanaugh and "the patriarchy which emboldens, rewards and protects them" (Lang 2018). The event organizer told *Time* that witchcraft has "always been practiced by the most downtrodden and the most harmed and the most at risk, disenfranchised people in society because they have no other form of recourse" (Lang 2018). Meanwhile, the 1960s-era radical feminist group W.I.T.C.H. was revived in Portland, and by 2017 had spread to 50 covens in the United States and Europe. In Boston, W.I.T.C.H. activists donned pointed black hats for protests, used tarot cards as political leaflets, and performed ritual binding spells on Trump. As one member explained, "The witch is a powerful figure when so many people feel like they're losing control" (Birnbaum 2017). Through rituals and theatrical protests, witchcraft becomes a means to express resistance and tap into a powerful legacy.

Charmed's reboot also coincides with a broader revolution in media, as television has taken on feminist visions of women's solidarity and activism. For example, in Freeform's *The Bold Type* (2017–present), an affable trio of young women explore feminism and sexual identity in their work for a glossy women's magazine. The vigilantes of AMC's *Dietland* (2018) and NBC's *Good Girls* (2018–present) use their wits and weapons to take down sexual predators. Comedy Central's idiosyncratic *Broad City* (2014–2019) mixes humor with pathos in its 2017 Halloween episode "Witches," in which the youthful duo reclaims their sexual power and joins a coven of quirky older women to resist Trump. On Netflix's *Chilling Adventures of Sabrina* (2018–2020), a "woke" teenage witch forms an intersectional feminist club called WICCA at her high school. This mixture of magic and feminism is familiar terrain: Scholar Susan Douglas notes that the witch has long been a means for television to capitalize on feminist movements, as 1960s sitcoms such as *Bewitched* (1964–1972) debuted when women read Betty Friedan and "girls took to the streets in an outpouring of female resistance against the status quo" (1994: 138).

The new *Charmed*, then, draws inspiration from television trends and the cultural climate in its address of contemporary gender politics. Rather than occupying a Victorian manor in San Francisco, sisters Mel (Melonie Diaz), Maggie (Sarah Jeffery), and Macy (Madeleine Mantock) live in the fictional university town of Hilltowne, Michigan. Their mother, Marisol (Valerie Cruz), was a women's studies professor and activist prior to her death, and the budding witches occupy the academy in student, teacher, and researcher roles. In addition to catering to a college-aged audience, *Charmed*'s new setting makes academic feminist insights accessible to a broader audience and recognizes the role of the university in shaping anti-rape activism. Significantly, it also frames the women as intelligent, especially as early plotlines show Macy's attempts to reconcile the world of magic with her scientific knowledge.

Jeffery claims that *Charmed* is timely as a source of representation for viewers "receptive to being on the right side of history" (Andreeva 2018). Accordingly, the series makes frequent references to real-life politics, even calling out Trump by name. In the pilot, whitelighter Harry (Rupert Evans) claims the election of Trump, "when the weakest of men reaches ill-gotten glory," signals the start of the apocalypse (1x1 "Pilot"). In a later episode, Mel compares Trump's obsessive Tweets to demonic activity. While comical, such dialogue resonates with audiences who feel alarmed or affronted by Trump's presidency and bemoan his acceptance by many Christian conservatives.

The series opens with a voiceover intoning, "This isn't a witch hunt; this is a reckoning," a warning to men who dismiss their accusers' accounts of misconduct (1x1). The phrase "witch hunt" has been used by celebrities Woody Allen and Liam Neeson, among others, to describe the #MeToo movement (Kumari 2018). In late 2018, Trump excessively used the term on

Twitter and in public appearances to characterize the Mueller investigation into Russian interference—a figure of speech that some practicing witches saw as insensitive (Kwong 2018; Chinoy, Ma, and Thompson 2018).

In the pilot, elder witch Marisol is propelled through an attic window to her death by an unseen force. Her daughters initially assume her death is connected to her political activity, namely spearheading a sexual harassment investigation at the university. As in many real-life cases, the charges don't stick—the elder white male professor in question, "a world-famous geneticist," dismisses the accusations as a baseless "witch hunt" (1x1; 1x4 "Exorcise Your Demons"). He brags that he has been cleared of all charges, even as he makes leering and inappropriate remarks to the women around him. He ultimately reveals himself to be an immortal demon who must be vanquished by the newly empowered *Charmed* sisters. The episode addresses #MeToo at multiple points: Mel, walking through a student lounge where couples are making out, loudly reminds the women that "when it comes to consent, you can change your mind at any time" (1x1). Evoking consent helps Maggie evade the deadly kiss of a demon who growls, "You already said yes," in the middle of an interaction. At the end, when the sisters relegate the professor demon to a corpse who then vanishes into thin air, a frightened male witness gasps, "What was that?" The sisters consider wiping his memory, per custom, but decide to let him live with the knowledge. "No one will believe another hysterical man," they reason. They link arms and triumphantly leave campus as an anti-harassment protest wages in the background (1x1).

In subsequent episodes, an evil entity inhabits the body of Asian American student Angela Wu, one of the vanquished professor's victims, rendering her a fearsome blood-sucking beast. The possessed Angela's first act is to behead a campus radio-show host while he is in the middle of a rant about radical feminism. (We later learn that the demon is only drawn to virgin blood, which indicates the host is part of the "incel" movement of men who blame their poor sexual fortunes on feminist gains.) Although the elders write off Angela as a lost cause who must be destroyed, the sisters refuse to give up on her. She is healed not only through the witches' willingness to use themselves as bait, but also Maggie's empathetic powers that enable her to connect with the vulnerable woman inside the beast. The episode emphasizes the need to listen to women and stand in solidarity with them. In a flashback, their mother Marisol encourages Angela to come forward with her accounts of the professor's harassment. "I will be here to support you," Marisol tells her. "You're not alone." In the present, Maggie uses her empathetic power to encourage Angela to fight back against the evil being that has taken over her body. "Tell yourself a different story, Angela," Maggie pleads. "You're strong enough" (1x4).

In a later episode, Mel and her new love interest Jada, an African American witch who is part of the underground coven Sarcana, meet in a bar to stop a serial rapist. "He's like your typical entitled predator," says Jada. "The sexual assault charges got dismissed because the judge didn't want to ruin his 'promising future.'" Jada and Mel watch as the young white man drops a "roofie" pill into his Asian American date's drink, then swoop in to defend the woman. Mel uses her signature power to freeze the people in place. Jada walks over and takes the man's head in her hands and, with a bemused look, whispers, "Justice now. Consequences now. It is so" (1x11 "Witch Perfect"). When Mel unfreezes time, the man finds the wine glass stuck to his hand, making it obvious he is trying to drug his date. His fellow bargoers react in disgust and call the police. Although played up for comedy, this intervention reflects many viewers' genuine interest in interrupting assault and bringing attackers to justice. In this scenario, the predator's nefarious deed literally sticks to him. Jada's reference to lenient judges evokes cases like Brock Turner's—or for that matter Brett Kavanaugh's—in which a man's bright future supersedes a woman's pain (Wootson 2017). It is significant that *Charmed* centers the experiences of everyday women of color in these #MeToo scenarios, as scholars have called for the movement to broaden its focus beyond "white, affluent, and educated women with access to a significant social media following and offline clout," whose experiences tend to be more easily believed and validated (Kagal, Cowan, and Jawad 2019: 134). That *Charmed*'s harassers and assailants tend to be white men also highlights racialized power dynamics in the workplace and romantic relationships.

Charmed addresses broader aspects of feminism and female representation as well. One episode combines Greek mythology with a #MeToo premise: Medusa is awakened when fraternity members share explicit photos of female students without their consent, and she stalks the Hilltowne campus turning male students to stone. While Medusa most often surfaces in mainstream popular culture as a "sexually ravenous" monster, Elizabeth Johnston argues that many feminist authors have re-envisioned her as a "powerful symbol of feminist rage" and a means to interrogate rape culture (2018: 184, 201). *Charmed* draws from this interpretation as Macy empathizes with Medusa, the witch-turned-demon who in the original myth was "raped, slut-shamed, and turned into a monster." While others turn away from Medusa and call for her beheading, Macy faces her with compassion. "You were cursed to cover up the crime of a powerful man, so that no one would ever see your pain. But I see it," Macy tells her. "Know that you are not to blame. … We will do everything in our power to right these wrongs" (1x15 "Switches and Stones"). Having truly been seen, Medusa recedes and her magic is reversed. This episode reminds us that sexual violence was present in the earliest mythologies, and posits the monstrous female as a response to longstanding injustice (Johnston 2017). At the end of the episode, Maggie takes concrete action, risking her sorority bid to report the guilty fraternity members.

Medusa is far from the only archetype that *Charmed* explores. Another episode engages contemporary media criticism by introducing a pixie who drives men to their death with her relentlessly perky agenda. The sisters discover that her heart has been stolen, rendering her a "literal Manic Pixie Dream Girl" who exists only to please others. The man behind the plan is a film student who is using the pixie to kill off his competition because he worries his chances of making it big in Hollywood are slim as a white male (the sisters roll their eyes at this claim). Mel magically compels him to confess his crime to the police and encourages the pixie to guard her heart. "We use something called the Power of Three to make us stronger," the sisters tell her. "Maybe you and the other pixies could team up and organize" (1x13 "Manic Pixie Nightmare"). The sisters rectify a power dynamic in which an aggrieved white male uses a less powerful female to do his bidding. Furthermore, the episode emphasizes the need for multifaceted roles for women, and for women to organize for self-preservation—a message reminiscent of the Time's Up movement that advocates for gender equality in Hollywood.

In the following episode, Macy accidentally brings a televisual duo of male witches from the 1990s to life and enters their fictional realm. The episode challenges the damsel-in-distress trope—as Macy rewrites the series' ending to save herself—and encourages more respectful behavior from the men, one of whom sports a leather jacket to match his macho persona. While she recognizes "woke wasn't a thing yet in the '90s," Macy tells them: "This whole misogynistic, brooding, bad boy thing is canceled" (1x14 "Touched by a Demon"). The 1990s reference could be a dig at the original *Charmed*, or at least a reflection on how the politics of representation have changed. In many recent action and science fiction narratives, women are the heroes who rescue themselves and others. However, recent pieces in *Variety* and *The New Yorker* acknowledge the persistence of a "bad boy" archetype that promotes toxic masculinity and encourages women to settle for subpar treatment (Botticello 2018; Ringwald 2018). These trends have influenced *Charmed*'s writers' room: While Maggie's relationship with her half-demon boyfriend Parker parallels Phoebe's relationship with Cole in the earlier series, the creators reportedly discussed how to avoid glamorizing a "bad boy" character (Swift 2018). Rather than relishing his dark side, Parker seems haunted by it, and his mild-mannered persona leaves some viewers to dismiss him as bland (Kirby 2018). As they grant complexity to pixies and rebels alike, *Charmed*'s creators break from established patterns of representation and promote equality in both romantic and workplace relationships.

However, *Charmed*'s first season is inconsistent in its treatment of sexual assault and trauma, which may undermine the overall feminist message. A *Gizmodo* critic complains strongly about the episode "Bug a Boo" (1x8), in which demonic insects use a dating app to abduct and impregnate victims. "At the end of each date … the bugs forcibly penetrate their victims through their mouths and paralyze them," she writes. "You see this happen, and it's incredibly disgusting. It looks, feels, and reads like sexual assault" (Elderkin 2018). She complains that the episode treats the "date rape" theme lightly through humorous dialogue and by erasing victims' memories, "effectively silencing their sexual trauma" (Elderkin 2018). While other viewers commenting online took the episode less seriously, perceiving the demonic insects as comical "Monsters of the Week," they nonetheless saw the insects' penetration of women's mouths as a sexual metaphor (Elderkin 2018; Primetimer 2018). Similarly, in the episode "Kappa Spirit" (1x6), sorority sister Lucy is goaded by a demon into attempting suicide. The spell is reversed and her memory of the incident is erased, but she is never offered psychological support for the underlying pain that has made her an easy target in the first place (Elderkin 2018). The episode glosses over the Kappas' implied history of suicides, "barely taking the time to address how these deaths would have affected the girls" (Panda 2018).

Strength in Differences

Marisol's advice to her daughters—"You're better together, your differences are your strengths, and nothing is stronger than your sisterhood"—evokes the power of female collectivity and the importance of diversity among feminists (1x1). *Charmed*'s diverse cast is a welcome change from the 1990s series and fits with the CW's "Open to All" marketing campaign, which was launched in the same season. "We are committed to making sure our viewers see themselves represented on screen, and that we also have diverse voices being heard behind the camera," network president Mark Pedowitz explained. "We want to be known as a place where all are welcome to be, and all are welcome to watch" (Turchiano 2018). He noted that 12 of the 17 CW series airing in 2018 were helmed by women and/or people of color. *Charmed*'s pilot also displays the hashtag of the #SeeHer initiative, an advertising industry effort to increase accurate and diverse portrayals of women in media (Nickolai 2018).

Building on her success with the Latino/a ensemble series *Jane the Virgin* (2014–2019), showrunner Jennie Snyder Urman has opted to cast women of color as the three leads and openly address racial issues. The original *Charmed*, in contrast, features a white family in the midst of multicultural San Francisco. When people of color did appear they were most often villains or sidekicks, such as police officer Darryl. The reboot's diverse cast not only adds to representation on television but has the potential to transform the ways in which viewers think about magic. Mantock herself spoke about the rarity of a series featuring three women of color. "I'm used to [auditioning] for things and hearing, in the end, 'They didn't want to go diverse,'" she told the *New York Times*. "That happened to me three times in the last year. Now I get to be the hero, and I get to do it with two other women who are sensitive to what's going on in the world" (Angelo 2018).

Charmed's treatment of race both defies and plays into common stereotypes. On the surface, the three sisters' professional roles are a welcome change from more common representations of Latinas as service workers or sexualized beings. Scholars and media advocates have long documented a "Latino Media Gap," in which the rapid growth of the Latino/a population far outpaces the representations of Latinos/as in media (Almeida 2016). Dana Mastro and Alexander Sink's historical analyses of popular television find that Latino/a representation has been "abysmally low" and that Latina characters are perpetually marked by their sexual allure, quick tempers, and strong accents (2017: 145–146). Furthermore, programs featuring Latino/a characters often lack specificity about their ethnic backgrounds and tend to favor light-skinned protagonists (Cepeda and Casillas 2016: 6). These omissions and stereotypes can reinforce prejudiced perceptions among non–Latinos, and erode the self-esteem of Latino/a youth (Mastro and Sink 2017). Scholars have also emphasized the importance of increasing Latino/a representation in acting and media production. For example, a 2019 USC Annenberg study on film representation urged Hollywood to provide avenues for lesser-known Latino/a actors to gain experience and visibility rather than over-relying on stars like Jennifer Lopez and Cameron Diaz (Smith, et al. 2019: 9–10).

Media critics have similarly lamented the lack of Latino/a representation both onscreen and in the industry. *Remezcla* reported in early 2018, "It is clear that TV shows about the wide variety of the Latino experience are more the exception than the rule. And when it comes to representation of Afro-Latinos, indigenous, or LGBTQ Latinx on TV, you'd have to look long and hard to find even a couple appearances. For the most part, Latino actors are still relegated to bit parts with few chances to break out" (Betancourt 2018a). In the Gay and Lesbian Alliance Against Defamation's (GLAAD's) analysis of 2018 primetime scripted broadcast programs, only 8 percent of series regulars were Latino/a. The CW led broadcast networks with 12 percent of its series regulars counted as Latino/a, largely due to *Jane the Virgin* and its *Charmed* reboot (GLAAD Media Institute 2018).

Given these statistics, some viewers resent *Charmed*'s decision to cast non–Latina actresses in Latina roles (Bastién 2018; Sanchez 2018). Only Melonie Diaz identifies as Latina. Of the other actresses, "Jeffrey identifies as African American and has noted that her mother is indigenous Canadian. Mantock is half Afro-Caribbean and half white" (Bastién 2018). A *Vulture* critic argues that "this gets into a thorny issue of both colorism and Hollywood's treatment of minorities as if we are interchangeable" (Bastién 2018). A podcaster contends that Latina and Afro-Latina women should have been cast, calling *Charmed*'s media tour "a blatant attempt to make money from the Latinx experience without employing us" (Sánchez 2018).

Nevertheless, the characters are cognizant of racial difference. Macy is the outsider, given up for adoption as a child and only now reunited with her biological sisters. She makes the strongest claim to black heritage and, in an early episode, chides Maggie for asking to touch her curly hair (1x8). When it is revealed in episode three that she is still a virgin in her late twenties, Macy explains how being one of only two women of color in a Connecticut boarding school has shaped her sexuality for life. "You had to solidify what type of minority you were, before they decided for you," she explains. "My friend Tasha became the sexy, funny one and I was always the smart, serious one. I've played that part for so long, I don't know how to be anything else" (1x3 "Sweet Tooth"). By downplaying her sexuality, Macy evades the hypersexualized Jezebel stereotype that has served to denigrate black women and justify their sexual subjugation (Rosenthal and Lobel 2016). The series' creators said they intended the plotline to dispel cultural shame around virginity, describing Macy as sexually empowered and aware of her own desires (Lenker 2019). However, as a woman who dresses conservatively and subtly loses her virginity midseason, Macy's character is less threatening than a sexually forthright black woman would be. Macy expands black female representation in her role as a brilliant scientist, but *Charmed*'s decision to make her a virgin and deemphasize her sexual desire reinforces the smart/sexy binary she faced in boarding school.

When Maggie discovers through genetic testing that she and Macy share the same black father, she begins to question what it means to have African American ancestry. Her plotline explores the meanings of race as both lived experience and cultural legacy: Maggie decides against applying for a race-based scholarship, given her advantages as a light-skinned woman who is newly aware of her black heritage. However, she intends to explore her cultural identity in tandem with the university's Black Student Union (1x18 "The Replacement"). The series signals Latino/a culture in subtler ways, such as Mel's prominent display of a Puerto Rican flag in her bedroom, occasional use of Spanish in rituals, and the family's tradition of serving *coquito* at Christmas. Mel does remind a friend that the family is Puerto Rican when asked if they can help with a Cinco de Mayo celebration. While some viewers may see the flag and Spanish-dialogue as window dressing and wish *Charmed* would go "full throttle" in its Latina representation, others have applauded the inclusion. A Puerto Rican critic told The CW on Twitter: "I'm going to be 39 in two weeks. I don't think I've ever seen my flag in a TV show before. And she's a #queer #boricua at that! Thank you. Thank you" (Betancourt 2018b). While subtle, *Charmed*'s emphasis on Puerto Rican heritage counters television's historic tendency to homogenize Latino/a experiences and downplay specific ethnic origins (Cepeda and Casillas 2016: 6).

However, *Charmed* does fall into a racialized notion of good and evil, saddling its most black-identified sister with a dark side and suggesting that she and other women are easily corrupted by power. Macy eventually learns of her "dark" origins, namely that she was stillborn and resurrected with demon blood, which has led to her estrangement from the family. Throughout the first season, she both battles her demon side and relies upon it for insight. Pricking her forehead with an acupuncture needle gives her knowledge about her mother's murder and other evil happenings, but gradually the darkness takes root in her body. Her eyes become pitch black, her emotions volatile, as she growls at and repeatedly attacks her sister Mel. She temporarily finds her balance with a yin-yang necklace and realizes that magic itself is neither good nor evil—it depends on who is wielding the power. In the series finale, however, Macy becomes the vessel for The Source of all magic. Her eyes glow orange and catlike and her aggression increases to deadly levels until she decides to relinquish her newly obtained power. While this plotline sends mixed messages about female power in general, it also plays into stereotypes of black female aggression. As a desexualized scientist, Macy's character evades the mammy and jezebel stereotypes that have long defined black representation in media. Yet in her demonic state she resembles the Sapphire, an "aggressive, dominating, angry, emasculating" stereotype of black women (Rosenthal and Lobel 2016). Historically, domineering black women have been blamed for issues such as poverty and single motherhood, as they supposedly deny black men their rightful place in the family. Macy herself is self-sufficient and unmarried, and as embodiment of The Source, she reverses a heroic decision by her boyfriend Galvin, committing a selfish act with disastrous consequences.

When *Charmed* was first promoted, Latina critics were dismayed to see the centrality of the Celtic *triquetra* symbol in a story about three Latina witches (Sánchez 2018) and complained that the dramatic special effects "don't look like the homegrown, intimate magic of Black, Indigenous, and

Caribbean spiritualities" (Villarreal 2018). Yet over the course of the season, the showrunners broadened the story to incorporate ethnically specific traditions. "Every culture has their own witchcraft traditions, and we really wanted to explore not just from a Salem witchcraft [perspective] but all kinds of different witchcraft that happens all around the world," executive producer Amy Rardin explains (Brockington 2018). *Charmed*'s syncretistic approach to magic mirrors the "cross-cultural borrowing" practiced by some feminist spirituality practitioners. Cynthia Eller notes that as white women incorporate other cultural influences into their spiritual practice, they risk misinterpreting these traditions and alienating women of color (1998: 235).

Charmed's creators make attempts at authenticity. In the fourth episode, the witches free Angela Wu from demonic possession by reading a Spanish spell authored by their mother, which Harry claims is based in Santería, an Afro-Cuban religion practiced in Latin America. The spell is apparently written by Mexican American writer Marcos Luevanos, whom the producers have described as "a real Latinx witch." As an editor for *The Mary Sue* complains, "that doesn't mean that he has been taught Santería, and it also matters when you consider that this is an Afro-Cuban/Afro-Latinx faith with no Afro-Latinx actors portraying the characters" (Princess Weekes 2018). Viewers responded positively to the spell, even though the actresses speak in "not-so-perfect Spanish" (Betancourt 2018b).

In other episodes, Macy seeks the advice of Vodou elder Mama Roz to understand why her African American love interest, Galvin (Ser'Darius Blain), seems to be repelled by her; her diagnosis of Macy's innate "darkness" leads her to discover her demonic origins. Galvin normalizes magical practice by explaining how the African variant of Vodou is part of his childhood: "When I was growing up, my grandma was always talking about her religion," he recalls. "Yoruba this, Yoruba that. Witches and demons. And she even said that she did a special spell on me when I was a baby to protect me from evil" (1x10 "Keep Calm and Harry On"). Galvin later treks to Africa to find magical artifacts to cure Macy's demon side. He is possessed while traipsing through the jungle and returns home, where he swiftly kills Mama Roz in a fit of rage. This is yet another moment in which *Charmed* characterizes a powerful black person as dangerous and animalistic.

In addition to addressing diverse magical traditions, *Charmed* also addresses racial tensions within feminism. Mel is initially a graduate student writing a thesis on intersectional feminism before she makes an abrupt decision to leave academia. Yet she puts theory into practice when she infiltrates the Sisters of Arcana, or Sarcana, a countercultural coven comprised of young women of color. Mel is warned that the Sarcana are seductive "terrorists" who may be responsible for her mother's death. Yet she becomes sympathetic to their cause as she starts a brief relationship with Jada (Aleyse Shannon), a black woman whose braids, body modifications, and gothic attire signal difference. Jada, for her part, characterizes the Elders—older witches—as heartless. "They have always been cold and out of touch. And in power for far too long. But all that's gonna change," Jada predicts (1x10). The fact that Mel is torn between the officially sanctioned magic of her elders and the girl gang Sarcana could be emblematic of generational and racial divides within feminism. For example, some third-wave feminists have touted their racial and sexual diversity as a means to distinguish themselves from second-wave feminists. In these debates, second-wave feminists are characterized as stodgy, primarily white, and fixated on gender concerns rather than supporting broader visions of equality (Grady 2018).

Although we eventually learn that an Elder is actually responsible for Marisol's death, the Sarcana make dangerous decisions as well. Ultimately both groups of witches are killed by demons, leaving the *Charmed* sisters in charge of the future of magic—and by association, the future of feminism. This twist reveals a bias in favor of youthful visions and new solutions rather than intergenerational wisdom. As in the earlier *Charmed* and other supernatural dramas of the 1990s and early 2000s, the rise of young witches depends upon the symbolic and literal death of their foremothers (Karlyn 2011, Sanders 2007).

Charmed also represents strides for lesbian representation. In 2018, The CW led the five broadcast networks in LGBTQ representation among series regulars, according to GLAAD (2018). Accordingly, Mel is an out lesbian in a committed relationship with her Asian American girlfriend Niko (Ellen Tamaki); their partnership is presented as a natural part of life, as they are shown in bed at the beginning of the pilot episode. "We want to really normalize gay and lesbian relationships," Diaz explains. "This is just her partner, and that's it" ("Charmed Stars" 2018). Accordingly, Mel is spared the "coming out" plotline that has historically defined LGBTQ stories in media. Although she discovers her powers to freeze time as she is sitting across from Niko, she conceals her growing abilities from her girlfriend, a burden that she describes as painful. "[Our mom] knew I was gay before I even figured it out. And she made sure I was always proud of who I was. So I've never had to hide who I am from the people I love. And now, here I am, in the closet," she complains to her sisters (1x3).

As a police officer, Niko is charged with investigating supernatural activities, a role that places her in grave danger. Thus, in the fifth episode (1x5 "Other Women"), Mel agrees to magically erase their entire two-year relationship to preserve Niko's safety. (The spell also erases Mel's teaching assistant position, which prompts her to drop out of graduate school.) Although Mel retains the memory of her romance, her grief over her vanishing girlfriend is muted and short-lived compared to her sisters' relationship drama. Viewers also complain that the erasure plotline has come too early in the series to carry sufficient emotional weight. As an outspoken lesbian-feminist Latina who helms the series, Mel's character is a powerful role model for young viewers. However, *Charmed*'s tendency to curtail her relationships and place her love interests in mortal danger plays into a broader televisual tendency to undermine queer characters.

LGBTQ characters and relationships often meet violent or tragic ends in media, a relic from the time when same-sex relationships were more censored in popular culture and condemned in everyday life. As late as the 2015–2016 season, critics decried television's tendency to kill off lesbian and bisexual characters once they have expressed their sexual attraction. Among other series, fans protested The CW series *The 100* (2014–2020), in which a budding lesbian relationship is cut short by gun violence. The doomed lesbian is a "tired but persistent figure who haunts lesbians and other women with the message that their lives and stories are expendable" (Millward, Dodd, and Fubara-Manuel, 2017: 10). Although Niko does escape the literal death that faced earlier CW heroines, she initially vanishes from *Charmed* as a regular character.

Niko does reappear in Mel's life six episodes later, as a private investigator trailing Jada's Sarcana activities (1x11). The flame between Mel and Niko is briefly reignited; they share a kiss and Mel gives her a magical protective ring. In this new arrangement, Mel feels free to disclose her powers to Niko. Their romantic connection is presented as a love that transcends time and supernatural disruption; however, Niko's health fails when she learns of her altered past. The women's relationship ends abruptly in the season finale, as Mel sadly waves goodbye to Niko from across a courtyard. Although Mel's straight sisters also suffer romantic losses in the season finale, they visibly display more grief and their breakups are not voluntary.

Emotion, Agency and Power

The *Charmed* reboot has been described as a celebration of female power, anger, and resistance. As Diaz describes her character: "They wanted Mel to be angry about [the current political situation] and frustrated. … This idea that I get to play somebody who feels the weight of that and embracing her anger is really cool. Because there's a lot to be angry about right now" (Betancourt 2018b). In real life, activists seeking to combine magic and politics find anger to be a valuable tool. In the Brooklyn hexes of Kavanaugh, participants performed a ritual of "righteous rage," using the anger to defend themselves and seek justice (Fink 2018).

However, the series sends mixed messages about female power and repeatedly undermines its protagonists' autonomy. In the pilot, the witches have their new powers explained to them by Harry, a British white male who ties them up, pokes fun at their character flaws, and chides them for interrupting his speech. Although he later becomes a much more sympathetic character and is a women's studies professor to boot, the initial power dynamic has led some viewers to compare *Charmed* to *Charlie's Angels* (1976–1981). Viewers note that although the original *Charmed* has a male whitelighter, he does not serve in an advisory role until the 14th episode, allowing the witches to discover their powers on their own terms ("So What's" 2018).

Like the original series, the sisters consider magic their birthright; however, they voluntarily choose to assume the role of witch, giving them greater agency. ["It's a fully pro-choice enterprise," Harry quips (1x1)]. Macy, in particular, seems to be motivated less by the common good than by advancing her science career and reconnecting with her sisters. The three sisters' powers closely resemble their predecessors', as the series grants Mel the ability to freeze time and Macy the ability to move objects with her mind. Maggie has the more passive power of empathy, in contrast to her predecessor Phoebe's powers of premonition. The women's powers expand and increase over the course of the season; for example, Maggie focuses her emotional power with a wooden pole that enables her to pierce a hole in an otherwise unstoppable demon.

Douglas writes that earlier television series featuring witches contain women's power through rules that dictate how and where they could use magic (1994). Similarly, the original *Charmed* places constraints on the women using magic for "personal gain." If a witch uses her abilities to enhance her beauty or avenge a wrong, she typically would face severe consequences. Although Harry warns Maggie about using magic for personal gain when she magically decorates for a sorority party, the concept is less dominant in the reboot. However, their magical powers do require moderation of female emotion. Early on, fiery Mel learns that anger blocks her power to freeze time, and she must assume a calm demeanor to perform magic. Maggie laughs and tells her, "Your powers are judging you" (1x1). In the finale, Macy realizes that taking on The Source enhances her rage and insecurity, and voluntarily gives up great power to return to her calm, gentle self. *Charmed* rightfully validates traditionally feminine characteristics such as empathy and collaboration. However, the idea that anger and self-assertion are counterproductive qualities ignores more contemporary feminist reclamations of female anger as the source of political change (Traister 2018). The sisters' struggles with anger also play into televisual stereotypes of Latinas as "hot-tempered" (Mastro and Sink 2017: 146).

Repeatedly the sisters learn that women in authority cannot be trusted, as they are betrayed by the Elder Charity, who has caused their mother's death and lied to them, and her sister Fiona, a newly freed witch whose personal mission is to end all magic. A sorority sister of Maggie's unwittingly cooperates with the demon trying to destroy them, and Harry is briefly replaced with a female whitelighter, a brisk young woman of color whom the *Charmed* ones dub a "mean girl" before she sacrifices herself to protect them (1x18). These plot twists suggest that women are as fallible and capable of evil as men, and are perhaps inevitable in a series with a majority female cast. However, *Charmed* essentially positions the sisters as the only "good" surviving witches and makes Harry the sole authority to be trusted, undermining the intended message of female solidarity and sisterhood.

In the dramatic end of the first season, demons slay all the female Elders, triggering the apocalypse. Blood rains from the sky and townspeople fall prey to a violent illness that the best doctors can't cure. While the witches—in combination with one last sacrificial act by Galvin—save the world from certain destruction, their heroic powers remain hidden from the public. Their relationships do not survive the first season, as Galvin dies, Parker leaves town, and Mel bids farewell to Niko. Such resolutions suggest that healthy relationships cannot co-exist with female power. While a happy ending for all three women may have seemed forced, their fate backs up Mel's suspicion that "love is just something we have to sacrifice" for witchcraft (1x5).

The *Charmed* ones will now govern without the guidance of Elders—aside from occasional appearances by their deceased mother Marisol—granting them greater control than they have at the beginning of the series. Yet, the series' decision to kill off all the Elders limits opportunities for intergenerational dialogue and portraying older women as powerful beings. As in the original *Charmed*, older women are relegated to the margins. In the end, Macy gives up the world-altering spell of The Source, declaring "no one should ever have that much power" (1x22 "The Source Awakens"). Instead, she seems content to rule politely with her sisters over magical beings such as pixies and satyrs. In a nod to the original series, she walks into the sisters' house, then turns to close the front door telekinetically, containing herself and her powers safely in the feminine space of the home. While *Charmed*'s first season makes imaginative leaps in tying witchcraft to intersectional feminism, it may take more time for the sisters to tap into their full power.

References

Almeida, Walyce. 2016. "Latinos Left Behind by Media Mergers, Finds Study Led by Frances Negrón-Muntaner." *Columbia News*, Jun 7. https://news.columbia.edu/news/latinos-left-behind-media-mergers-finds-study-led-frances-negron-muntaner.
Andreeva, Nellie. 2018. "'Charmed' Star Sarah Jeffery Hits Back at Reboot Critics, Touts Its 'Positive Effect.'" *Deadline*, May 27. https://deadline.com/2018/05/charmed-star-sarah-jeffery-hits-back-reboot-critics-touts-positive-effect-rosponse-holly-marie-combs-1202398676/.
Angelo, Megan. 2018. "The Witches of 'Charmed' Are Out to Slay Demons. and the Patriarchy." *The New York Times*, Oct 7. https://www.nytimes.com/2018/10/05/arts/television/charmed-reboot-jennie-snyder-urman-witches.html.
Bastién, Angelica Jade. 2018. "Charmed Reboot Review: A Hollow Celebration of Sisterhood." *Vulture*, Oct 12. https://www.vulture.com/2018/10/charmed-the-cw-reboot-review.html.
Betancourt, Manuel. 2018a. "Is Latino Representation on TV Actually Getting Better?" *Remezcla*, Jan 5. https://remezcla.com/features/film/latino-representation-television-2017/.
_____. 2018b. "This Week's 'Charmed' Featured a Santería-Based Spell & Twitter Is (Mostly) Loving It." *Remezcla*, Nov 5. https://remezcla.com/features/film/cw-charmed-reboot-nycc-panel-santeria/.
Birnbaum, Molly. 2017. "W.I.T.C.H. Women's Movement—Behind the Pointy Hats." *Topic Magazine*, Oct 2017. https://www.topic.com/witches-brew.
Botticello, Mike. 2018. "John Leguizamo on Hollywood's Future: No More 'Bad Boys Club Behavior.'" *Variety*, Sept 16. https://variety.com/2018/scene/news/john-leguizamo-hollywoods-future-no-more-bad-boys-club-behavior-emmys-metoo-times-up-1202943649/.
Brockington, Ariana. 2018. "'Charmed' Team on Exploring Brujeria, Current Issues Without Lecturing." *Variety*, Sept 9. https://variety.com/2018/tv/news/charmed-brujeria-ability-to-read-minds-leading-with-issues-1202933972/.
Cepeda, Maria Elena, and Dolores Inés Casillas. 2016. *The Routledge Companion to Latina/o Media*. New York: Routledge Press.
"'Charmed' Stars Talk Reboot Backlash." 2018. n.d. *Variety*. Accessed May 24, 2019. https://variety.com/video/charmed-reboot-stars-backlash-comic-con/.
Chinoy, Sahil, Jessia Ma, and Stuart A. Thompson. 2018. "Trump's Growing Obsession with the 'Witch Hunt.'" *The New York Times*, Aug 22. https://www.nytimes.com/interactive/2018/08/22/opinion/trump-cohen-mueller-investigation.html, https://www.nytimes.com/interactive/2018/08/22/opinion/trump-cohen-mueller-investigation.html.
Douglas, Susan J. 1994. *Where the Girls Are: Growing Up Female with the Mass Media*. New York: Three Rivers Press.
Elderkin, Beth. 2018. "*Charmed* 'Bug a Boo' Recap: Doesn't Acknowledge Sexual Assault." *Gizmodo*, Dec 3. https://io9.gizmodo.com/the-latest-charmed-depicted-sexual-assault-and-failed-t-1830821195.
Eller, Cynthia. 1998. "Affinities and Appropriations in Women's Spirituality." In *Spellbound: Women and Witchcraft in America*, edited by Elizabeth Reis, 221–46. New York: Rowman & Littlefield.
Fink, Jenny. 2018. "'A Tool for Resistance and Resilience': Witches Hosting Hex on Kavanaugh, Rapists, Patriarchy." *Newsweek*, Oct 12. https://www.newsweek.com/witches-hosting-hex-brett-kavanaugh-rapists-patriarchy-new-york-ritual-1167843.
Gay and Lesbian Alliance Against Defamation Media Institute. 2018. "Where We Are on TV Report." *GLAAD.org*, 2018. https://www.glaad.org/whereweareontv18.
Grady, Constance. 2018. "The Waves of Feminism, and Why People Keep Fighting Over Them, Explained." *Vox*, Jul 20. https://www.vox.com/2018/3/20/16955588/feminism-waves-explained-first-second-third-fourth.
Johnston, Elizabeth. 2017. "'Let Them Know That Men Did This': Medusa, Rape, and Female Rivalry in Contemporary Film and Women's Writing." In *Bad Girls and Transgressive Women in Popular Television, Fiction, and Film*, edited by Julie A. Chappell and Mallory Young, 183–208. Cham, Switzerland: Palgrave Macmillan.

Jones, Marcus. 2018. "'Charmed' Star Holly Marie Combs Dragged the Show's Reboot and Fans Are Here for It." *BuzzFeed News*, Jan 16. https://www.buzzfeednews.com/article/marcusjones/charmed-star-holly-marie-combs-dragged-the-shows-reboot-and.

Kagal, Neha, Leah Cowan, and Huda Jawad. 2019. "Beyond the Bright Lights: Are Minoritized Women Outside the Spotlight Able to Say #MeToo?" In *#MeToo and the Politics of Social Change*, edited by Bianca Fileborn and Rachel Loney-Howes, 133–49. Cham, Switzerland: Palgrave Macmillan.

Karlyn, Kathleen Rowe. 2011. *Unruly Girls, Unrepentant Mothers: Redefining Feminism on Screen*. Austin: University of Texas Press.

Kilkenny, Katie. 2018. "'Charmed' Creators Explain 'Wish Fulfillment' of Show in Trump Era." *The Hollywood Reporter*, Oct 14. https://www.hollywoodreporter.com/live-feed/charmed-creators-explain-wish-fulfillment-show-trump-era-1152152.

Kirby, Meaghan. 2018. "*Charmed* Recap: A Shocking End Twist Reveals a Traitor Close to the Charmed Ones." *Entertainment Weekly*, Nov 26. https://ew.com/recap/charmed-season-1-episode-7/.

Kumari, Kayla. 2018. "*Charmed* Reboot Vanquishes Bad Men in Its Sharp, Campy Pilot." *The A.V. Club*, Oct 14. https://tv.avclub.com/charmed-reboot-vanquishes-bad-men-in-its-sharp-campy-p-1829742891.

Kwong, Jessica. 2018. "Donald Trump Has Witches 'Mad' and 'Rolling Their Eyes' at His 'Witch Hunt' Mueller Investigation Tweets: Report." *Newsweek*, Dec 17. https://www.newsweek.com/donald-trump-witches-mad-witch-hunt-1262253.

Lang, Cindy. 2018. "Brooklyn Witches Host Hex Brett Kavanaugh Ahead of Midterms." *Time*, Nov 2. http://time.com/5442528/brett-kavanaugh-hex/.

Lenker, Maureen Lee. 2019. "'Charmed' Creators Open Up About Macy's Virginity, Erasing Shame Through Pop Culture Representation." *EW.Com*, Mar 3. https://ew.com/tv/2019/03/03/charmed-creators-talk-macy-virginity-representation/.

Mastro, Dana, and Alexander Sink. 2017. "Portrayals of Latinos in the Media and the Effects of Exposure on Latino and Non-Latino Audiences." *Race and Gender in Electronic Media: Content, Context, Culture*, Edited by Rebecca Ann Lind, 144–160. New York: Routledge Press.

Millard, Anna. 2018. "The Internet Thinks Alyssa Milano Is Casting a Spell on Brett Kavanaugh." *Refinery 29*, Sept 29. https://www.refinery29.com/en-us/2018/09/212682/alyssa-milano-witch-kavanaugh-hearing-viral-photo.

Millward, Liz, Dodd, Janice G., and Fubara-Manuel, Irene. 2017. *Killing Off the Lesbians: A Symbolic Annihilation in Film and Television*. Jefferson, N.C.: McFarland.

Nickolai, Nate. 2018. "The CW and #SeeHer Announce New Partnership." *Variety*, Oct 11. https://variety.com/2018/tv/news/the-cw-seeher-partner-launch-event-seeher-award-1202976149/.

Panda. 2018. "Charmed: Kappa Spirit." *Doux Reviews*, November. https://www.douxreviews.com/2018/11/charmed-kappa-spirit.html.

Princess Weekes. 2018. "*Charmed* Finally Breaks Away from Its Euro-Centric Magical Roots." *The Mary Sue* (blog), Nov 5. https://www.themarysue.com/charmed-euro-centric-magical-roots/.

Ringwald, Molly. 2018. "What About 'The Breakfast Club'?" *The New Yorker*, Apr 6. https://www.newyorker.com/culture/personal-history/what-about-the-breakfast-club-molly-ringwald-metoo-john-hughes-pretty-in-pink.

Rosenthal, Lisa, and Marci Lobel. 2016. "Stereotypes of Black American Women Related to Sexuality and Motherhood." *Psychology of Women Quarterly* 40 (3): 414–27. https://doi.org/10.1177/0361684315627459.

"S01.E08: Bug a Boo." 2018. Charmed (2018), Primetimer, Nov. 24. https://forums.primetimer.com/topic/87917-s01e08-bug-a-boo/.

Sánchez, Kate. 2018. "Not So Charming: 'Charmed' Reboot Isn't What It Seems." *But Why Tho?*, Oct 9. https://butwhythopodcast.com/2018/10/09/not-so-charming-charmed-reboot-isnt-what-it-seems/.

Sanders, Hannah E. 2007. "Living a Charmed Life: The Magic of Postfeminist Sisterhood." In *Interrogating Postfeminism: Gender and the Politics of Popular Culture*, edited by Yvonne Tasker and Diane Negra, 73–99. Durham, N.C.: Duke University Press.

Smith, Stacy L., Marc Choueiti, Ariana Case, Katherine Pieper, Hannah Clark, Karla Hernandez, and Jacqueline Martinez. 2019. *Latinos in Film: Erasure on Screen & Behind the Camera Across 1,200 Popular Movies.* Los Angeles: USC Annenberg Inclusion Initiative. http://assets.uscannenberg.org/docs/aii-study-latinos-in-film-2019.pdf.
"So What's the Verdict on *Charmed*?" 2019. *Reddit*, Feb 3. https://www.reddit.com/r/CharmedCW/comments/amkhb0/so_whats_the_verdict_on_charmed/.
Swift, Andy. 2018. "*Charmed* Recap: Season 1 Episode 9 Ending Explained—Harry's Fate." *TV Line*, Dec 10. https://tvline.com/2018/12/10/charmed-recap-season-1-episode-9-ending-explained-harry-dead-alive/.
Traister, Rebecca. 2018. *Good and Mad: The Revolutionary Power of Women's Anger.* New York: Simon & Schuster.
Turchiano, Danielle. 2018. "The CW Launches #CWOpenToAll Campaign to Promote Inclusion." *MSN*, Oct 14. https://www.msn.com/en-us/tv/news/the-cw-launches-cwopentoall-campaign-to-promote-inclusion-watch/ar-BBOo8lv.
Villareal, Vanessa Angélica. 2018. "The Commodification of Witchcraft Spells Trouble." *Bitch Media*, Nov 23. https://www.bitchmedia.org/article/commodification-witchcraft-sephora.
Wootson, Cleve R., Jr. 2017. "The Judge in the Infamous Brock Turner Case Finally Explains His Decision—a Year Later." *Washington Post*, Jul 2. https://www.washingtonpost.com/news/grade-point/wp/2017/07/02/the-judge-in-the-infamous-brock-turner-case-finally-explains-his-decision-a-year-later/?noredirect=on&utm_term=.950a5934e3ab.

From Witchcraft Activism to Witch Hunt Sentiments
The Changing Political Landscape in American Horror Story[1]

Johanna Braun

The Witch is back. Anyone who has been following public discourse in the past couple of years in the United States can witness an increased interest in all kinds of witchcraft and magic, notably the "trending" of one buzzword, "witch" and, to a greater extent, the term "witch hunt" on social media. As a result of or in correlation with this trend, the figure of the witch is celebrating a colorful revival in a wide range of cultural productions. Pop-stars perform as witches, or make explicit references to witchcraft, as did Katy Perry at the 2014 Grammy awards, Azealia Banks on social media (Quinn 2016), and Beyoncé in her visual album "Lemonade" (2016). Artistic practices have not been left untouched by this phenomenon either, as witchcraft and magic have been increasingly mobilized in contemporary (performance) art and activism (Scott 2016; Yates Garcia 2016). Several books were recently published that focus on this intersection of magical resistance, or witchcraft activism in the United States (Hughes 2018; Salisbury 2019). The liberal feminist website "Broadly" regularly publishes articles such as "How the Socialist #Feminists of WITCH Use Magic to Fight Capitalism" and, in June 2017, even *Vogue* celebrated "Witchy Week" to mark the summer solstice. This increased public interest in witchcraft has also led to a colorful comeback of the figure of the witch on the big screen, with highly popular movies such as *Maleficent* (2014), *Into the Woods* (2014), *The Witch* (2016), *The Love Witch* (2016), the recent re-telling of *Blair Witch* (2016), and *Suspiria* (2018), to name a few, and this phenomenon is also manifested on stage with the Broadway musical *Wicked* (2003–present), which continuously tours internationally and is based on the two witch characters from *The Wizard of Oz* (1939).

This recent revival and celebration of the witch can be regarded partly as a continuation of "witchcraft activism" groups, such as W.I.T.C.H., a feminist protest group that was founded on Halloween in 1968 by members of the New York Radical Women group (and was resurrected by the protest group Chicago Coven in 2015). Discussions surrounding the witch as a feminist icon of the 1970s in the United States are already covered by Silvia Bovenschen in her text "The Contemporary Witch, the Historical Witch and the Witch Myth: The Witch, Subject of Appropriation of Nature and Object of the Domination of Nature" (1978). Bovenschen explores the growing interest in the witch as a figure of protest within and in the reception of feminist movements in the 1970s. Most of the aforementioned recent productions represent the witch in the vein of Bovenschen and W.I.T.C.H. as an empowered and empowering figure that questions, challenges and threatens power structures, re-inscribing the witch into a history of repression as well as empowerment. However, within that framework, this representation of the witch undergoes production and distribution within the capitalist mechanism that continues to promote a whitewashed history of the figure (Federici 2004). Therefore, building on Silvia Federici's *Witches, Witch-Hunting, and Women* (2018), this essay looks at how the recent attention paid to interpersonal and institutional violence against white women, women of color, and queer women has occurred alongside an expansion of capitalist social relations.

American Horror Story references, in obvious ways, many of the abovementioned discussions on gender and sexuality and race in the current political climate via its portrayal of witches. In this investigation, I will take a closer look at season three, *American Horror Story: Coven* (2013–2014, from here on referred to as *Coven*) and season eight, *American Horror Story: Apocalypse* (2018, from here on referred to as *Apocalypse*), where witches are the main focus of the narratives, to trace how the discussions and the themes of the series have significantly shifted from *Coven*—which was produced and distributed at the beginning of this new wave of interest in witchcraft and magic as a form of empowerment—to *Apocalypse*, which was produced and aired after the inauguration of Trump, and can be situated in a post–#MeToo context, where men in powerful positions frame themselves as wrongful victims of a so-called "witch hunt" by countless accusers of sexual abuse. Therefore, *American Horror Story* can be seen as an interesting illustration of how the debates surrounding the figure of the witch have transformed in recent years.

A Short Introduction to the American Horror Story *Universe*

To give a brief insight into the multilayered universe of *American Horror Story:* this is an American anthology horror television series, created by Ryan Murphy and Brad Falchuk, and each season is conceived as a self-contained miniseries. The primary focus of this series is revealed by its title straight away: it features countless cultural and historical references that are especially significant to the United States, and each season focuses on a different iconic trope of American (horror) history. This essay is interested in the third season, *Coven*, which features Miss Robichaux's Academy for Exceptional Young Ladies, a boarding school for young witches in present day New Orleans, which, at the time of airing, was 2014; and the eighth season, *Apocalypse* (2018), set in a bunker in a remote location in a post-apocalyptic landscape in the United States.

Iconic locations are used as backdrops and American historical figures make their appearances, with pointed references to current public political debates. *American Horror Story* introduces iconic historical characters (inspired by historical and fictional sources) to an American audience, such as the boy-next-door killer in reference to the mass shooter from the Columbine shootings (*Murder House*); Nellie Bly; Ed Gein; Lizzie Borden (*Asylum*); Marie Laveau; "The Axeman of New Orleans" (*Coven*); and the most notorious serial killers in American history, H.H. Holmes, Aileen Wuornos, John Wayne Gacy, Jeffrey Dahmer, the "Zodiac Killer," and the "Night Stalker" Richard Ramirez (*Hotel*). *Coven*, for instance, incorporates several flashbacks, including the infamous Salem Witch Trials of 1692 and the horrendous murders by the serial killer Delphine LaLaurie in the 1830s. These characters are introduced to storylines that deal with time-specific issues, such as mental health reform (*Asylum*), reality TV and fake news (*Roanoke*), racism and systematic segregation in New Orleans (*Coven*), the growing influence of corporate America on political and cultural developments, online trolling, election sabotage, or the rise of alt-right anti-feminist movements (*Coven, Cult, Apocalypse*).

As we can see in this brief summary, which includes only some of the many references to current and historical instances, the creators and writers of *American Horror Story* are very much aware of the prevailing currency of historical material for a contemporary audience and the historical threads that can be projected onto current instances, thus forming continual public discussions throughout American history. In performing this projection, *American Horror Story* follows the premise of Silvia Federici's argument that current debates do not arise out of an ahistorical vacuum but are firmly embedded in their historical framework. Therefore, this essay is informed by scholarship that connects television to its cultural and historical context.

Literature on American Horror Story *and Activism*

Three volumes were published that are dedicated to the series and investigate different angles on how the series engages in current theoretical and public debates: Rebecca Janicker's edited volume *Reading* American Horror Story: *Essays on the Television Franchise* (2017), which includes two chapters on *Coven*; Richard Greene and Rachel Robison-Greene's edited American Horror Story *and Philosophy: Life Is but a Nightmare* (2018); and Harriet E.H. Earle's edited volume *Gender, Sexuality and Queerness in* American Horror Story (2019) which neither dedicates an essay to *Coven* nor *Apocalypse,* and both seasons only get mentioned in passing in two of the volume's contributions. Conny Lippert's essay "Nightmares Made in America: *Coven* and the Real American Horror Story" in *Reading* American Horror Story asks what being American is in *Coven* and how the show negotiates questions of race and oppression, while firmly embedding *Coven* in the American gothic genre. In "The Season of the Witch: Gender Trouble in *American Horror Story: Coven*" (2017), Elisabete Lopes draws a link between *Coven* and a female gothic tradition. In doing this, both authors set *American Horror Story* in a gothic television tradition. Kyle Ethridge's essay "The Minotaur, the Shears and the Melon Baller: Queerness and Self-Mortification in *Coven*" in *Reading* American Horror Story, analyzes a group of *Coven*'s protagonists using critical tools from queer theory and the emergent field of monster theory to explore themes of desire and violence throughout this particular season. Ethridge observes that *Coven* introduces new and more "mature" characters into the witch trope while facilitating a more complex discussion of the witch's political and social dimensions (101). As *American Horror Story* works through historical figures and cases that were instrumental in shaping the current representation of witchcraft in American pop culture, this essay is informed by scholarship that has investigated the cultural and political dynamics that lead to and have shaped the public discourse of historical significant instances of witch trials in the United States—the Salem witch trials in particular and witchcraft discussions in colonial New England in general (e.g., Rosenthal 1993, McMillan 1994, Breslaw 1996, Reis 1997, Adams 2008, Games 2010, Le Beau 2010, Reed 2015), and also beyond (e.g., Johnston/Aloi 2007, Davies 2013 and Davies 2017).

With this in mind I want to take a closer look into *Coven* and *Apocalypse* and how they use the figure of the witch, drawing on historical sources (and blurring fictional and historical accounts) to comment on present political and social discussions in the United States surrounding the emergence of the #MeToo movement.

Coven *and the Reawakening of Witchcraft Activism*

Coven's plot centers on a coven of witches, living in a classic Garden District colonial mansion in New Orleans, who are direct descendants of the survivors of the witch trials in Salem, Massachusetts, in 1692. The narrative's main focus is Fiona Goode's (Jessica Lange) return to the Academy as she, the current Supreme (the coven's leader) struggles with her recent decrease in power, portending that the New Supreme is already on her way to replace her. Her daughter Cordelia (Sarah Paulson), the current headmistress of the Academy, the Academy's new students, and Fiona's nemesis Voodoo Queen, Marie Laveau (played by Angela Bassett and based on the historical figure of the same name) deal with this shift in power relations within the Coven itself and New Orleans at large. These power struggles reveal a string of intergenerational, racial, and class conflicts among the groups of women that point to the historical inflictions and their prevalence into the present time of these debates.

The ongoing exclusion and marginalization of black witchcraft practitioners (led by Marie) by the white coven (led by Fiona) point to the continuing exclusion of the histories and perspectives of women of color in feminist movements. This exclusion is apparent in the #MeToo movement, when actress Alyssa Milano, who launched the hashtag in relation to the Harvey Weinstein case and to encourage victims of sexual abuse to share their stories on social media, neglected to name Tarana Burke, the originator of the hashtag. Burke, a social activist and community organizer, has been promoting the #MeToo movement since 2006 in order to raise awareness of sexual abuse and provide a platform to women of color to share their personal stories of harassment. Although *Coven* does not refer to Burke-Milano directly, the ongoing exclusion of women of color, and the shared histories of American women independent of their ethnicity and race, are highlighted in the series.

The racial tension in *Coven* is played out between Fiona and Marie. In a flashback it is revealed that, in the 1970s, a former Supreme and Marie divided their territory in New Orleans in a truce and the lines have been firmly set since then. This prevailing segregation is illustrated in the headquarters of the respective covens: While the Academy is situated in a grand historic colonial mansion in the prosperous Garden district of New Orleans, Marie runs a simple hair salon in a predominately black neighborhood in the ninth ward, one of the districts worst hit by Hurricane Katrina. In *Coven*, this systematic and historically defined, racially and colonially motivated segregation is traced back to the Salem Witch Trials in the 1690s in New England, when, in the aftermath of the trials, white witches fled south, claiming territory that was already occupied by black witchcraft practitioners.

This centuries-long conflict is tied to the historical figure of Tituba, a slave who allegedly practiced witchcraft in Salem.[2] In *Coven*, Tituba is portrayed as the source who brought witchcraft to America. At one point, Marie reminds Fiona about the origin of "white witchcraft": "Everything you got, you got from us," and that Tituba was taught by the Shamans of a Native American tribe, a circumstance that therefore connects her practiced witchcraft to an older local tradition that predates the colonial witchcraft of the white witches of New England (3x2 "Boy Parts"). In vehemently denying this legacy, Fiona reveals her ignorance and anti-black sentiments. Nevertheless, Fiona continually frames her disregard as classist, not racist. This conflict is also picked up by the Academy's student Queenie (Gabourey Sidibe), a young black fat-positive woman, who is torn between the coven of only white women—except her—and the BIPOC-centered coven of Marie. Marie reminds Queenie that she belongs to them, instead of the white colonial witches who "stole witchcraft from the slaves" (3x4 "Fearful Pranks Ensue"). Later, Fiona makes the racist immortal Madame Delphine LaLaurie (played by Kathy Bates and based on the eponymous historical figure, who tortured, mutilated, and murdered slaves in her New Orleans mansion in the 1830s) the slave of Queenie. The two women start to cultivate an unlikely friendship. Nevertheless, it is problematic that Queenie bears the burden of educating Delphine and that this unlikely bond cannot prevail over Delphine's overwhelmingly racist and ignorant worldview (3x7 "The Dead"). This circumstance is also a pivotal point of discussion during the emergence of the #MeToo movement, when BIPOC women had to educate and inform their white peers about the differences in experiences of sexual abuse and violence perpetrated on women of color and about the lack of public acknowledgment of racial exclusion in debates.

It is also problematic to note that, although Marie and Queenie are pivotal characters in the series, especially in connection to the racial tensions, both actresses are only credited as supporting characters, despite the fact that they appear in more episodes than most of the lead characters, including Kathy Bates. Through this production decision made through the many complex dynamics and ideologies of the players involved, it becomes notable that even in a TV show that centers on the ongoing exclusion and separation of BIPOC women, a highly separatist view regarding whose appearance and labor are more visible and valued is still promoted and distributed.

Only in realizing that they have a shared interest in survival can Fiona and Marie finally join forces to defeat the witch-hunters who have been persecuting both groups for centuries (3x10 "The Magical Delights of Stevie Nicks"). In acknowledging that they have indeed a shared history of oppression by white men in power, the women work together in fighting this system of oppression. This unity of white women and BIPOC women shares commonality with a conflict that takes center stage in the #MeToo movement, when white women are forced to face the fact that they also have turned a "blind" eye to the struggles of women of color and that, if continuing mechanisms of exclusion and inequity are to be challenged, white women need to acknowledge this discrepancy so that American women can unite and mobilize. The ability of both coven leaders to unite their communities against the systematic oppression and violence of the white supremacists of The Delphi Trust of witch hunters demonstrates how their shared interests trump the historical violence that made their cooperation difficult in the first place.

The Delphi Trust (of which Cordelia's husband is a member) is a secret society of witch hunters before the time of Salem (3x9 "Head"). The Delphi Trust, which is also known as The Cooperative, is masked as a transnational asset management company that plays on the staples of corporate America. The president of the Trust is an evil CEO who trains his son to be a witch hunter during a father-son hunting trip in the woods. A white supremacist conspiracy, involving the Trust, operates transnationally and over centuries. The first episode of *Coven* also features an event at a fraternity house that is associated with The Delphi Trust: a group of young men drug and gang-rape Madison Montgomery (Emma Roberts), a student of the Academy, during a fraternity party, and video tape the ordeal with a smart phone (3x1 "Bitchcraft"). The contemporary fraternity house, as a site of violence, echoes several recent #MeToo discussions on sexual abuse at American universities. *Coven*, with the settings of The Trust and fraternity house, then situates the #MeToo movement in a white male supremacist culture, and women, by banding together and recognizing their differences, are empowered to resist this toxic masculinity.

Coven's final episode ends with Cordelia's rise to power as the new Supreme. She gives a television interview in which she reveals the existence of witches to the world, calling for young witches to recognize their power and to unite. With Queenie and Zoe next to Cordelia, this new Academy represents a more inclusive feminism that departs from the previous "whitewashed" feminist movements, welcoming a new generation of witches to the boarding school. The episode concludes with Cordelia's speech to the press:

> We are not a cult. We don't proselytize, we have no agenda, we're not recruiting. Women who identify as witches are born as such, and their abilities—which we call powers—are part of who they are, part of their DNA, if you will. [...] There are so many young witches who have resisted their calling because they're afraid of how they may be perceived, or what's expected of them. [...] When you hide in the shadows, you are less visible, you have less protection. We'll always be targets for the ignorant [3x13 "The Seven Wonders"].

The speech concludes with an address to potential new students: "There is a home and a family waiting for you." While this episode was produced and aired before the #MeToo movement broke out in the fall of 2016, we can still find interesting parallels in the use of (social) media to unite the interest of women in the United States to speak out against systematic oppression. Being reminded again of Federici's argument, this illustrates that neither the #MeToo movement nor such recent cultural productions as *Coven* arise out of an ahistorical vacuum, but are firmly embedded in their historical framework. *Coven* comments pointedly on the debates of its time: white supremacy within feminist discourses, the rise of alt-right anti-feminist movements, and the continual historical racial tension in the United States.

The Permeable Line Between Witches and Witch Hunters: Apocalypse *and Trump*

Set in 2020, *Apocalypse* follows the events leading up to the end of the world and takes place in the underground shelter "Outpost 3" operated by "The Cooperative." The shelter is located somewhere in the United States after a nuclear holocaust wipes out most of the population, except for people who are able to afford to buy their way into the shelter and those who are selected for their genes.

Continuing where *Coven* left off, *Apocalypse* introduces a group of warlocks, who see themselves as disenfranchised and oppressed by witches. The warlocks place their hopes on the new rising "Alpha," Michael Langdon (Cody Fern), who is the Antichrist and will ultimately supplant the Supreme in their hierarchy. For the first time in history, a man will lead the warlocks and witches to "take their rightful place" at the top of magical powers and put "an end to ages of female dominance" (8x4 "Could It Be … Satan?"). The coven is then confronted with the possibility that a man could take over as the next Supreme, a role exclusively held by women for generations. Here, *American Horror Story* paints an apocalyptic picture of how a world in which men view themselves as disenfranchised by women will surely bring about its own end, and echoes in evident ways the current sentiments of especially young white men in a post–#MeToo era.

In contrast to the previous mostly optimistic outcome of *Coven*, *Apocalypse* follows the current post–#MeToo climate, in which powerful mostly heterosexual white men in American politics and society inflict great devastation upon women and society. These men, by repeatedly proclaiming that the sexual harassment cases were a "witch hunt," generated a renewed cultural and political resonance for the figure of the witch and used it productively to proclaim allegedly unjust prosecution. In response to the "Magical Resistance" movement, which includes collective activities such as casting the #bindtrump spell in an effort of self-defense, Donald Trump has used the term "witch hunt" to play the victim, and to portray his opposition as vicious witch hunters, as in the Salem Trials. According to the *New York Times*, Trump used the term "witch hunt" more than 110 times on Twitter, in the period between May 2017 and 2018 (Chinoy, Ma, and Thompson 2018). In 2018, he also used the term "rigged witch hunt" 84 times between January to August 2018 alone (Paschal 2018). As of March 2019, according to the Factba.se database, Trump used the term over 261 times during his presidency (Milbank 2019). In turn, the *New York Times*, for example, printed the term "witch hunt" more than 336 times in 2018 alone, which more than triples the rate of its use prior to 2016 (Beecher Field 2018). Yet the same time, Trump and his allies still use "witch" to vilify women; his targets include Hillary Clinton, Nancy Pelosi, Elizabeth Warren, and Dianne Feinstein. During the 2016 presidential election campaign, Hillary Clinton was repeatedly defined as a witch by Trump supporters: Clinton was "the wicked witch of the Left," pictured with "classic" Wizard-of-Oz features such as green skin, pointy hat, and broomstick, and her opponents even claimed she smelled of sulfur, aligning her, therefore, with stereotypical representations of witches (Sollée 2017). As we can see, the use of the term, "witch," is versatile enough for Trump to use it on himself when he wants to play the victim and also to use it on women when he wants to vilify them.

Trump is not the only powerful white heterosexual male to be involved with the term, "witch." On October 20, 2018, at a bookstore called Catland that describes itself as "Brooklyn's premiere #occult bookshop & spiritual community space" in New York, witches held an event to "hex" the then Supreme Court Justice nominee, Brett Kavanaugh, who faced several accusations of sexual assaults during his Senate confirmation hearings. Kavanaugh uses the same tactics as Trump. While many online and real witchcraft rituals were cast on Kavanaugh, his supporters framed him as a witch. The email blast from the Republican National Committee included the phrase "STOP THE WITCH HUNT AGAINST JUDGE KAVANAUGH." Senator Lindsay Graham mocked a Kavanaugh protestor by suggesting, "Why don't we dunk him in the water and see if he floats?" (Beecher Field 2018) and headlines like "Journalism Hits New Lows in Kavanaugh Witch Hunt" (Hunter 2018) reveal the prevailing sentiment of a witch hunt during the hearings.

Further, the #MeToo and #TimesUp movements are often described as ruthless and unfounded witch hunt allegations. Woody Allen, commenting on the Harvey Weinstein case and the emerging #MeToo movement, in a climate where allegations against Allen himself regularly find their way into public debates, proclaims: "You do not want it to lead to a witch hunt atmosphere, a Salem atmosphere, where every guy in an office who winks at a woman is suddenly having to call a lawyer to defend himself. That's not right either" (Abramson 2017). As we are able to see before, these discussions are evidently echoed in *Apocalypse*—such as the representation of powerful men who paint themselves as disenfranchised and oppressed victims of marginalized groups of people (e.g., women and people of color)—and depart significantly from the main themes in *Coven*.

Eventually, Mallory (Billie Lourd) is revealed to be the New Supreme and to have the power of time-warping to defeat Michael and save the world. She then travels back in time to kill Michael Langdon in 2015, and thereby erasing most of the storyline of Outpost 3. Right after, Mallory's voice-over wonders: "The devil isn't just going to give up. And in changing the past, a part of me will always wonder what it truly means for the future," and it is then revealed that the coming of the Antichrist is still not prevented (8x10 "Apocalypse Then"). In a flash-forward scene, which is set in 2020, the young couple Emily (Ash Santos) and Timothy (Kyle Allen), who are "selected for their exceptional DNA" to participate in the survival program at Outpost 3 and seem out of place in the early episodes prior to being killed shortly at the mass murder, return and meet in this alternative timeline during a protest march. It turns out that the couple is the Devil's plan B in case anything goes wrong with Michael, and they are destined to conceive the new Antichrist. Fast forward: In 2021, Timothy and Emily are about to welcome a baby boy named Devan and, come 2024, they leave the three-year-old boy alone with a babysitter whom they then find brutally murdered in the child's bedroom. The dates colliding with the upcoming presidential elections of 2020 and 2024 portend the continuously looming potential of "repeating" the past and the coming of an apocalyptic future in the wake of the #MeToo movement and the vehement backlash that has followed since.

The Rise, Defeat and Rise of a New (Post-)Apocalyptic Order

The two seasons of *American Horror Story* coincide with several explicit uses of the term witch and witch hunt in recent public discussions during or in the wake of the #MeToo movement. At a time when women's rights are under attack, the figure of the witch is being used as a queer-feminist symbol of power, both rhetorically and in actual practices of witchcraft rituals. The aim of this essay is to bring the complex and often scattered dots of *American Horror Story*'s universe together in understanding how it comments on and incorporates pressing public discussions of its time. Witchcraft, in this vein, is often understood as a means of fighting against social, economic, and environmental injustices and allying with the marginalized and oppressed, as outlined in the many "witchcraft activism" endeavors at the beginning of this essay, a strategy that is clearly echoed in *Coven* and *Apocalypse*. As illustrated in this essay, *Coven* is informed by the growing public interest in the witch as an empowered and empowering figure, while also pointing to the historical and ongoing economic and systemic oppression of women and people of color. In the wake of the #MeToo movement, *Apocalypse* in turn mocks powerful white heterosexual men who go to the extreme of creating an apocalypse in order to maintain the status quo when their positions of power are threatened.

Notes

1. This essay was written as part of Johanna Braun's postdoctoral research project "The Hysteric as Conceptual Operator," funded by the Austrian Science Fund (FWF): [J 4164-G24].

2. For more on Tituba, especially on the issue of race, please refer to Rosenthal 1993, Breslaw 1996, Cakirtas 2013.

References

Abramson, Alana. 2017. "Woody Allen: You Don't Want a Hollywood 'Witch Hunt' in Wake of Harvey Weinstein Scandal." *Time*, Oct 15 Accessed May 1, 2019. time.com/4983126/woody-allen-harvey-weinstein-scandal/.

Adams, Gretchen A. 2008. *The Specter of Salem: Remembering the Witch Trials in Nineteenth-century America*. Chicago: University of Chicago Press.

Baxstrom, Richard, and Todd Meyers. 2016. *Realizing the Witch: Science, Cinema, and the Mastery of the Invisible*. New York: Fordham University Press.

Beecher Field, Jonathan. 2018. "This Is Not a Witch Hunt." *Boston Review*, Oct 30. Accessed May 1, 2019. bostonreview.net/politics/jonathan-beecher-field-not-witch-hunt.

Beeler, Karin. 2008. *Witches, and Psychics on Screen: An Analysis of Women Visionary Characters in Recent Television and Film*. Jefferson, NC: McFarland.

Benshoff, Harry M., and Sean Griffin. 2004. *America on Film: Representing Race, Class, Gender, and Sexuality at the Movies*. Oxford, UK: Blackwell.
Bovenschen, Silvia. 1978. "The Contemporary Witch, the Historical Witch and the Witch Myth: The Witch, Subject of Appropriation of Nature and Object of the Domination of Nature." *New German Critique* 15: 83–119.
Breslaw, Elaine G. 1996. *Tituba, Reluctant Witch of Salem: Devilish Indians and Puritan Fantasies*. New York: New York University Press.
Çakirtaş, Önder. 2013. "Double Portrayed: Tituba, Racism and Politics." *International Journal of Language Academy* 1: 13–22.
Chinoy, Sahil, Jessica Ma and Stuart A. Thompson. 2018. "Trump's Growing Obsession with the 'Witch Hunt.'" *New York Times*, Aug 23. Accessed May 1, 2019. www.nytimes.com/interactive/2018/08/22/opinion/trump-cohen-mueller-investigation.html.
Clark, Anne Victoria. 2018. "Beyoncé's Former Drummer Accuses Her of 'Extreme Witchcraft'" *Vulture*, Sept 21. Accessed May 1, 2019. www.vulture.com/2018/09/beyoncs-former-drummer-accuses-her-of-extreme-witchcraft.html.
Clover, Carol. 1992. *Men, Women and Chainsaws: Gender in the Modern Horror Film*. Princeton, NJ: Princeton University Press.
Creed, Barbara. 1993. *The Monstrous-Feminine: Film, Feminism, Psychoanalysis*. New York: Routledge.
Davies, Owen. 2013. *America Bewitched: The Story of Witchcraft After Salem*. Oxford, U.K.: Oxford University Press.
Davies, Owen (ed.). 2017. *The Oxford Illustrated History of Witchcraft and Magic*. Oxford, U.K.: Oxford University Press.
Doty, Alexander M., and Patricia Clare Ingham. 2014. *The Witch and the Hysteric: The Monstrous Medieval in Benjamin Christensen's Häxan*. Brooklyn, NY: Punctum books.
Ethridge, Kyle. 2017. "The Minotaur, the Shears and the Melon Baller: Queerness and Self-Mortification in Coven." In *Reading American Horror Story*, edited by Rebecca Janicker, 85–103. Jefferson, NC: McFarland.
Federici, Silvia. 2004. *Caliban and the Witch: Women, the Body and Primitive Accumulation*. Brooklyn, NY: Autonomedia.
Games, Alison. 2010. *Witchcraft in Early North America*. Lanham: Rowman & Littlefield.
Gerrard, Steven, Samantha Holland and Robert Shail (eds.). 2019. *Gender and Contemporary Horror in Television*. Bingley, UK: Emerald Publishing.
Grant, Barry Keith. 2015. *The Dread of Difference: Gender and the Horror Film*, 2nd ed. Austin: University of Texas Press.
Greene, Heather. 2018. *Bell, Book and Camera: A Critical History of Witches in American Film and Television*. Jefferson, NC: McFarland.
Greene, Richard, and Rachel Robison-Greene (eds.). 2018. American Horror Story *and Philosophy: Life Is but a Nightmare*. Chicago: Open Court.
Harriet E.H. Earle (ed.) 2019. *Gender, Sexuality and Queerness in* American Horror Story. Jefferson, NC: McFarland.
Higley, Sarah Lynn, and Jeffrey Andrew Weinstock. 2004. *Nothing That Is: Millennial Cinema and the Blair Witch Controversies*. Detroit: Wayne State University Press.
Hunter, Derek. 2018. "Journalism Hits New Lows in Kavanaugh Witch Hunt." *Daily Caller*, Oct 2. Accessed May 1, 2019. dailycaller.com/2018/10/02/journalism-lows-kavanaugh-witch-hunt/.
Jackson, Kimberly. 2016. *Gender and the Nuclear Family in Twenty-First-Century Horror*. New York: Palgrave Macmillan.
Janicker, Rebecca (ed.). 2017. *Reading American Horror Story: Essays on the Television Franchise*. Jefferson, NC: McFarland.
Johnston, Hannah E., and Peg Aloi (eds.). 2007. *The New Generation Witches: Teenage Witchcraft in Contemporary Culture*. Farnham: Ashgate.
Krzywinska, Tanya. 2000. *A Skin for Dancing In: Possession, Witchcraft and Voodoo in Film*. Trowbridge, England: Flicks Books.
Le Beau, Bryan F. 2010. *The Story of the Salem Witch Trials*, 2nd ed. Upper Saddle River, NJ: Prentice Hall.

Lippert, Conny. 2017. "Nightmares Made in America: Coven and the Real American Horror Story." In *Reading* American Horror Story, edited by Rebecca Janicker. 182–199. Jefferson, NC: McFarland.

Lopes, Elisabete. 2017. "The Season of the Witch: Gender Trouble in American Horror Story-Coven." In *Re-visiting Female Evil: Power, Purity and Desire*, edited by Melissa Dearey, Susana Nicolás, and Roger Davis, 113–39. Boston: Brill-Rodopi.

McMillan, Timothy J. 1994. "Black Magic: Witchcraft, Race, and Resistance in Colonial New England." *Journal of Black Studies* 25, 1: 99–117.cMil.

Milbank, Dana. 2019. "Trump Is Right. This Is a Witch Hunt!" *The Washington Post*, Mar 18. Accessed May 1, 2019. washingtonpost.com/opinions/trump-is-right-this-is-a-witch-hunt/2019/03/18/a2487b14–49bf-11e9-b79a-961983b7e0cd_story.html?utm_term=.75ee7b0dc7af.

O'Reilly, Julie D. 2013. *Bewitched Again: Supernaturally Powerful Women on Television, 1996–2011*. Jefferson, NC: McFarland.

Paschal, Olivia. 2018. "Trump's Tweets and the Creation of 'Illusory Truth.'" *The Atlantic*, Aug 3. Accessed May 1, 2019. www.theatlantic.com/politics/archive/2018/08/how-trumps-witch-hunt-tweets-create-an-illusory-truth/566693/.

Reed, Isaac A. 2015. "Deep Culture in Action: Resignification, Synecdoche, and Metanarrative in the Moral Panic of the Salem Witch Trials." *Theory and Society* 44, 1: 65–94.

Reis, Elizabeth. 1997. *Damned Women: Sinners and Witches in Puritan New England*. Ithaca: Cornell University Press.

Rosenthal, Bernard. 1993. *Salem Story: Reading the Witch Trials of 1692*. Cambridge, UK: Cambridge University Press.

Scott, Izabella. 2016. "Why Witchcraft Is Making a Comeback in Art." *Artsy*, Sept 6. Accessed May 1, 2019. www.artsy.net/article/artsy-editorial-why-witchcraft-is-making-a-comeback-in-art.

Sollée, Kristen J. 2017. *Witches, Sluts, Feminists: Conjuring the Sex Positive*. Berkeley: ThreeL-Media, Stone Bridge Press.

"Witchy Week." 2017. *Vogue*, Sept. Accessed May 1, 2019. www.vogue.com/tag/misc/witchy-week.

Quinn, Dave. 2016. "Azealia Banks Cleans Blood-Stained Room She's Used to Practice Witchcraft for 3 Years: 'Real Witches Do Real Things.'" *People Magazine*, Dec 30. Accessed May 1, 2019. https://people.com/music/azealia-banks-witchcraft-brujeria-peta-statement/.

Yates Garcia, Amanda. 2016. "The Rise of the L.A. Art Witch." *CARLA*, Nov 30. Accessed May 1, 2019. contemporaryartreview.la/the-rise-of-the-l-a-art-witch/.

Re-Remembering the Past
Hauntological Feminist Memories of Salem in Chilling Adventures of Sabrina

Brydie Kosmina

The first trailer for Netflix's *Chilling Adventures of Sabrina* (fittingly released just before Halloween 2018) features a scene from the second episode where Sabrina Spellman (Kiernan Shipka) stands in a muddied white nightgown and declares: "My name is Sabrina Spellman, and I will *not* sign it away" (1x2 "The Dark Baptism"). This scene aligns *Sabrina*'s narrative with that of another famous American text which is (ostensibly) about witches: Arthur Miller's *The Crucible*, in which the protagonist, John Proctor, chooses to die rather than falsely admit to witchcraft "because it is my name!" (1956: 124). *Sabrina*'s trailer recalls the Salem myth and its position within American popular culture. It is my contention that the first season of Netflix's *Sabrina* draws on feminist cultural memories of Salem to present a reconsideration of American historical narratives and memories. Details of Salem recur throughout the show, acting as a ghostly historical echo to the present-day fantasy narrative. I use "ghostly" deliberately, picking up the myriad meanings of spectrality, and I use Derrida's notion of hauntology to analyze how the ghosts of the Greendale 13, witches killed in early witch trials in the fictional town, haunt the show figuratively as well as literally, and the irruption of these ghosts collapses distinctions of linear time to present a desire for a herstorical future.

The Salem trials are recognized as a crucial foundation myth in the "making of modern America," and have long been used metaphorically to comment on America in the present day. Occurring in the Puritan frontier town of Salem (now called Danvers), Massachusetts, in 1692 and 1693, the trials have been written about by historians as resulting from religious beliefs and upheavals, colonial anxieties, environmental catastrophes, racist prejudices, and heteronormative patriarchy (I would posit that each of these historiographical approaches is useful, and should be considered simultaneously). Despite the different approaches, it is generally accepted that the trials began when two young girls in the house of the Rev. Samuel Parris fell ill, and were determined to be afflicted by witchcraft. A slave in the Parris household, Tituba, was soon blamed for the girls' torment, and, unusually, Tituba confessed to using magic to try to heal the girls: this was taken as evidence of her malicious witchcraft. Two other women in the town, Sarah Osborne and Sarah Good, were accused of colluding with Tituba. More young girls began to suffer from supernatural afflictions, and more people began to be accused of witchcraft over the following months. Over the course of the next year, between 100 and 150 people were jailed for witchcraft (approximately fifty of these confessed to their crime), dozens more were accused without facing trial, and 20 people (14 women and six men) and two dogs were executed for witchcraft. Nineteen of the people were hanged, and one, Giles Corey, died during torture aimed at forcing a confession. The hysterical air of the trials in the Court of Oyer and Terminer has resonated in cultural memories of the trials, and often Salem is used as a cultural metaphor to comment on American historical consciousness, paranoia, in-fighting, and mass hysteria. In *Sabrina*, however, the Salem trials are not used metaphorically, but as historical precedent. The witches of Salem are given back their magic, and are rewritten as genuinely magical women in service to the Dark Lord, murdered for their religion. The Salem narrative is used to reinforce and underscore the witch trials of the same year that took place in Greendale, the (fictional) town in which *Sabrina* is set. Salem becomes an ur-myth for the series, as a fantasy of feminist revenge for the Salem trials (and for the persecution of women more broadly) is played out in Greendale.

Collective memories of the Salem Witch Trials have been utilized for cultural critique and the trials have long been metaphorically used in the American literary canon. As Gretchen A. Adams writes in *The Specter of Salem: Remembering the Witch Trials in Nineteenth-Century America*:

> [T]he long, strange career of the Salem "witches" as an American cultural metaphor is an artefact of an equally long-held and complex collective memory of the trials of 1692. Always linked to cultural anxieties, the metaphor has meanings that shift to suit contemporary realities. But from a narrative created to give meaning to the recent community ordeal after the trauma of the trials themselves through its evolution into a useful prescriptive metaphor, the memory of Salem has always held at its core meanings meant to mark the boundaries of generally accepted beliefs and behaviors [2013: 157].

Memories and cultural myths of the Salem trials shift in accordance with contemporary cultural needs and critiques. The cultural metaphor of the Salem trials acts as a recurring symbolic prism through which the history and culture of America can be refracted, revisited, and revised.

Looking at the way that history has transitioned to cultural myth is a process investigated by memory studies scholars. Memory studies as a discipline emerged during the mid-twentieth century, primarily in response to the Holocaust. Maurice Halbwachs, a French sociologist whose work *On Collective Memory* was published after his death in Buchenwald and translated into English in the 1990s, is often seen as the first key figure in the field. Halbwachs posited that "no memory is possible outside frameworks used by people living in society to determine and retrieve their recollections" (1992: 43), as the individual mind "reconstructs its memories under the pressure of society" (1992: 51). Memory, according to Halbwachs, is collectively constructed. The individual's memories as well as collective memories adhere to communal reconstructions of events. This socialized form of memory is crucial in constructing social group identity in the present, as memory contributes to historical narratives of collective pasts (particularly of trauma), from which identity can be constructed. Collective memory thus defines group identity, while group identity reciprocally exerts pressure on collective memories of the past. Pierre Nora, a French historian who further developed Halbwachs' work in his own seminal work, *Realms of Memory*, sums up this reciprocal relationship, writing that "[m]emory wells up from groups that it welds together" (1996: 3). The redefinition of group identity according to shifting cultural norms, values, and necessities "requires every social group to redefine its identity by dredging up its past" (1996: 10). Therefore, collective memory is not necessarily "true" or "historically accurate" (terms which are, rightfully, viewed with some suspicion in postmodernity), as memory can and will be distorted to support, and in response to, ideological needs and norms of group identity at a given time.

Halbwachs acknowledges the symbolic meaningful nature of memory for group identity, writing that "[a]s soon as each person and each historical fact has permeated this [social, collective] memory, it is transposed into a teaching, a notion, or a symbol and takes on a meaning. It becomes an element of the society's system of ideas" (1992: 188). Memory "yield[s]" to the needs and reflections of the present-day social group because "these ideas [memories] represent, if you will, the consciousness that society has of itself in its present situation" (Halbwachs 1992: 183). "Social beliefs," therefore, "have a double character. They are collective traditions or recollections, but they are also ideas or conventions that result from a knowledge of the present" (Halbwachs 1992: 188). Much as memory is simultaneously welling up from social groups while welding them together, it is also a means of engaging and interacting with the past, while responding to and reinterpreting the present. This process of reinterpretation opens the collective memories of a group up to revision according to ideological necessity in the present-day. The "values and ideals" of a chosen group are exemplified by their collective memory, and, more specifically, certain narratives and memories are "retrieved, manipulated, and mobilized" for the purpose of shaping present-day collective identity (Karlsson 2010: 47). Prominent memory studies scholar, Jan Assmann similarly writes that "[t]hrough its cultural heritage a society becomes visible to itself and to others. Which past becomes evidence in that heritage and which values emerge in its identificatory appropriation tells us much about the constitution and tendencies of a society" (1995: 133). Although this manipulation of collective memories is usually discussed in relation to nationalism and identity, it is equally applicable to other identity groups, particularly groups neglected from "official" national or majority group identities, but whose group identity is equally reliant on collective memory/ies. LGBTQI+ communities, feminist groups, ethnic and diaspora communities, working class communities, regional groups, and so many more, are all social identity groups with specific collective memory/ies, which are often used to bolster the group against the majority, "official" narrative of group identity and memory.

Historical writing has been viewed as a means of redressing perceived injustices or bringing to light long-ignored historical events, a function which Karlsson refers to as the "moral use of history" (2010: 48). Feminist historiography of the witch trials in fifteenth-century Britain and the seventeenth-century American colonies falls into this category. Historians have written about the witch trials using a number of different theoretical frameworks, with clear changes discernible in witchcraft historiography, transitioning from Rankean and Whig history which emphasizes the role of literate elite groups in perpetrating the trials (groups such as the clergy, the monarchy and other governmental figures) (Trevor-Roper 1956; Broedel 2013; Williams 1995), to Marxist and social history which changes the focus to the peasantry and middle classes' experiences of the trials, and points to widespread popular religious and cultural beliefs and institutions as the causes of the trials (Federici 2004; Ginzburg 1966; Demos 2008). From social history emerged women's history, and soon after, feminist history, which has had the most impact on how the trials are viewed by lay audiences. Feminist historians have addressed the (now shocking) failure of previous historians to deeply interrogate the gender coding of witchcraft, and, in doing so, repositioned the witch trials in the Western cultural imagination.

The trials across Europe and North America have come to be seen in the popular cultural historical consciousness and feminist discourses as the violent product of patriarchy, and as an attempted gynocide. In *Gyn/Ecology*, for instance, radical feminist Mary Daly writes that "the intent [of the European witch trials] was to break down and destroy strong women, to dismember and kill the Goddess, the divine spark of be-ing in women. The intent was to purify society of the existence and of the potential existence of such women" (1978: 183). Similarly, in *Woman Hating*, Andrea Dworkin uses a feminist psychoanalytic approach when looking at the hysteria and violence of the witch trials:

> we are dealing with an existential terror of women, of the "mouth of the womb," stemming from a primal anxiety about male potency, tied to a desire for self (phallic) control; men have deep-rooted castration fears which are expressed as a horror of the womb. These terrors form the substrata of a myth of feminine evil which in turn justified several centuries of gynocide [1974: 134].

Reading the witch hunts through a radical feminist historiographical lens positions the events as a "brutal means by which patriarchy exerted control over women and sought to curb the perceived threat posed to men's dominance of early modern society by women's allegedly rapacious sexuality," as Alison Rowlands succinctly argues (2013: 450). Feminist historiography of the witch trials has been so successful in reshaping memories of the trials that the accepted view of the trials in popular culture today is as an attack on women, particularly women who threatened patriarchal dominance. Collective memories of the witch from the trials are now of "an independent adult woman who does not conform to the male idea of proper female behavior" (Larner 1994: 253). In reclaiming the history of the trials, the witch has consequently become an "engine of activism" (Sollée 2017: 47), and "a symbol for active and dominant women" (Toivo 2008: 10) in modern day feminist discourses and in popular culture representations of the symbol.

Literature functions as a repository for collective memories, fictionalizing and narrativizing historical events for the maintenance of memory. For instance, feminist narratives of the witch trials that bolster feminist principles in the present are identifiable in popular culture texts like *Sabrina*. Aleida Assmann's work on cultural and collective memory is crucial in understanding how cultural memories of historical events transition to fiction. In "Texts, Traces, Trash" Assmann argues that texts (or "letters" as she puts it) can be "'read' as clues to important historical changes in the structures of cultural memory" (1996: 124). Ann Rigney's notion of textual afterlives is similarly useful in tracing how popular culture functions as a repository of memory. Rigney proposes the idea of a text's (or symbol's) social life as the mnemonic fragments of the past that return over and over again in popular culture. Using the metaphor of memory's social life and afterlife, Rigney addresses the "underlying portability that enables them [stories, memories, symbols] to move into different media and social contexts" (2012: 12). Thus, feminist memories of the witch trials transition to popular literature and film, and the afterlives of this revisionist historiography haunt the symbol of the witch, who becomes a figure of radical feminist potential.

In Season One of Netflix's *Chilling Adventures of Sabrina* (2018), this hauntological feminist revision of the history of the Western witch trials, specifically of the 1692–3 Salem trials, is the foundation of the series and imbues the depiction of witchcraft in *Sabrina* with an inherent feminist radicalism. Following the initial paratextual link to Salem myths in the trailer, the show also foregrounds the Salem trials as foundational from early in the first episode, demonstrating the textual afterlives of the trials that dominate *Sabrina*. Miss Mary Wardwell, Sabrina's teacher and "unofficial town historian" (1x1 "October Country"), outlines Greendale's witchcraft history to a young girl she rescues from the side of the road (who is revealed to be more malevolent than we first expected). "Everyone knows about the witch hunt in Salem," Wardwell says, "but there was one right here in Greendale, 1692. 13 witches were hung [sic] in the forest, and their angry spirits have haunted the woods ever since" (1x1). The Greendale witch trials not only occurred the same year as the infamous Salem trials, but the setting of *Sabrina*, the fictional town of Greendale, is a mirror to Salem. While it is unclear where exactly in America the town is located, there is a definitive New England aesthetic to the town of Greendale. The environment recalls this area, particularly the dense woods that surround the town. Before her Dark Baptism, Sabrina plans to tell her mortal friends that she is "being transferred to some posh boarding school in Connecticut" (1x1), positioning Greendale somewhere in the New England region. The Spellman house-and-mortuary is also modeled after the House of Seven Gables in Salem, creating a material intertextual link to the physical environment of Salem and New England.

Later in the same episode, Sabrina, trying to explain to her mortal boyfriend Harvey about her witch heritage, says:

> SABRINA: Harvey, do you remember, at the beginning of the school year, what Miss Wardwell told us about ye olde Greendale? How there were witch trials, like in Salem, but no one ever talked about them or wrote about them? There are no gravestones, no monuments?
> HARVEY: Hazily, yeah…
> SABRINA: That's because the witches didn't want anyone to know. So that the coven could keep living in Greendale, privately, undisturbed, through the centuries. So that *we* could [1x1].

Despite the coven's attempts to hide the history of witchcraft in Greendale, memories of Salem bleed through, and details of the trials in Salem recur throughout the narrative. George Hawthorne, the tyrannical principal of Baxter High (who is discussed in more depth later) is named for the only Salem judge not to repent for his actions, John Hathorne (patrilineal grandfather to renowned author Nathaniel Hawthorne). Hawthorne is not the only figure from the Salem trials to be name-checked: Miss Wardwell is named for Samuel Wardwell, one of the men executed for witchcraft, while the Putnam family recalls Ann Putnam, one of the afflicted girls who began the panic in Salem. Sabrina's familiar names himself Salem, to Aunt Zelda's disgust (1x1), while Zelda's own familiar, Vinegar Tom, is named for the 1976 Caryl Churchill play, *Vinegar Tom*, which is set during the Salem trials and examines the gender dynamics of the events. Sabrina's lawyer, Daniel Webster, recalls the short story "The Devil and Daniel Webster," by Stephen Vincent Benét and the 1941 film adaptation, *All That Money Can Buy*, directed by William Dieterle. Feminist revisionist cultural memories of the idea of the witch hunt also abound in the show. For instance, when Sabrina asks Principal Hawthorne to investigate the football team to find her friend Theo's[1] tormentors, he questions her, asking, "Are you suggesting a witch hunt?" to which Sabrina, with a secret family history of persecution, primly replies "I don't care for that term" (1x1). These small details of the Salem trials act as signposts to the deeper preoccupation in the series with revisiting and revising cultural memories of the Salem witch trials, and the feminist impulse driving this reconsideration.

The reconsideration of Salem in the show transforms 1692 Puritanical zealotry into modern-day toxic masculinity and patriarchal "boys' clubs." Theo Putnam, one of Sabrina's best friends and a transgender student at Baxter High, is constantly physically and verbally assaulted by the school football team's players. A particularly violent attack on Theo prompts Sabrina to ask Hawthorne to intervene, a request he refuses as he does not want to incite a "witch hunt," as discussed above (1x1). Lamenting to Miss Wardwell, Sabrina says:

> SABRINA: It's this town, this school, there's a culture of—
> WARDWELL: —Puritanical masculinity? And Principal Hawthorne is the most intolerant, the most buffoonish, the most misogynist of all. When will the world learn? Women should be in charge of everything [1x1].

The violent misogyny of Greendale's boys and men is directly aligned with the Puritanism of Salem's judges and jurors. It is no coincidence that Principal Hawthorne is named for one of the Salem judges, who perpetrated the atrocities against the people (predominately women) of Salem in the name of religious duty. However, *Sabrina* revises the Salem narrative around Puritanical patriarchy and the violent ends women and queer people who suffer under it usually meet. Sabrina, her friends Roz, Theo, and other students at Baxter High form the Women's Intersectional Cultural and Creative Association (WICCA) to protect and fight for the marginalized students who are not protected by the school's administration. Sabrina even describes WICCA as "women protecting women, sort of like a coven" (1x1).[2] Sabrina goes on to cast a spell causing Hawthorne to be attacked by thousands of spiders, his greatest fear (1x1). In *Sabrina*'s revision of Salem, witchcraft and Wicca are not the reason for the victims' persecution: they are the answer to it.

Sabrina's trial in front of the Court of Witches similarly recalls memories of Salem and other witch trials in Western history. After Sabrina runs away during her Dark Baptism, the coven chases her, trying to bring her back to complete the ritual and pledge her soul to Satan (1x2 "The Dark Baptism"). Following this, the Church "sues" Sabrina for failing to fulfill her "contract" with Satan, which is positioned as a pseudo marriage (1x3 "The Trial of Sabrina Spellman"). Father Blackwood, the High Priest of the Church of Night and lead prosecutor, even accuses Sabrina of "leading on" Satan, pointing out that the crime Sabrina has been charged with, "Breach of Promise," is traditionally leveled at bridegrooms who leave their brides at the altar (1x3). Blackwood argues that Sabrina, having arrived at her Dark Baptism in her mother's wedding dress and having engaged in a "courtship" with the Dark Lord prior to the ceremony, has, in effect, promised herself to Satan (legally, and, it is implied, sexually) (1x3). Sabrina, Blackwood and the Church of Night argue, is "asking for it." Prudence, Sabrina's frenemy at the Academy of Unseen Arts, even claims that Sabrina "cocktease[d] [...] the Dark Lord" (1x4 "Witch Academy"). The witch trial in *Sabrina* thus has the same air of injustice as the Salem trials, and reads as a legal attack on women who refuse to submit to patriarchal domination. Where feminist memories of Salem position the women who faced the Court of Oyer and Terminer as victims of Puritanical patriarchy, Sabrina's trial is about her refusal to submit to Satanic patriarchy and sexual violence.

What these examples demonstrate is that *Sabrina* is interested in retelling and reconsidering cultural memories of Salem, and, thus, of witchcraft, of femininity, and of violence in present-day America. However, in revisiting Salem and the witch trials, *Sabrina* rewrites these cultural memories, with a specific aim of enacting feminist revenge for the women lost to patriarchal violence. Revenge is a recurring theme in *Sabrina*: Sabrina takes revenge on the bullying football players at Baxter High (1x1, 1x2); the students at the Academy of Unseen Arts who died as a result of the harrowing ritual (essentially hazing) seek revenge against the bullies of the school (1x4); and, later in the season, two of the students at the Academy, Agatha and Dorcas, perform a spell designed to kill Sabrina's boyfriend, Harvey Kinkle, and his brother, Tommy (1x7 "Feast of Feasts"). The Kinkles are descended from witch hunters, and killing the Kinkles is an act of vengeance and "blood atonement" for the deaths of the coven's ancestral witches

(1x8 "The Burial"). These episodes of intergenerational revenge culminate in "The Witching Hour" (1x10) when the witches of Greendale return to the town, seeking revenge against the witch hunters of the town, and against the coven which abandoned them to their deaths. Viewing revenge as a feminist act can be problematic: for instance, feminist literary scholars (particularly working in the horror genre looking at rape-revenge narratives) have debated the morality of violent revenge as a means of redressing patriarchal oppression. Nevertheless, the revenge of the Greendale 13 reflects the feminist desire for (admittedly violent and troubling) justice for the witches lost in Salem, and for all the women lost to patriarchal violence throughout history.

The Greendale 13, Sabrina's family explain, were witches murdered at the height of the American witch hunts, abandoned to their deaths by their coven:

> ZELDA: After the witch trials of Salem, all the witches in this part of the country were terrified.
> HILDA: Trouble was brewing in Greendale, and people ... mortals were identifying and arresting witches, including the original 13. And while they sat in their cell, the other witches met and decided—
> ZELDA: —The 13 would be sacrificed. To appease the mortals' bloodlust. While those 13 women were tortured and hung, the rest of the witches ... burned their poppets and buried their cauldrons.
> AMBROSE: They were scapegoats to quell the rising witch hysteria [1x10].

The hysteria, paranoia, fear, and injustice of the Salem trials are mirrored here, but with an additional layer: the executed women were not only attacked by the people of their town, but were abandoned by their own coven. Thus, when Wardwell calls the ghosts of the murdered witches back, she exhorts them to "claim your revenge. Go forth, sisters. Take to the sleeping streets. Reacquaint yourself with the town you so despise" (1x10). Theo's ancestor, Dorothea Putnam, who cut down the women and buried them when no one else would, appears as a ghost to Theo, and says that the 13 has "come for vengeance" (1x10) against the people of Greendale and against the coven who left them to die. Consequently, the Greendale 13 reflects a feminist impulse to take revenge for historical injustices against women in the witch trials. The specters of Greendale's executed witches stalk the town, embodying the specter of Salem that haunts the narrative of *Sabrina* and American popular culture, the specter of women's and feminist history which haunts the masculinist historical record, and which literally haunts the town of Greendale. Memories of Salem in *Sabrina* are thus imbued into the ghosts of the murdered women.

Sabrina, however, not only uses and revises memories of Salem for feminist vengeance, but forces a modern acknowledgment of responsibility.

Zelda, Sabrina's stiff, rule-following, Satan-praising aunt, points out that the Spellmans and the coven are complicit in the execution of the 13:

> ZELDA: It's a bloody mess what happened to the Greendale 13. The most ignoble chapter of the Church of Night's history, but it is our history and we cannot deny it. [...] The coven could have come together to save the 13, but they.... *We*, our ancestors, decided not to risk it [1x10].

Zelda accepting personal responsibility for the violent failures of her ancestors is in line with feminist historiographical writing about Salem. The injustices of patriarchy do not exist solely in the past: they continue to haunt the present, and we must take responsibility for them. However, in defeating the Greendale 13, Sabrina sets them alight with hellfire at the very tree which they were first hanged from. In burning the Greendale 13 at their own stake, and "re-executing" them, *Sabrina* continues the cyclical retelling and recycling of memories of Salem in popular culture: the witches will forever return to haunt the present, as the myth is forever renewed to serve new cultural purposes. They must continually be executed for the myth to maintain its potency as a cultural metaphor, a re-execution of past victims of patriarchy which troubles feminist herstorical readings of the text.

The ghosts of the Greendale 13 thus function as a mechanic for blurring temporalities. The haunting presence of these ghosts mirrors the haunting of feminist revisionist histories of Salem, which haunt the American historical record, just as the ghosts of the women who suffered under patriarchy (and who continue to suffer under global hegemonic patriarchy) haunt modern-day feminism. On top of this, cultural memories of Salem haunt American popular culture in many ways: the foundation myth of frontier paranoia, mass hysteria, and mob violence continue to haunt American popular literature and film, and the Salem narrative serves a multitude of metaphoric purposes in American popular discourses. The ghost is a central figure in the show's first season, which ends with the haunting and re-execution of the witches seeking revenge for their past oppression. The haunting of the final episode imbricates the revenge the witches seek with the responsibility for the past that Zelda and the Spellmans must assume, and the more just future free of patriarchy that the show envisions.

Ghosts are not empty, transparent vessels: they contain their own meanings, and thus the imbrication of memory, haunting, ghosts, and witches in *Sabrina* renders the trauma of the past and feminist reclamations and responses to this trauma a specter forever haunting the present. To discuss the specter, and the eternal haunting presence (or *present-ce*) of the past, recalls Jacques Derrida's hauntology. In *Specters of Marx: The State of the Debt, the Work of Mourning, and the New International* (1994)

Derrida proposes the term hauntology to describe the process of living with ghosts of the past, an eternal past-presence which is both present and absent, the past and the present, and even the future. Writing specifically about the ghosts of Marx, Marxism, and communism following the fall of Soviet communism in the late twentieth-century, and in response to Francis Fukuyama's *The End of History and the Last Man* (1992), Derrida asks:

> *What* is a ghost? What is the *effectivity* or the *presence* of a specter, that is, of what seems to remain as ineffective, virtual, insubstantial as a simulacrum? Is there *there*, between the thing itself and its simulacrum, an opposition that holds us? Repetition *and* first time, but also repetition *and* last time, since the singularity of any *first time* makes of it also a *last time*. Each time it is the event itself, a first time is a last time. Altogether other. Staging for the end of history. Let us call it a *hauntology* [1994: 10].

The postmodern condition is a process of "learning to live [with the specter][...]. And this being-with specters would also be, not only but also, a *politics* of memory, of inheritance, and of generations" (1994: xviii–xix). Memory can, in this reading, be understood as means of living with the specters of the past, marked by absence (memory exists as collective spectral recollections of a time no longer accessible) and by presence (memory/ies shape the present and, consequently, the future).

This question of the futurity of the specter is also discussed by Derrida, who writes that the specter is "[t]urned toward the future, going toward it, it also comes from it, it proceeds *from* [*provient* de] the future[...]. Even if the future is its [the specter's] provenance, it must be, like any provenance, absolutely and irreversibly past" (1994: xix). A "spectral moment," argues Derrida, is "a moment that no longer belong to time" (1994: xix). This collapsing of time, which Katy Shaw calls "the interconnected nature of past, present, and future," is the key feature of hauntological practice (2018: 109). The specter "dissolv[es] the separation between now and then," and therefore hauntology dually reflects a "compulsion to repeat the past, and an anticipation of the future" (Shaw 2018: 2). Similarly, Chris Hughes writes that "[h]auntology is the idea that there is something from the past which is always present in the present; and, also, that this something is waiting for its return to a future to come [...]. The specter is thus both past and future" (2012: 15). The ghost irrupts into the present, collapsing any boundaries between past and future into the one spectral moment.

Learning to live with the specter, as Derrida asks us to, consequently becomes a matter of justice: "[o]f justice where it is not yet, not yet *there*, where it is no longer, let us understand where it is no longer *present*, and where it will never be [...]. It is necessary to speak *of the ghost*, indeed *to the* ghost and *with* it [...]. No justice [...] seems possible or thinkable without the principle of some *responsibility*, beyond all living present, within that which disjoins the living present" (1994: xviii). A spectral haunting "demands justice or, at the very least, a response from the haunted subject" (Shaw 2018: 107). The specter collapses distinctions of past, present, and future, and, in this collapsing, consequently "demand[s] actions and decisions from the living" for the future (Shaw 2018: 12). As Mark Fisher notably argues, "[t]he future is always experienced as a haunting: as a virtuality that already impinges on the present, conditioning expectations and motivating cultural production" (2012: 16). To responsibly live with the specter is to respond to it, and to take future action as a result of this response.

What I propose, therefore, is that the Greendale 13 should be read hauntologically. As the ghosts of witches, they are marked by both their witch identity (and the myriad meanings that the witch now contains, following feminist reclamation of the symbol) and by their spectrality. The memories of Salem that recur throughout the narrative of Season 1 of *Sabrina* are marshaled in the denouement to serve a hauntological feminist purpose. The ghosts of the witches, collapsing the distinction between past, present, and future, seek retribution for their murders, and, metaphorically, for the deaths of other wronged victims of the trials; their irruption into the present reflects an imbrication of memory, ghosts, revenge, justice, and feminist fantasy. The ghosts seek revenge for their own deaths, but they also symbolically seek vengeance for the victims in Salem and in other witch trials, and for the erasure-death of women from *his*tory. The witch-ghosts thus symbolically function as the spectral embodiment of feminist revisions of the past, and as the returned victims of past patriarchy.

The irruption of the specter in the narrative of *Sabrina* (and, consequently, into cultural memories of Salem) also forces us to look to the future. The ghosts in *Sabrina* haunt the town and the narrative as symbols of a desire for a feminist future which has been lost, or, perhaps, has not yet happened. In playing with cultural memories of the Salem myth, *Sabrina* enters in an ongoing reconsideration of America's patriarchal past and conversation about a feminist future. In presenting a feminist revision of Salem in the present-day, the specters which haunt Greendale allow the collapsing of modal notions of time, and the past returns to the now. Consequently, the past can be rewritten, and, crucially, so can the future. *Sabrina* presents an attempt to live with the specter of the witch, as Derrida asks us to, and to respond to and speak with the ghosts of the past for a more *just* future, one free from the patriarchal persecution of the past, and as the return of a vengeful imagined feminist future.

Notes

1. In Season One, Theo is called Susie, and is referred to using female pronouns. In Season Two, Susie changes their name to Theo, and I have referred to them throughout this paper by that name. Lachlan Watson, the non-binary actor playing Theo, uses they/them pronouns, and talks about Theo in interviews using those same gender-neutral pronouns, and I have therefore followed their lead.
2. This is prior to Theo's transition.

References

Adams, Gretchen. 2013. *The Specter of Salem: Remembering the Witch Trials in Nineteenth-Century America*. Chicago: University of Chicago Press.
Assmann, Aleida. 1996. "Texts, Traces, Trash: The Changing Media of Cultural Memory." *Representations* 56: 123–134. doi: 10.2307/2928711.
Assmann, Jan. 1995. "Collective Memory and Cultural Identity." Trans. John Czaplicka. *New German Critique* 65: 125–133. doi: 2307/488538.
Broedel, Hans Peter. 2013. "Fifteenth-Century Witch Beliefs." In *The Oxford Handbook of Witchcraft in Early Modern Europe and Colonial America*, edited by Brian P. Levack, 32–49. Oxford: Oxford University Press.
Daly, Mary. 1978. *Gyn/Ecology*. London: The Women's Press.
Demos, John. 2008. *The Enemy Within: Years of Witch-hunting in the Western World*. New York: Viking.
Derrida, Jacques. 2006 [1994]. *Specters of Marx: The State of the Debt, the Work of Mourning, and the New International*. Translated by Peggy Kamuf. New York and London: Routledge Classics.
Dworkin, Andrea. 1974. *Woman Hating*. New York: E.P. Dutton.
Federici, Silvia. 2004. *Caliban and the Witch*. New York: Autonomedia.
Fisher, Mark. 2012. "What Is Hauntology?" *Film Quarterly* 66, 1: 16–25. doi: 10.1525/fq.2012.66.1.16.
Ginzburg, Carlo. 1966. *The Night Battles: Witchcraft and Agrarian Cults in the Sixteenth and Seventeenth Centuries*. Translated by John Tedeschi and Anne Tedeschi. London: Routledge and Kegan Paul.
Halbwachs, Maurice. 1992. *On Collective Memory*. Translated by Lewis A. Coser. Chicago: University of Chicago Press.
Hughes, Chris. 2012. "Dialogue Between Fukuyama's Account of the End of History and Derrida's Hauntology." *Journal of Philosophy: A Cross-Disciplinary Inquiry* 7, 8: 13–26. doi: 10.5840/jphilnepal201271813.
Karlsson, Klas-Göran. 2010. "The Uses of History and the Third Wave of Europeanisation." In *A European Memory?: Contested Histories and the Politics of Remembrance*, edited by Małgorzata Pakier and Bo Stråth, 38–55. New York: Berghahn Books.
Larner, Christina. 1994. "Was Witch-Hunting Woman-Hunting?" In *The Witchcraft Reader* 2nd ed., edited by Darren Oldridge, 253–256. London and New York: Routledge.
Miller, Arthur. [1953] 1968. *The Crucible*. Middlesex, England: Penguin Books.
Nora, Pierre. 1996. *Realms of Memory: Rethinking the French Past, Volume One: Conflicts and Divisions*. New York: Columbia University Press.
Rigney, Ann. 2012. *The Afterlives of Walter Scott: Memory on the Move*. Oxford: Oxford University Press.
Rowlands, Alison. 2013. "Witchcraft and Gender in Early Modern Europe." In *The Oxford Handbook of Witchcraft in Early Modern Europe and Colonial America*, edited by Brian P. Levack, 449–467. Oxford: Oxford University Press.
Shaw, Katy. 2018. *Hauntology: The Presence of the Past in Twenty-First Century English Literature*. Cham, Switzerland: Palgrave Macmillan. doi 10.1007/978-3-319-74968-6.
Sollée, Kristen J. *Witches, Sluts, Feminists: Conjuring the Sex Positive*. Berkeley, U.S.A.: ThreeL Media.

Toivo, Raisa Maria. 2008. *Witchcraft and Gender in Early Modern Society: Finland and the Wider European Experience*. Hampshire U.K. and Burlington, U.S.A.: Ashgate.

Trevor-Roper, Hugh. 1969 [1956]. *The European Witch-Craze of the Sixteenth and Seventeenth Centuries and Other Essays*. New York: Harper Torchbooks.

Williams, Gerhold Schultz. 1995. *Defining Dominion: The Discourses of Magic and Witchcraft in Early Modern France and Germany*. Ann Arbor: University of Michigan Press.

Good Witch, Bad Witch
Identities and Ethics

Declawing the Jungle Cat

Caging Feminine Power on the CW's The Secret Circle

Charity A. Fowler

From enchantress to hag, wise woman to servant of Satan, fairy-tale villain to feminist icon: the image of the witch is complicated, particularly in Western culture. This complexity of the witch shows in the multiplicity of her representations in popular culture. After a couple of decades where the domesticated witch could be living next door, the Satanic Panic of the early 1980s led to a resurgence of the "horror witch" which erased any feminist connections pop culture witches of the 1960s and 1970s had (Greene 2018: 150, 167). However, in her history of witches in American film and television, Heather Greene claims that in the mid–1990s, the teen witch film, *The Craft* (1996), the live action adaptation of *Sabrina the Teenage Witch* (1996–2003), and Alice Hoffman's novel, *Practical Magic* (1995), marked a turning point toward more empowered witches, and paved the way for shows like *Buffy the Vampire Slayer* (1997–2003) and *Charmed* (1998–2006) (Greene 2018: 167). While all of these texts have some problems in representation, Greene argues they nevertheless "demonstrate a change in the cinematic treatment of witchcraft and women's agency" (Greene 2018: 169).

In marking *The Craft*, *Sabrina* and *Practical Magic* as setting out a path to a new era of cinematic and televisual witches, however, Greene's analysis misses L.J. Smith's *The Secret Circle* trilogy[1] published in 1992.[2] Greene is not alone in failing to consider *The Secret Circle*'s place in the history of witches in popular culture (see Gibson 2006; Moseley 2002; Winslade 2001; Cush 2007). Like Smith's other trilogy, *The Vampire Diaries* (1991), chronologies of supernatural YA literature often overlook *The Secret Circle*, and its influence on the genre goes unremarked. But, like how *The Vampire Diaries* helped create and solidify the patterns and tropes in

YA vampire literature still seen today, *The Secret Circle* is one of the seminal teen witch narratives, and bridges the gap caused by the Satanic Panic between second-wave feminism's reclamation of the witch and the explosion of teen witches consuming Silver Ravenwolf's *Teen Witch: Wicca for a New Generation,* as well as those fictional texts which are rooted more in third-wave or postfeminism, like *Sabrina* and *Charmed* (Projansky and Vande Berg 2000; Wolfe 2007; Miller 2007; Moseley 2002). In short, what Greene claims *The Craft* did in shaping this new era of the teen witch, *The Secret Circle* did four years earlier and with a more positive representation of witchcraft. However, much of what makes *The Secret Circle* so powerfully feminist disappeared when Kevin Williamson adapted it into a television show on the CW in 2011.

In this essay, I analyze both versions of *The Secret Circle* against one another, focusing on how the changes made in the process of adaptation affect the performance, representation, and combination of gender, sexuality, and power. Ultimately, I argue that the adaptation strips *The Secret Circle* of its subversive and queer elements, as well as its explicit connection to and celebration of second-wave feminist spirituality, turning it instead into a more hegemonic representation of third-wave or postfeminism in two main ways: first, by removing the spiritual elements and values from the text entirely, and secondly, by changing the characters and plot in ways that disempower the female characters and constrain them through external and internalized patriarchal discourse within the text. Given that the television adaptation of *The Secret Circle* is now the more familiar text, this reassertion of patriarchal power over the narrative not only is troubling to see replicated repeatedly on television, but also continues to obscure the contribution *The Secret Circle* novels made to the shift in representation of witches, teen and otherwise, on television and beyond.

Both versions of *The Secret Circle* tell the story of Cassie Blake, a 16-year-old girl who moves to the town where her mother grew up and discovers that she is a witch. So are the children of her mother's friends, and they need her to join their Circle[3] to complete it. Both versions also have at their core a mystery about what happened to the previous generation of witches, half of whom died when the teens were still infants, and both require the witches to face down witch hunters and the malevolent force that is Cassie's father—Black John, in the novels; John Blackwell, in the show—who wants to control them and use their power in his quest for power, vengeance, and domination. Eschewing the love triangle, both versions instead create a complex love quadrangle (books) or pentagon (TV) among characters, and conflict in both Circles often arises over disagreements about the use of their power.

However, while the broad strokes of the narratives are the same, the adaptation makes significant changes which modify both tone and representation. The two most obvious changes are in setting and characters. The adaptation changes the setting from New Salem, Massachusetts, to Chance Harbor, Washington, which affects the historicity of the narrative and its deep connection to the historical persecution of witches.[4] Additionally, the adaptation slashes the number of Circle members from 12 to 6 and drastically changes the characterizations of those it retains. A less obvious, but critical, change is in the depiction of the many facets of feminist witchcraft present in the original text. In the novels, the Circle's witchcraft represents the mythic tradition behind the surge in neopaganism, and, further, is firmly based in the values of feminist spirituality, but the television show abandons any spiritual elements for more dramatic supernatural elements like demons, dark magic, and secret societies of witch hunters governed by a Council. Because the power of the feminist reclamation of the witch is at the heart of much of my analysis, I begin there.

"Earth and water, fire and air, see your daughter standing there"

The Goddess Within

The original *Secret Circle* trilogy builds its representation of witchcraft on the mythic foundation both Gerald Gardner and the feminist witches in the 1970s were seeking (or creating a narrative hypothesis for): a pre–Christian religion, rooted in old knowledge and ways of knowing passed down in secret through generations. The witches in *The Secret Circle* do not call themselves Wiccan or say they are Dianic practitioners, because their witchcraft predates Alastair Crowley, Gerald Gardner, Z Budapest, and Starhawk by centuries, maybe longer. They "[dig] up the old traditions and [wake] the Old Powers" via each family's Book of Shadows, and old letters and journals, piecing together the shape of it, the proper rituals and observances, the herbal lore and spells, bit by bit, much like feminist activists, historians, archaeologists and theologians, comb through archives and ruins searching for the "glorious matriarchal past" (Goldenberg 2004: 207). Only, while little hard evidence of this past, or of pagan rituals, exists in our world, it flourishes in that of the original *Secret Circle* trilogy.

That said, as a fictional narrative, *The Secret Circle* has no "real" past, and, thus, Smith must have either invented the novels' witchcraft or based it upon some practices or beliefs in our world. And what Smith clearly patterns the witchcraft in the novels on is the feminist witchcraft and spirituality that developed in the 1970s. In particular, the witchcraft in the novels closely aligns with Dianic Craft, which, in turn, draws a great deal from Gardnerian Wicca. All three incorporate and rely heavily on things like casting a circle while calling on the four elements, correlated to the cardinal directions; celebrating sabbats and esabats, and worshiping the Triple Goddess (Griffin 2005: 63). When it comes to gender, Dianic Craft and Gardnerian Wicca split: Gardnerian Wicca believes in sexual polarity for magic, while Dianic Craft is a single-sex faith: no men allowed. Similarly, many Wiccan groups worship both the god and goddess, but in the Dianic faith, the goddess rules alone. The witches in *The Secret Circle* combine these two in a way that privileges the young women in the group but acknowledges the young men are "just as important" as the women "in a different way" (Smith 2009: 217).

The Circle is matriarchal in nature; the knowledge of their craft is passed down mainly through matriarchal lines. When they need assistance, they turn to the crones in their families—their grandmothers and great-aunts—for guidance; only women may be chosen as leaders[5]; there are seven girls to five boys and they celebrate the goddess in many forms, while the only male deity to get a mention is Herne, and only on Samhain. Like in Dianic Craft, the goddess rules alone: Herne, or the Horned God, may be her consort, but her power is supreme. The witches in *The Secret Circle* also practice a clearly nature-based faith, working with herbs, crystals, oils, colors and the elements, also like Dianic Craft. Finally, in a clear invocation of Dianic Craft and its honoring of the goddess Diana, the name of the Circle's leader is Diana.

Feminist witchcraft believes that the goddess is immanent, rather than transcendent, and is located within each of its practitioners; each woman is divine (Scarboro and Luck 1997: 76; Van Fossan 2012: 78; Gordon 1995: 9). In some covens, the goddess has a multiplicity of faces and roles, meaning that there are many ways to approach and connect with her (Scarboro and Luck 1997: 72). *The Secret Circle* novels reflect this, quite explicitly. On the walls of Diana's bedroom hang six art prints of various goddesses which the novels revisit several times. Each time, Cassie notes more details until she and the reader see how each female member of the Circle represents a specific facet of the immanent goddess: Suzan represents Aphrodite, the goddess of love; Deborah epitomizes Artemis, the huntress; Faye, predatory, jealous, and power-hungry, embodies Hera, queen of the Gods; Melanie, the voice of reason in the group, reflects Athena, the goddess of wisdom; Laurel, with her love of plants, connects with Persephone, who loved them, too; and Diana represents the goddess she was named for, Diana, the Queen of the Witches (Smith 2008: 302–3). In the last scene of the trilogy, Diana plans to add a seventh print to her wall—the Muse, looking inspired, the spirit of the arts, which is the costume Cassie chooses for Halloween (2009: 388). Thus, Cassie, too, finds herself in an ancient symbol of feminine power. Notably, the male characters have no such correlation. With its matriarchal leadership and focus on feminine spirituality, then, the text offers the girls something empowering that it doesn't specifically offer the male members, but Cassie notes that "all the guys in the Circle were undisturbed by the girls' rights and privileges. They didn't feel threatened," unlike many men would in a society operating under patriarchal ideals (Smith 2009: 217).

The Circle in the CW's adaptation has no such spiritual grounding, neither in feminist witchcraft nor in any recognizable form of Wicca. While the witches do call on the quarters and elements when casting a circle, we only see them do this once—when they first bind their Circle (1x2 "Bound"). They do use protective circles around dangerous objects, but rather than casting a ritual circle, they use unspecified materials, possibly salt, to draw these circles on the ground, which references more demonology than feminist witchcraft. It feels as if the show picks and chooses things like crystals and herbs and occasional protection circles and uses them as set dressing to remind us these are witches, not aliens or mutants. While, technically, like the books, they came to Chance Harbor from Salem, the only real connection they have to their past are the professional witch hunters. They may use the elements in their spells, if necessary, but it's rare, and none of them have any special connection to them, nor any other higher power. The goddess is absent in any reverential form. They have two Books of Shadows, but they use them to find spells they need at the moment or ways to exercise more power, not to learn about their heritage. They have no sense of the Wiccan Rede—"An it harm none, do as you will"—or the rule of three—what you send out into the world comes back to you threefold, that provide ethical guidance within neopagan and feminist spiritualities (Griffin 2005: 63). Along with this, their practice seems mostly gender neutral. The girls have no greater insight, or connection. Their Circle has no priest or priestess, and while there are four girls and only two boys, this seems more chance than tradition.

"Are you a planning to be a good witch or a bad witch?" Monism vs. Dualism

Unlike Abrahamic faiths and patriarchal ideology, "Wicca is monistic, not dualistic" (Jarvis 2008: 44). This means that it sees everything as part of a unified whole, a totality, rather than divided into binaries like "good" and "evil." Along with the Wiccan Rede this emphasizes responsibility rather than strictures and sin. *The Secret Circle* novels seem to largely take this view, at least regarding witchcraft and magic. When explaining to Cassie how their parents want them to stay away from magic because it's too scary and wicked, Diana argues that it can be used for good as easily as not (Smith 2008: 192). Power is power; what matters is what you do with it. In the climactic battle with Black John, the Circle members call on both creative and destructive natural forces for Power: the sun and the darkness, the waves and the rocks, fire and ice, lightning and dew. It is from the natural world and their attunement with it that they draw their magic—these are the "Old Powers" they have woken and can call on. Further, as discussed more below, Cassie's final vision sees the Circle as interconnected with the totality of life—a monistic view. Black John is a villain and his magic and energy are dark because of his choices, not because of some inherent evil in him or magic.

However, while magic in general seems to be neutral in the television show, "dark magic" is a separate, more powerful thing that only some witches have. It allows even witches bound in a Circle to use individual magic, but, by its very nature, it prompts the witch who has it to do harmful things with it, and the more the witch uses it, the more it will lead him or her down the dark path (1x16 "Lucky"). For example, when Cassie thinks Adam has betrayed her trust, she instinctively uses her dark magic to lash out, almost killing him before she realizes what she's doing (1x11 "Fire/Ice"). The Circle members, thus, see "dark magic" as a separate, inherently evil, force from their own magic, and one only Cassie wields for most of the show: "Miss Innocent here is full of dark magic, evil magic," Faye reminds them (1x11). Despite this, Cassie takes increasingly unethical actions, up to the point of almost killing Diana, deliberately and without her consent, to activate Diana's dark magic (1x22 "Family"). Dark magic, along with the existence of demons, then, serves both to polarize the world into a dualism missing in the novels, and often absolves the "good" characters of responsibility for their actions, in contradiction to the tenets of Wicca and feminist spirituality.

The Good of the Many...

One defining characteristic of third-wave feminism and postfeminism is the focus on the individual and on choice over collective action. These are feminisms where women seek personal freedoms and individual solutions to problems, where women find their individual voice, rather than joining in a collective one (Projansky and Vande Berg 2000: 15; Wolfe 2007: 91). Conversely, second-wave feminism's focus was on coming together to collectively work for large-scale social change, not individual emancipation (Wolfe 2007: 92). This tension between the individual and the collective is a central theme in both versions of *The Secret Circle*, but they resolve in very different ways first when they bind or complete their Circles, and again in how the two narratives end.

In both versions, the witches are more effective, magically, as a group, than they are on their own, but their reasons for wanting to complete, or bind, their Circles come from different motivations. In the novels, the witches want a complete Circle simply because of how much more power having twelve members of the Circle will give them; "You know we need twelve to get anything done," Diana points out (Smith 2008: 176). However, while this communal magic is stronger, individual witches "can do quite a lot on their own" (Smith 2008: 177). Once the Circle initiates Cassie as the twelfth member, the witches can choose to do magic on their own, in small groups, or as a full Circle, with each additional witch's power added to the spell making it stronger. They can be both individual *and* collective.

Conversely, the television show forces the witches to be individual *or* collective. An unbound witch can do magic on his or her own, sometimes very powerful magic, but the witches believe that magic is unstable and hard to control. For example, Faye summons a storm she can't control that nearly kills her one night, and another, lashes out at another girl and kills her by throwing her down onto rocks[6] (1x1 "Pilot"). On the other hand, a bound Circle is much more powerful, but to access that power, they must sacrifice their individual magic. Diana does not share this with the others, so when they agree to bind the Circle, mostly convinced by Faye's disasters, they are angry and shocked to find out the next day that they cannot do even simple spells they'd taken for granted without another witch there (1x2). Further, because they have no experience working collectively, just two witches working together still can do very little for a long time. Faye is furious at having her individual magic stripped away without her consent, and she spends the rest of the show trying to get it back. As soon as the Circle is bound, demons and ghosts start to come after them, the witch hunters start hunting them, and John Blackwell comes to town to claim them. The benefits of giving up their individual power to work as a group often seem not worth the cost, and when their Circle is broken in the final episode and they get their individual magic back, it is only Cassie and Diana's combined dark magic that saves the day, Cassie is the only one who wants to rebind the Circle in the aftermath (1x22). However, Cassie, with her dark magic, can still do individual magic while bound, so she sacrifices nothing to be part of the collective: she and Diana, with their dark magic, can be both individuals and part of the collective. The others' powers are subsumed. The series ends with the Circle broken and most of them relieved to be free of it.

Meanwhile, in the novels, the same truth holds through consistently: no matter what individual witches can do, the Circle is stronger together. They are only able to defeat Black John when they have the complete Circle and all add their individual talents to the collective whole. With only eleven of them, they hurt him, but he rallies. Only when Faye adds in her voice and power to theirs can they summon enough power to destroy Black John (Smith 2009, 374–76). And instead of the broken Circle and scattered individuals the television show finishes with, the novels end with the Circle whole and planning what to do with their newfound power, with, among the "fun" suggestions, ideas including collective social action in environmentalism and improving relations with the non-witches of New Salem. (Smith 2009: 388). The last passage reads, in part: "They were all connected, all part of one another, and the light shone around them to touch the earth and sky and sea.... With her inner vision, Cassie saw that the Circle was part of something bigger, like a spiral that went on and on forever, encompassing everything, touching the stars" (Smith 2009: 389–90).

Femininity and Desire: Subversion vs. Caging

Writing about the power in witches, words, and witchy words, Naomi Goldenberg confesses:

> Witchcraft attracts me because it is rife with magical discourse that encourages us to play with fire. We all recognize magic words when we hear them, and witchy words have magic ... the word witch has magic ... because it brings to mind what every patriarchal institution shuts out: namely, fantasies of maternal, sexual power in all of its complicated, messy, marvelous manifestations [2004: 205].

The Secret Circle novels reflect this subversive, playful spirit, especially as compared to most YA novels, known for their tendency toward latent conservativism which polices girls by "correcting 'aberrant' femininity" (Moseley 2002: 405). They embrace multiplicity in gender performance and sexuality, delight in inherent queerness, and allow space for unconstrained, unruly desire.

Many scholars have argued about the failure of the televisual and cinematic teen witches of the 1990s and 2000s to represent consistent feminist values. In analyzing *Sabrina,* for instance, Sarah Projansky and Leah R. Vande Berg conclude that the show "offers empowering representations of independent girls who have access to equality and engage in cross-gender behavior," while still "constraining those representations within narratives that emphasize beauty, male attention, and taking responsibility for others" (2000: 16). Similarly, Catriona Miller argues that *Charmed* rejects the second-wave feminist reclamation of the "dangerous, powerful, bloody, sexual" witch and replaces it with a postfeminist sensibility focused on producing a "clean and orderly (ladylike) self," with fixed, patriarchal boundaries constraining the Halliwell sisters (2007: 72–73). Looking at a wide variety of teen witch films and television shows, Rachel Moseley concludes the same: the "[u]nconventional wild female space of feminist witchcraft has been transformed. It has become a powerful, girly, sexualized space—a postfeminist space" (2002: 418). While she doesn't specifically mention *The Secret Circle*, Marion Gibson laments, "It might certainly have been expected that late twentieth- and early twenty-first-century texts would offer more of a challenge to this state of affairs" (2006: 102). However, while the novels do offer this challenge, like many of the other teen witch shows of the last 20 years, the CW's *The Secret Circle* falls far short of the promise within its source material. Beyond divorcing itself from the empowering connection to feminist witchcraft, a large part of this results from the fundamental changes the adaptation makes to the main female characters, changes which alter the implicit and explicit messages in the text.

Faye Chamberlain is the "bad-girl" witch of both the novels and television show. In both, she is capricious, a little wild, and reckless, motivated by power and pleasure. However, this is where the similarity ends. In the books, Faye is strong, fearless, and dominant. Cassie is terrified of her at first, and describes her in predatory terms, likening her nails to the talons of a bird of prey three times in the first two novels, and also describing her frequently as one of the large cats: for example, her smile is reminiscent of a "crouching jungle cat," and she works "her long, red-tipped fingers like a cat exercising its claws" (2008: 77, 81). Her predatory nature extends to her sexuality: she is beautiful and sensual, chooses boys who are a challenge, and usually gets them, then discards them when she grows bored. She is a young woman in charge of her body and her sexuality—the embodiment of the type of feminine power and sexuality that Stephen King once said taps into a "historically specific male fear of women" and the type of woman who is "dangerous" to hegemonic femininity (Moseley 2002: 411; Antinora 2010: 121).

In the CW's adaptation, Faye is still wild and hostile to Cassie, but she changes from this confident, dangerous young woman to an insecure girl obsessed with Jake Armstrong,[7] the boy who used, abused, and abandoned her two years before the start of the show (1x6 "Wake"). When he returns to town, however, she dresses as provocatively as she can to go see him, determined to make him regret leaving her. However, he just insults and dismisses her, saying, "You're always so damn clingy, Faye" (1x6). The whole relationship, as well as his consistent denigration of her, becomes more problematic considering their respective ages. In the present, Faye is 16, and Jake is 19, meaning when he seduced and abandoned her, she was 14, and he was 17. Below the age of consent, she was clearly not emotionally prepared for a sexual relationship, as Melissa confirms later in the episode. Finding Faye high on something, balancing on the pier railing, Melissa tries to talk her down, reminding Faye that she was so damaged by Jake's treatment of her two years ago that it "almost put her in a psych ward" (1x6). Although Melissa begs Faye to stay away, Faye refuses to heed her, chasing after Jake for most of the rest of the season. In a related change to her character, when asked how many guys she has slept with during a game of "Truth or Dare," she replies, "Two," and when they all look stunned, adds, "Ooh ... guess I'm not the super slut you all think I am" (1x8 "Beneath"). This slut-shaming is antithetical to third-wave feminism and reflects the ingrained patriarchal norms about confining female sexuality. Combined, this all significantly disempowers Faye, casting her as a victim—prey instead of predator—and turns the subversive witch, taking pleasure where she pleases, heedless of patriarchal authority, into a girl who throws herself at her abuser until he finally decides they should be together at the end of the season.

If Faye is declawed in the adaptation, Diana gains hers. Throughout the novels, Faye and her friends describe Diana as the "Princess of Purity." While Cassie's connotation is more positive, she, too, uses the same word to describe her: "Diana resembled something from a fairy tale or legend more than a real person. But the goodness and—well, *purity* that shone out of Diana's eyes were very real indeed" (Smith 2008: 303–4). She is the light to Faye's darkness, literally: she is blonde and fair, where Faye has black hair and golden skin, and her ceremonial shift is white, while Faye's is black. She is kind to everyone. Even the non-witches, who hate the rest of the Circle, treat her like a princess. Even when she finds out that Cassie and Adam—the love of Diana's life—are soulmates and in love, her first instinct is to step aside and let them be together. She only waits to do so because they beg for another chance to not betray her trust, and she realizes how important her love and trust are to them. But when the time comes, she gives them her blessing to be together: in fact, she insists on it (Smith 2009: 386).

The CW's Diana is not nearly so pure. She is bossy and a little controlling, happy to drink and party with the other teens, and far more sexually adventurous. When she discovers Adam's father believes Adam and Cassie are destined to be together, she becomes jealous and bitter, even though Adam loves and wants to be with Diana, and Cassie fully supports that. But Diana begins consistently picking fights with Adam, accusing him of being jealous of Jake and Cassie's friendship, when he is just as plausibly angry because Jake has stolen a lot of money from Adam's father, and he's worried about Cassie, after what Jake has done to Faye. But Diana continues to try and prove that Adam is jealous, going so far as to dare Cassie to kiss Jake during Truth or Dare, just so she can test Adam to see if it upsets him (1x8). Ultimately, she breaks up with him, even as he tries to make their relationship work. Afterward, she tries to stay friends with Cassie, but the rift between Adam and her becomes a rift between the Circle and her and she tells Cassie that after they deal with the witch hunters, she's out (1x19 "Crystal"). Unlike in the books, her devotion to the Circle and the others breaks, even more so when she finds out that she, too, has dark magic. Unlike Cassie, she doesn't want to use it, but merely possessing it taints whatever "purity" she might have retained from the novels.

Cassie, too, undergoes a profound shift from page to screen. A shy girl, desperately longing to make friends in a new town, a sensitive writer, easily cowed, Cassie begins the novels seeming in many ways like a classic Gothic heroine: somewhat passive, reacting rather than acting, finding herself in danger and needing to be rescued (M. J. Smith and Moruzi 2018: 9). However, even from the start, the text reveals there is more to her than that. The day she first meets Adam, she protects him from witch hunters, finding him a place to hide, and then telling the hunters he has gone in the opposite direction. She sticks to her story, even when she sees one of them has a gun and another grabs her and twists her wrist, injuring her. Later, when bullied by Faye, and before knowing she is a witch, she instinctively draws upon the power of Earth to ground her and give her strength. Her progress fluctuates, but each novel sees her getting stronger until she leads her Circle against the evil that is her father and defeats him.

Meanwhile, the CW's Cassie is a loner with no desire to join the Circle or make friends with them. Rather than finding Faye intimidating, Cassie calls her out from the start, and never backs down from a fight with her. Cassie is the one who wields dark magic first, and she steps into a leadership role in the Circle almost immediately, simply by virtue of an assertive personality. Unlike her book counterpart, her mistakes cause far more harm than anything she does to save them. She is neither innocent nor shy. When Faye asks her if she's ever going to go for a guy who isn't sleeping with someone else, Cassie finds Jake alone and makes a move on him, saying she's been accused of doing a lot of things, so maybe she should try at least one of them (1x8). Her growth over the season is in her desire to connect to others and coming to value them as her family, as she loses more and more of her blood family, but, like Diana and Faye, she goes through no fundamental change over the course of the series.

These changes to Faye, Diana and Cassie, combined with the loss of the other four female characters from the novels, also alter the representational and "witchy" nature of the novels and render the CW's *The Secret Circle* into a typical teen drama. While the changes to Faye and Diana might make them more "realistic" characters, they do so by making them more like every other teenage girl on TV, eliminating what is unique about them and destroying the allegorical relationship to one another the novels create. Faye is no longer dark and dangerous—she's a stereotypical petulant bad girl. In the novels, Diana may arguably be too good to be true, but she is the light to Faye's darkness. When she is turned into a character more concerned with her boyfriend than her Circle, the light in the series all but disappears. In the novels, the two characters are balanced—first cousins, they are both descendants of the same family line, two sides of the same coin. Contemplating reincarnation and an ancestor of theirs she had seen in a vision, Cassie even wonders if a reincarnated soul can split into two (Smith 2009: 388). At first glance, this may seem simplistic, but this is not a reiteration of the Madonna/Whore dichotomy; rather, the text does not value one over the other—both are absolutely necessary for the community's survival. Cassie becomes the epicenter of their balance, both light and dark, and together they represent a form of the Triple Goddess, and, at the novels' end, they lead the Circle as a triumvirate. While the changes in Cassie for the TV adaptation may have arisen out of a fear that her quiet, inner strength that overcomes her anxiety and insecurity isn't "plucky" enough for a teenage heroine in 2011, eliminating the concepts of opposition and balance from the narrative strips a great deal of its richness and is another severed connection to the feminist witchcraft tradition.

This severing of connection is also evident in the adaptation's loss of the other four female characters from the novels: Suzan, Melanie, Laurel, and Deborah. In some ways, the girls in the books are archetypal, but with their elemental, archetypal characteristics, they also are, like the prints on Diana's wall, a study in the many ways to be a woman, all of which the novel argues are valid. From pure to wickedly sensual, obsessed with boys to scornful of heterosexual romance, quiet to exuberant, practical to mystical, the text celebrates them all and shows the strength they can have when they accept and value what each brings to the table. The adaptation's elimination of this diversity in the presentation of womanhood leaves us with girls who are far more hegemonic and homogenous; this is even more true when considering the loss of Deborah, specifically. Drawing on Alexander Doty, Projansky and Vande Berge argue that "the more the show insists on heterosexuality in the face of close female relationships, the more material there is available for a spectator who reads from a 'queer' perspective" (2000: 24). This can be true for books, as well, and, in *The Secret Circle* novels, even the "insistence" on heterosexuality is tenuous. While, admittedly, all the explicit romances are heterosexual, Deborah is clearly coded as queer, especially for novels from the early 1990s: her hair is short, she rides a motorcycle, she abandons dances to play poker with the boys in the boiler room, and Suzan implies that she never notices boys. She skips out on a party where Faye and Suzan are seducing pizza delivery boys to offer Cassie a ride on her motorcycle, where she takes her all over the island, sharing her favorite places (2009: 23–28). Notably, when the show tries to recreate this pizza party, Cassie leaves to be with Adam, which, retrospectively, paints her ride with Deborah in the novels even more colors of queer (1x14 "Valentine"). Cassie, too, can be read as at least bi-curious—she notices the other girls' beauty in extreme detail, is fascinated by Deborah and finds their ride one of the most exhilarating experiences of her life, and is drawn to Faye's allure in ways that make her uncomfortable with herself. Nothing is explicit, but the queerness is easy to find. Conversely, the show is stringently heterosexual in a way that seems to cut off even queer appropriation, and this lack of queerness further reinforces the patriarchal feminine ideal.

"The boy is mine": Hegemonic Femininity

While the characters in the novels are far from perfect, Melissa and the television versions of Faye, Diana, and Cassie reflect many of the shortcomings of postfeminism, including a femininity constrained within the traditional feminine ideal valued by patriarchal forces. The "powerful and painfully present unruly witch" is gone, domesticated—still sexy, but respectably so, for the most part, and confined to heterosexual romance (Moseley 2002: 421–22). In analyzing *Sabrina the Teenage Witch* (1996–2003), Projansky and Vande Berg argue that "the show … narratively assent[s] to the traditional feminine notion that the whole purpose of striving for beauty is to acquire the attention of males" (2000: 29). In a patriarchal society, girls learn that part—sometimes, even most—of their power rests in their ability to attract men. Already problematic in substance, this limited scope of power leads to competition rather than cooperation between women, separating them from support and rendering them even more vulnerable to patriarchal power (Shugart, Waggoner, and Hallstein 2001: 205). While the novels have a couple of scenes of the girls getting ready for school dances, and hoping the guys find them attractive, this never leads to competition, nor does any male attention they do receive become more than momentarily flattering. Throughout the novels, five or six of the seven girls are single, and, although Cassie's feelings for Nick and Adam are always there, they never dominate the larger narrative—the relationships she builds with the women receive far more time. Rather, the real competition in the books is not for male sexual attention, but actual power—the leadership of the Circle.

As seen above with the individual characters, however, a strong focus on heterosexual relationships, including a lot of competition over boys, is a continuous issue in the television show. Even Faye and Melissa, who have no serious interest in the same guy, find themselves drawing on magic to compete for the attention of the school's star hockey player (1x18 "Sacrifice"). This friction over boys prevents the girls from ever coming together in the way they do in the books. Even worse, the girls define themselves by and focus their happiness on boys. At first, Melissa and Nick's relationship consists of him using her for sex and mocking her when she signals she wants more. Just when he decides to open up and take a risk with her, he dies, and Melissa grieves for him the rest of the season. I've already detailed Faye's obsession with Jake, above. Diana, too, defines herself against Adam, completely lost when she loses him, even though it is her own doing. She very quickly falls for a mysterious young man who is at least 21 (five years older than her), and, after no more than three dates, runs away with him at the end of the series, leaving her Circle and female friends behind (1x22).

The replacement of sexual agency with sexual victimhood, constant insecurity over boys and a willingness to be treated badly by them, competition instead of cooperation, the elimination of queerness—all these changes in the adaptation weaken the original feminist rhetoric of the text. The characters may not have been as fleshed out in the novels, due to Cassie's limited point of view, but neither are they flat—they are symbolic, and their symbolism stands for much of the more radical and liberating doctrines of second-wave feminism. Meanwhile, the girls in the show are often aware of their lack of love and dysfunctional relationships, but fall right back into the same confining, regressive behaviors that leave them disconnected from each other, themselves, and any higher connections at the end of the narrative. Faye is the only one who seems to learn to value her connection to the others at the end, blowing off Jake to celebrate the return of their individual magic with Melissa. However, since her choosing Melissa is only for one night—she and Jake kiss before she goes off with Melissa—this moment of possible growth is too brief to shift the rest of the narrative.

Conclusion

Writing for *Vogue* about the exclusion of the original *Secret Circle* novels from the canon of '90s teen witches, Julia Felsenthal contends that *The*

Secret Circle "never imprinted on the culture as firmly as it should have." Acknowledging that it did get adapted into a television series, she adds, "If you happened to catch any of it, please disregard everything you think you know." The show could have been so much more, but I disagree with Felsenthal about the impact the novels made. They may have been consciously forgotten in the intervening decades, but the novels' legacy lives on, unacknowledged. Indeed, seeds of *The Secret Circle* novels can be seen in much of what came after: *Practical Magic*, *The Craft*, *Buffy the Vampire Slayer*, and *Charmed*, among others, all rely on themes and tropes that *The Secret Circle* novels brought to teen-witch narratives. Further, the novels provide a template for teen witches that offers the possibility for what Nickianne Moody contends is the role of the representation of the teenage witch in media and society: "a cultural interest in using fantasy to challenge and subvert emerging and prevailing social norms particularly those, which are so contradictory regarding gender and generational politics and power" (2005: 57). At the same time, she argues that there is a "commercially successful contract" between producers and audiences, not that all teen witches be the same, but that there are ways they should be represented in narrative (2005: 59). Perhaps it was that unspoken agreement the TV version of *The Secret Circle* was trying to fulfill in replicating the problems with other witch narratives. But those narratives were a decade before, and *The Secret Circle* failed on television.

Meanwhile, the same subversive elements that make the novels so interesting turn up, albeit in different forms (less goddesses and crystals, more Satan and blood) in Netflix's highly successful *Sabrina*: what it means to be a woman with power; what the price is; what responsibility it brings; the knowledge that there will be powerful men who want to take your power and use it to increase their own, or who will try to destroy you if you step too far out of line; how a support network of other women, sisters, can save you; that competition, selfishness, and pride get you nowhere, but cooperation and collective action can save you from your Satanic (or evil, twice-resurrected, super-powerful witch) father. It may have taken nearly a quarter of a century, but as we move forward in this one, hopefully more shows will use the teenage witch not to show yet more images of "girl power" allowed to expand only to the boundaries of hegemony, but to challenge and subvert the foundations of an oppressive ideology and revive the discourse that builds bridges instead of walls between women. And, hopefully, when they do, we can recognize both the debt such depictions owe to the seeds planted by Smith's novels and that being a failed adaptation may be one reason the CW's *The Secret Circle* was also a failed television show.

Notes

1. The original trilogy consists of *The Initiation*, *The Captive* and *The Power*, all published in 1992, and is a complete narrative. After the television show aired in 2012, the later novels in the series came out, but although, due to various contract details, the later novels bear Smith's name as author, they are, in fact, written by Aubrey Clark, after Alloy fired Smith. Therefore, since the television show is adapted from the original trilogy, I only consider those first three novels in my analysis in this essay.
2. While Greene's study focuses on film and television, she includes a thorough discussion of the influence of the original, book versions of *The Witches of Eastwick* and *Practical Magic* and other print texts that became TV shows or movies.
3. Their word for coven.
4. This is an interesting avenue of criticism to pursue, but, as it falls outside of discussions of gender and power, I have left it for another time. However, it is significant enough to bear mentioning for further inquiry.
5. They do not use the term High Priestess, but the role is the same.
6. The girl is able to be revived by one of the older witches, so none of the teens are aware the girl actually died, but the audience is.
7. Jake is not in the books, but a new character added for the show, to replace his brother Nick. While Nick carries the same name as the book character, like Faye, Diana, and Cassie, he has nothing in common with the book version either.

References

Antinora, Sarah. 2010. "The Simpsons, Gender Roles and Witchcraft: The Witch in Modern Popular Culture." *452°F. Electronic Journal of Theory of Literature and Comparative Literature* 3: 115–30.
Cush, Denise. 2007. "Consumer Witchcraft: Are Teenage Witches a Creation of Commercial Interests?" *Journal of Beliefs & Values* 28, 1: 45–53. https://doi.org/10.1080/13617670701251439.
Felsenthal, Julia. 2017. "Before There Was Twilight, Harry Potter, and Goop-Approved Crystals, There Was the Secret Circle." *Vogue*, June 19. https://www.vogue.com/article/the-secret-circle-young-adult-witch-fiction.
Gibson, Marion. 2006. "Retelling Salem Stories: Gender Politics and Witches in American Culture." *European Journal of American Culture* 25, 2: 85–107. https://doi.org/10.1386/ejac.25.2.85/1.
Goldenberg, Naomi R. 2004. "Witches and Words." *Feminist Theology: The Journal of the Britain & Ireland School of Feminist Theology* 12, 2: 203–11. https://doi.org/10.1177/096673500401200207.
Gordon, Rebecca. 1995. "Earthstar Magic: A Feminist Theoretical Perspective on the Way of the Witches and the Path to the Goddess." *Social Alternatives* 14, 4: 9.
Greene, Heather. 2018. *Bell, Book and Camera: A Critical History of Witches in American Film and Television*. Jefferson, NC: McFarland.
Griffin, Wendy. 2005. "Webs of Women: Feminist Spiritualities." In *Witchcraft and Magic: Contemporary North America*, edited by Helen A. Berger, 55–80. Philadelphia: University of Pennsylvania Press.
Jarvis, Christine. 2008. "Becoming a Woman Through Wicca: Witches and Wiccans in Contemporary Teen Fiction." *Children's Literature in Education* 39, 1: 43–52. https://doi.org/10.1007/s10583-007-9058-0.
Miller, Catriona. 2007. "'I Just Want to Be Normal Again': Power and Gender in Charmed." In *Investigating Charmed: The Magic Power of TV*, edited by Karen Beeler and Stan Beeler, 67–78. New York: I.B. Tauris.
Moody, Nickianne. 2005. "Modern Apprenticeships for Girls: The Teenage Witch Convention in Young Adult Fiction." In *Children's Fantasy Fiction: Debates for the Twenty First Century*, 57–73. Liverpool: Association for Research in Popular Fictions, John Moores University Press.

Moseley, Rachel. 2002. "Glamorous Witchcraft: Gender and Magic in Teen Film and Television." *Screen* 43, 4: 403–22.

Projansky, Sarah, and Leah R. Vande Berg. 2000. "Sabrina, the Teenage…? Girls, Witches, Mortals, and the Limitations of Prime-Time Feminism." In *Fantasy Girls: Gender in the New Universe of Science Fiction and Fantasy Television*, edited by Elyce Rae Helford, 13–40. Lanham, MD: Rowman & Littlefield.

Scarboro, Allen, and Philip Andrew Luck. 1997. "The Goddess and Power: Witchcraft and Religion in America." *Journal of Contemporary Religion* 12, 1: 69–79. https://doi.org/10.1080/13537909708580790.

Shugart, Helene, Catherine Egley Waggoner, and D. Lynn O'Brien Hallstein. 2001. "Mediating Third-Wave Feminism: Appropriation as Postmodern Media Practice." *Critical Studies in Media Communication* 18, 2: 194–210. https://doi.org/10.1080/07393180128079.

Smith, L.J. 2008. *The Initiation and the Captive Part I*. 1st HarperTeen pbk. ed. The Secret Circle. New York: HarperTeen.

———. 2009. *The Captive Part II and the Power*. 1st HarperTeen pbk. ed. The Secret Circle. New York: HarperTeen.

Smith, Michelle J., and Kristine Moruzi. 2018. "Vampires and Witches Go to School: Contemporary Young Adult Fiction, Gender, and the Gothic." *Children's Literature in Education* 49, 1: 6–18. https://doi.org/10.1007/s10583-018-9343-0.

Van Fossan, Dolly. 2012. "Feminist Witchcraft: A Radical Woman's Religion." *Journal of Theta Alpha Kappa* 36, 2: 71–85.

Winslade, J. Lawton. 2001. "Teen Witches, Wiccans, and 'Wanna-Blessed-Be's': Pop-Culture Magic in Buffy the Vampire Slayer." *Slayage: The Online International Journal of Buffy Studies* 1, 1. https://www.whedonstudies.tv/uploads/2/6/2/8/26288593/winslade_slayage_1.1.pdf.

Wolfe, Susan J. 2007. "Charming the Elders: Girl Power for Second-Wave Feminists." In *Investigating Charmed: The Magic Power of TV*, edited by Karen Beeler and Stan Beeler, 90–100. New York: I.B. Tauris.

The Witches of the West and the Boundaries of Goodness

Lindsey Mantoan

In 1975, Margaret Hamilton, famous for playing the iconic Wicked Witch of the West in the 1939 MGM film *The Wizard of Oz*, appeared on the *Mister Rogers* show. Hunched and in a pink button-down dress, she was at the time seventy-three years old and a grandmother of three. She guested on the show in an effort to demystify her role as the Wicked Witch, so that children might not be so scared of her; the fear and dread from children encountering her in real life had pained and saddened Hamilton for decades. A life-long advocate for children and education, Hamilton had been a schoolteacher prior to landing her role in the classic film, and she shared stories with Mr. Rogers about dressing up as a witch for Halloween as a young girl. Mr. Rogers pointed out that "girls *and* boys like to play witches. A witch is a fine thing to play." Indeed, the dialogue and action of this carefully crafted seven-minute segment framed the Wicked Witch as a character Hamilton puts on, rather than who she is; she discussed how challenging it was for her to eat lunch during filming without messing up the makeup on her hands and face, Rogers helped Hamilton don parts of the Wicked Witch's costume, and Hamilton switched back and forth from her own slightly warbly voice to the high-pitched cackle of the Wicked Witch. She offered audiences an empathetic reading of the Wicked Witch of the West's behavior:

> Sometimes the children feel that she's a very mean witch. And I expect she does seem that way. But I always think that there are two things about her. She does enjoy everything she does, whether it's good or bad. She enjoys it. But she's also what we refer to as frustrated. She's-she's very unhappy because she never gets what she wants. [...] I just think that sometimes we think that she's just mean and a very bad person. But actually, we have to think about her point of view.

Hamilton confessed that children often asked her why she was so mean to Dorothy, and she reminded audiences of *Mister Rogers' Neighborhood*: "It's just pretend." Mr. Rogers chimed in with: "All witches don't have to be bad, either."

Indeed, this last assertion generally gets lost in the cultural imaginary about *The Wizard of Oz*, where the Wicked Witch of the West seems to signify all witches and Glinda, although called a "good witch," signifies more as a fairy, with her floating orb and tiara. Hamilton's Wicked Witch joins a long genealogy of terrifying magical women who prey on children for power, youth, beauty, and pleasure. From Hansel and Gretel's witch, who wants to consume the little children, to Snow White's witch, who wants to be the fairest of them all, witches seldom have names and almost always use enchantment for violence against children. Yet with the blockbuster popularity of Gregory Maguire's 1995 novel *Wicked: The Life and Times of the Wicked Witch of the West*, and Stephen Schwartz and Winnie Holzman's 2003 Broadway musical adaptation *Wicked*, the image of the Wicked Witch has been recuperated—or at least, complicated. Dozens of adaptations of L. Frank Baum's original Oz narrative, the first and arguably only U.S. fairy tale, rethink the original story's framing of a certain kind of America—particularly U.S. politics regarding class, race, gender, and the urban/rural divide—and also a certain kind of witch.

Oz has often been a site where the U.S. imaginary can work through questions of identity—both national and personal—and values. NBC's dystopian *Emerald City* (2017) suggests that patriarchal persecution of women has created the conditions for Oz's downfall. Amazon's *Lost in Oz* (2015–2018), a brightly animated show aimed at children, puts forward two arguments: that female friendship is necessary for the security and prosperity of the community, and almost every villain can be saved. In both of these adaptations of the Oz narrative, the Witch of the West figure makes mistakes and has a dark side, but cannot be said to be evil, and also demonstrates goodness, too. This essay explores multiple representations of the Witch of the West against the backdrop of values related to good and evil, looking specifically at Mistress West in *Emerald City* and West in *Lost in Oz*. I ask: which behaviors fall under the category of "mistakes," which ones are counted as "evil," and how do gender and magic influence these value judgments? How does the figure of the Witch of the West intersect with other witches, the Dorothy figure, and the Wizard, especially in terms of who is granted forgiveness, who is written off as irredeemable, who is allowed a position of prominence in the community, and who is isolated or abandoned? And, haunting all these questions, is: what do these women say about fantasies of U.S. utopia, home, and belonging? In what follows, I present an overview of the Oz narrative and its cultural importance and a genealogy of its adaptations. I analyze the figure of the Witch of the West and her evolution in narratives across multiple media. I then offer a focused investigation of *Emerald City* and *Lost in Oz* as two recent television representations of this mercurial character.

Witches West, East, South and North

Part of the appeal of Oz narratives are their dual nature as both fairy tale and distinctly U.S. story. L. Frank Baum's children's book *The Wizard of Oz* reflects his desire to broaden the fairy tale genre into America, and this story in all its incarnations raises questions of both personal and national identities. By leaving rural Kanas and traveling to Baum's Oz, a world filled with color and magic, "one is forced to become aware of what is absent in America" (Zipes 2006: 128). Given the proliferation of adaptations of Dorothy's journey through Oz, Baum's work "paved the way for later writers to experiment even more with the potential of *sequel* fairy tales to present radical alternatives to social reality" (Zipes 2006: 127). These iterations, whatever the media, position themselves against not only the original, but also against markers of U.S. identity; according to Ryan Bunch, for example, the MGM film *The Wizard of Oz* translates "the already powerful symbolic national mythology of Baum's book into participatory expressions of American identity through embodied performance" (Bunch 2015: 54). Critics starting with Henry Littlefield in 1964 theorize that Baum's story stakes a position in the nineteenth-century debate about U.S. monetary policy, with the Yellow Brick Road representing the gold standard, Dorothy's iconic shoes representing silver (MGM made them ruby, but they were silver in the original), and Oz itself named for the periodic table abbreviation of the element gold. Others theorize that the Scarecrow stands in for U.S. farmers and the Wicked Witch represents westward expansion. While some interpretations might be more supportable than others, they all grapple with economic and political questions about the past and future of the U.S.

Thus, Oz narratives reflect both U.S. values as well as the multifaceted considerations of psychology endemic to fairy tales. Common misconceptions about fairy tales include the notions that they are children's stories (adults revel in them and their origins in the court of Louis XIV and exclusive Parisian solons explain in part why they feature explicit sexual references, rape, and voyeurism), and that they always teach lessons. Rather, most scholars of folk and fairy tales agree that their appeal lies in their power to help people young and old grapple with unconscious longings and fears. Psychoanalysts in particular are drawn to fairy tales, with Bruno Bettelheim's foundational *The Uses of Enchantment: Meaning and Importance of Fairy Tales* fixating on penis envy, fear of castration, and Oedipal longings.

Like most fairy tales, the Oz narrative is familiar in its narrative structure of protagonist leaving home, having an adventure, and returning forever altered. Dorothy exhibits the bravery and grit typically reserved for male heroes, although Alissa Burger writes that "Dorothy's desire to return home reaffirms her traditional gender role," and explains that female adventurers must commit to themselves to the domestic sphere, happily sacrificing their love of adventure and affirming instead their place in the home (Burger 2010: 125). The Scarecrow might weep when Dorothy prepares to return to Kansas at the end of the story, and Dorothy herself might feel a pang of loss as she bids goodbye to her new friends, but the narrative leaves no room for doubt that Dorothy has come to prefer the rural house she has once tried to run away from to the magical realm of Oz.

If goodness in women means that they selflessly long for home, narratives framing ambitious women as evil signal society's anxiety about the loss of traditional gender roles. The Wicked Witch stands in for female threats to male authority, and Baum's Wizard tells Dorothy: "One of my greatest fears was the Witches, for while I had no magical powers at all I soon found out that the Witches were really able to do wonderful things.... The Witches of the East and West were terribly Wicked, and had they not thought I was more powerful than themselves, they would surely have destroyed me" (Baum 2011: 144). The Wizard offers no explanation or evidence of the Witches' wickedness, however, and Dorothy, and by extension the readers and audience for this story, are meant to accept the word of a male charlatan rather than attempt to understand the perspective of powerful women. Burger explains this effect: "The Wicked Witch is defined by her desire alone, which makes her uncontrollable; she is the personification of excessive female power, terrifying and horrific" (Burger 2010: 127). Reflective of a society that sought to control women by relegating them to the domestic sphere, Baum and MGM's creation of the Wicked Witch serves as an outlet for Dorothy's repressed female desire for power which then gets sublimated by the witch's demise, signaling the maturation of a girl into domestic womanhood and eventual motherhood.

Many subsequent iterations of the Oz narrative refigure female ambition as not inherently evil, but as a complex set of behaviors that might make a character "good" or "bad" depending on her methods and objectives. *The Wiz*, for example, offers a varied understanding of witches and their behavior that retains the clear line between good and evil while also providing more backstory and voice to the Wicked Witch of the West, here named Evillene. While the 1978 film launches Dorothy's journey to Oz from Harlem rather than the Midwest, the 2015 NBC Live version retains the rural nostalgia present in Baum's story; regardless of the version, however, *The Wiz* "make an African-American claim on a presumptively white

American fairy tale" (Bunch 2015: 61). In the NBC Live musical, Mary J. Blige's Evillene is afforded the opportunity to sing, the primary currency of musicals. Evillene might have epic vocals, but she also embodies capitalist greed at the expense of humane conditions; she is essentially a slave-owner whose demise results in the liberation of African Americans who burst out singing the show-stopping number "Brand New Day." She's not evil because of her ability to control magic and threaten the Wizard's patriarchal authority; her wickedness stems from her human rights abuses. Good Witches abound in this adaptation; Addapearle (Amber Riley) and Glinda the Good Witch of the South (Uzo Aduba) guide Dorothy through Oz and then back home, and their soulful ballads reflect the nostalgia for home and family that so defined the original MGM film.

While *The Wiz* retains the original narrative's binary good/evil values system, subsequent imaginings of the story foreground moral grayness, moving past the narrative's—and by extension, society's—harmful and limiting subject positions for women (innocent young girl, power-hungry crone). The earliest significant embrace of ethical nuance in Oz can be located in Gregory Maguire's *Wicked: The Life and Times of the Wicked Witch of the West* (1995) and Stephen Schwartz and Winnie Holzman's stage musical *Wicked* (2003). Here, the Wicked Witch of the West bears a portmanteau name Elphaba, taken from the first sounds of each name in "L. Frank Baum." The witches of *Wicked* include Elphaba's best friend Glinda the Good (formerly Galinda) and her sister Nessarose, the Wicked Witch of the East. Foregrounding Elphaba's evolution from awkward outcast to political activist, *Wicked* subverts the classic narrative of Dorothy's journey through Oz—Dorothy, in fact, doesn't even appear on stage in *Wicked*. An explicitly political piece, *Wicked* centers on Elphaba and Glinda's relationship and also features a subplot in which talking Animals are more and more marginalized in Oz, to the point that they lose their ability to speak. Advocating for Animal rights, Elphaba seeks assistance from the Wizard, only to learn that he's the one orchestrating the Animals' downfall. Elphaba and Glinda adopt different tactics in response to the Wizard's villainy; Glinda seeks power through celebrity and becomes a leader beloved by all of Oz in order to work for change within the system, while Elphaba embraces her scapegoat status in order to fight the status quo. Burger describes this incarnation of the Witch of the West thus: "Elphaba has alternating moments of selflessness and ambition, refusing a singular, fixed identity. She is a flawed and imperfect woman: as such, Elphaba defies easy categorization as 'good' or 'evil,' necessitating a more complex reading of gender identity" (Burger 2010: 64). Elphaba's character both demonstrates expanding societal views of the roles available to women and provides a platform through which to continue opening possibilities for women.

If Dorothy and the Wicked Witch are diametrically opposed in Baum's story and MGM's film, and Dorothy's quest puts her in relation to a variety of male characters who need her help, recent Oz adaptations center on female relationships and investigate the ways in which friendship and romance might queer U.S. identity. Stacy Wolf cogently and persuasively demonstrates that the conventions of the musical frame Elphaba and Glinda's relationship as the queer romance at the center of the story. She argues that the multiple duets the women sing, the way their voices interact—crisscrossing each other in harmonies off-set by powerful unison moments—and their physical positions on the stage vis-à-vis each other and the scenery, match the trajectories of the heterosexual couples that dominate musical theater (Wolf 2010). I contend below that audiences see echoes of this queered female relationship in Amazon's *Lost in Oz*—in both narratives, witches make mistakes and sometimes have questionable motives, but the story refuses to vilify them and instead invites audiences to love them through the affection directed at them by another woman in the narrative.

Continuing the trend of representing morally complex magical women, Sci-Fi's 2007 3-episode miniseries *Tin Man* reconsiders the Oz narrative in terms of sisterhood, home, and collaboration. D.G. is wrenched from Kansas via tornado, but she soon learns that she's the daughter of a deposed Queen; the O.Z., or Outer Zone is her real home; and her sister Azkadellia has claimed the throne and seems utterly evil. D.G.'s journey in *Tin Man* is as much through her memories as it is through the O.Z., and as she cracks the magic sealing them off from her consciousness she sees visions of the past, including her impetuous decision as a child that led to Azkadellia being abducted and possessed by the shape-shifting "Evil Witch of the Dark." Adult D.G.'s objective becomes as much about saving her sister as about saving the O.Z. Overtly sexualized and focused entirely on increasing her power, the "wicked witch" Azkadellia seems for the first half of the series to be unredeemable. Yet Burger argues, "While Azkadellia is perceived as powerful and evil, her possession reframes her as one of the most powerless characters in the film, with almost no agency or power other than the brief moments when she is able to resist the witch within, moments that are characterized by exhaustion, terror, and great sadness" (Burger 2012: 72–73). The audience's orientation shifts from antipathy and revulsion for Azkadellia to pity and sorrow. The final moment of the conflict sees Azkadellia and D.G. hold hands while repelling the Witch; their combined strength and sisterly love save not only one sister but also the entire realm. The narrative converses with *Wicked* in that both foregrounds female friendship as a political force for change.

Writing about the original *Wizard of Oz* film, Raymond Knapp finds,

"The function of Oz, within the larger story, is to provide its child a place of empowerment [...] a place where she can be taken seriously and can fight back against adults who threaten her and wrong her." He considers "the film to function as an *American* fairy tale: it is not enough just to *be* good and deserving [...] one must also *act*" (Knapp 2006: 140). The flip-side of Knapp's argument is also true for contemporary narratives set in Oz: it is not enough villains to *be* bad. These recent adaptations blur lines between good and evil and place characters in gray areas. New adaptations set in Oz often seek to recuperate stereotypes associated with witches, transforming them into an activist and martyr (*Wicked*), a guilt-plagued brothel owner suffering from addiction (*Emerald City*), a caring sister whose body is possessed by an evil demon (*Tin Man*), or an adolescent teenager who loves Dorothy so much that her magic cannot function properly without her (*Lost in Oz*). With these reimaginings of Oz stories, the Wicked Witch of the West is no longer the stuff of nightmares, and by breaking open the figure of the witch to allow a fuller range of characteristics, these adaptations message to audiences that magic in the hands of women is not inherently evil, that characters of all genders can be complicated and nuanced, and that female ambition can benefit the entire community. These representations work against misogyny and patriarchy in a country were both remain firmly entrenched systems that structure politics, economics, and social dynamics.

Lost in Oz, Female Friendship, and Access to Redemption

Pitched at a young audience ages 4–12, Amazon Prime's original animated series *Lost in Oz* draws on what has become an established genealogy of sisterhood, female friendship, and arguably queer resonances between two female leads in Oz. As in most adaptations of the Oz narrative, Dorothy is a young girl from Kansas swept away to a magical land via tornado. The futuristic Oz she finds herself in suffers from a magic crisis and Glinda the Good is missing. Dorothy quickly befriends West, a precocious young witch; Ojo, an oversized Munchkin; Reigh, a conspiracy-theorist hacker Lion; and Scarecrow, Glinda's former advisor. The team encounters a series of villains, many of whom confront their mistakes and repent as their interactions with Dorothy and her crew change them. These villains include Fitz the Magician, a grade-school-aged sorcerer stealing magical elements (magic in this world comes solely from physical gems and stones) and King Roquat, a tyrannical child who bullies everyone. The two villains who are written off as unredeemable are General Guph, a narcissistic bully, and possibly Langwidere, a charismatic and powerful witch who turns out to be West's aunt. Eventually, Glinda is restored to her rightful place as leader of Oz, Langwidere is confined inside a painting, and the show undoes the binary understanding of home typical of most Oz narratives; it's clear Dorothy considers both worlds hers.

Dorothy's character across Oz adaptations has been much more static than the witches have been. Audiences learn near the end of Season One that this Dorothy is the great-granddaughter of the original Dorothy Gale; thus, this adaptation follows *Tin Man*'s lead in making the Dorothy at the center of its story a direct descendant of the well-known girl from Kansas who first took audiences to Oz. (In *Tin Man*, DG's father leads to her a portal that transports her to Kansas of the past, where she meets who he describes as: "Your greatest grandmother. The original slipper. First to make it through to the OZ from the other side" [*Tin Man* 1x3].) In *Lost in Oz*, Dorothy learns of her ancestor's deeds through Langwidere, who seeks revenge for the destruction wrought on her family by the original Gale. *Lost in Oz*'s Dorothy demonstrates bravery, loyalty, and commitment to doing what's right. Like her namesake, her goodness is never in doubt. Dressed in jeans, a white t-shirt, a red sweater, and white-and-blue checked Vans that harken back to the original MGM Dorothy's gingham dress, Dorothy appears as an accessible "everybody" figure for a contemporary adolescent audience.

Her foil in *Lost in Oz* is West, another 11-year-old girl descended from another iconic Ozian family. West, super skinny and goth, with asymmetric, purple hair, longs to master magic, to expand the boundaries of what science and sorcery can create. Filled with angst and snark, West flirts with darkness and mocks Dorothy's goodness. She sometimes confuses ambition and villainy, the way many representations of strong women do; yet when West dances too close to the edge of harming others for her own gain, Dorothy guides her toward recognizing that magical and scientific advancements don't have to come at the expense of the community. This dynamic between the two, that West might easily pursue power at the expense of goodness were it not for Dorothy, gets established in the first episode. Although she asks Dorothy to "bug off" in their first encounter, by the end of Episode One the two girls are saying the same thing at the same time. Under the influence of magic, West starts to teeter too close to darkness, and Dorothy rescues her. West tells her new friend, "I guess I lost myself there for a minute," to which Dorothy responds, "Found you!" Their friendship hits numerous bumps; West occasionally insults Dorothy and her pride prevents her from admitting how much she's come to care about her. And yet the climax of Season One, when Langwidere threatens to kill Dorothy, sees West rush to her friend's side with no weapon, no magic, and no plan. She grabs Dorothy's hand and, instead of dying together, their physical connection enables West to create magic from thin air—sparks and color emanate from their two hands clasped together and even though she has no physical magical elements, West magically repels Langwidere.

West's heretofore unheard of magical abilities serve as a metaphor for female development and parallels coming out narratives. After that powerful moment when she overcomes her aunt, another tornado takes Dorothy away and West struggles to conjure magic at will; she's unable to create even sparks until she starts talking about Dorothy. At night, she dreams about Dorothy and magic erupts out of her in her sleep, awakening her horrified mother, Cyra. A witch in her own right and formerly besties with Glinda and Dorothy's mother, Cyra firmly believes in the limits of magic. She has restricted use of her own powers to what amounts to massage therapy, and her lack of ambition serves as a direct contrast to Lanwidere's thirst for power. She instructs West not to tell anyone she once produced intrinsic magic and vows to make sure it never happens again. Nevertheless, it happens to West again at school the next day; she falls asleep in class and when Dorothy appears in her dreams again, magic bursts from her and fills the classroom.

A psychoanalytic reading of West's nocturnal fantasies and the literal sparks they create suggest sexual desire for her friend Dorothy. While Cyra's efforts at closeting West fracture her sense of self, her friend Ojo, like any good queer ally, gathers books and conducts research to help West be who she is. Glinda advises her Cyra to let West out of the closet, saying, "If she represses her magical ability, it will come out of her in dangerous ways" (2x2 "Magic from Nothing"). The threat of the dangerous consequences of self-denial lurking in the background—that the internal damage of closeting herself might manifest in external violence to herself or others—is alleviated by Ojo's support.

If West and Dorothy's friendship reads, like *Wicked*'s Elphaba and Glinda's, as potentially queer, then West's relationship with Langwidere reads as an older mentor abusing her apprentice. Langwidere manipulates West through spectacular displays of magic and dissembling about the consequences of their magic on those around them. Langwidere seeks to convince West that their talent and intelligence grant them moral authority over the less-skilled commoners around them (a little like Grindelwald and Dumbledore, minus the sexual tension). Where West's mother is a heavy-set, unfashionable woman who views magic with caution, Langwidere is gorgeous and displays her magic with abandon, adding to the myriad ways in which she's a compelling and dangerous mentor. What Salmon Rushdie writes of the original witches of Oz resonates here:

Of course, Glinda is "good" and the Wicked Witch is "bad"; but Glinda is a trilling pain in the neck and the Wicked Witch is lean and mean. [...] Glinda simpers upon being called beautiful, and denigrates her unbeautiful sisters; whereas the Wicked Witch is in a rage because of the death of her sister, demonstrating, one might say, a commendable sense of solidarity. We may hiss at her, and she may terrify us as children, but at least she doesn't embarrass us the way Glinda does [qtd. in Burger 2010: 77].

With West embarrassed by her mother and disappointed in Glinda (by the end of the series, it's clear that this Glinda is a badass, but it takes a while for West and the audience to see this side of her), it's easy for Langwidere to successfully appeal to West's deep thirst for knowledge. The show doesn't judge West for her desires and ambitions and it frames her many misdeeds as mistakes that can be remedied. Arguably her biggest mistake is putting her faith in the wrong mentor, and her ability—with Dorothy's guidance—to eventually see through Langwidere's schemes demonstrates her maturity; adolescents learning who to select and who to avoid as a role model is part of growing up. *Lost in Oz's* values reflect twenty-first century parenting styles that emphasize not inherent goodness or wickedness, but rather actions and their effects. This kind of progressive storytelling benefits all kids, helping them to move past essentialist views of identity as rooted in good and bad, with girls solidly in the domestic sphere and boys able to occupy multiple spaces, into more expansive understandings of possibility and ways to resist oppression.

On the spectrum of good to bad, West resides in the middle, with Dorothy pulling her to altruism and community values and Langwidere yanking her towards a world where wicked witches dominate all Ozians. Sheldon Cashdan writes that "the witch embodies unwholesome aspects of the self that all children struggle against" (1999: 17). Certainly, West possesses all the wicked traits her aunt does, and the narrative wants young audiences to understand that it's okay to be ambitious, to want to push the limits of science (and magic)—even to have a dark side—as long as friendship (or perhaps romance) helps them put their skills in the service of their community and not themselves. Langwidere herself isn't entirely dismissed by the narrative as unredeemable; though she languishes in a painting for the foreseeable future, the show's continued efforts to rehabilitate villains suggest that, were the narrative to continue, even this wicked witch might find her way back into the community.

Emerald City, *Masculine Science and Feminine Magic*

NBC intended its 2017 *Emerald City*, a much bleaker and more adult adaptation of the Oz story than the others I've mentioned, as an answer to HBO's *Game of Thrones*; alas, the show proved too expensive to maintain with the paltry fan-base it generated and the network cancelled it after ten episodes. Rather than the colorful and celebratory OZ of MGM, or the adolescent playground of *Lost in Oz*, this magical land is dystopian. The Wizard (Vincent D'Onofrio) rules the city through his supposed mastery of science; opposing him is Mistress North (Joely Richardson), whose given name is Glinda and who runs an orphanage, and Mistress West (Ana Ularu), who has no other name and operates a brothel while blissed out on opium. *Emerald City*'s Dorothy (Adria Arjona), a twenty-something Latina nurse, lands in Oz in a police car and immediately grabs a gun. In self-defense, she murders Mistress East, who has never seen a gun before, by convincing her to point the pistol at her own head and pull the trigger. This Dorothy isn't the selfless do-gooder we're used to, and her actions in Oz set into motion seas of violence. The conflicts in this adaptation are primarily gender-based, with the women using magic to defend themselves from the Wizard's efforts to exterminate them.

Historic patriarchal fears of witchcraft stemmed, according to Diane Purkiss, from fear of magic "as that unseen and infinitely extended aspect of [the witch's] body which can do harm beyond her apparent bounds" (1996: 2). In the twenty-first century, audiences more willingly view witches' magic as that which could do *good* beyond her apparent bounds. Writing about Maguire's *Wicked*, Christopher Roman argues: "Whoever can name what is evil or wicked proves to be the one with the power as rhetoric proves to be the ultimate political tool" (2009: 210). And yet, the Wizard of *Emerald City* protests so frequently that magic is the source of all evil in Oz, and he raises an army for the sole purpose of eradicating Oz's population of witches, that ultimately his assertions about witches lead audiences to the reverse conclusion; those who proclaim wickedness in others might be the guiltiest of it themselves. For a show that erases the line between wholly good or wholly evil, *Emerald City* eventually holds up the women who can do magic as preferable to the charlatan whose political strategies involve mass manufacture of guns and genocide (although the show was in production well before Trump was elected president, the parallels between him and the Wizard are striking).

Emerald City treats its characters as flawed, morally gray figures; nevertheless, Glinda more fully occupies the role of wicked witch than Mistress West. Unlike her evil progenitor or her angsty school-girl incarnation in *Lost in Oz*, Mistress West has given up most of her power in order to stay in the Wizard's good graces. Having been complicit in the Wizard's purge of young witches a few years ago, Mistress West now holds Glinda's disdain as the Mistress North continues to wage a quiet war against the Wizard. From her fortress in the North, Glinda governs acolytes she sends as so-called "advisors" to spy on the Wizard; dressed in robes with massive wimples around their faces, these women look to modern audiences like Margaret Atwood's handmaids, and with that obvious visual association, audiences wonder about the extent to which Glinda controls their fate. With her all-white clothes and hair, this Glinda is arguably as terrifying to adult audiences as Hamilton's green Wicked Witch was to children; Glinda's carefully cultivated appearance of purity and goodness reeks of hypocrisy and suggests a hidden agenda of violence and manipulation. When audiences learn in Episode Seven that she's been abusing young girls with magical abilities, pushing them past their capacities and leaving them mentally disabled in an effort to train an army of witches to overthrow the wizard, her exterior image of goodness disintegrates and her moral decay becomes visible.

Thus, *Emerald City* dismantles the traditional correlation between a witch's external appearance and her internal moral goodness; beauty, whiteness, and modesty do not equal purity, and blackness, ugliness, and cleavage do not equal wickedness. Glinda joins a new club of Ozian witches that includes her sister West in this adaptation, Azkadellia in *Tin Man*, and Langwidere in *Lost in Oz*, all of whom wear low-cut and/or tight clothing and are confident in their sexuality as one of their many sources of power, but whose appearance does not signal their morality. Burger writes that "The body of the Wicked Witch is also forced to stand in for the sociocultural tensions surrounding magic, witchcraft, and mysterious and uncontrollable female power" (2012: 75). The evolution of the body of a witch coincides with the rise of smart, sexy witches in popular culture. Burger says of Margaret Hamilton's Wicked Witch that she "commands the gaze of the viewer; she is impossible to look away from" (2012: 77). Audiences were captivated by Hamilton in part because of disgust and horror; now they're captivated the sex appeal of witches. From the women of *Charmed* and Willow on *Buffy*, witches no longer inspire the same cultural anxiety they did a century ago, but are instead seen as desirable—whether or not they are wholly good.

But *Emerald City* does something unique and politically progressive with the body of a witch. Although addicted to drugs and clearly a hot mess inside and out, Mistress West manages to uncover perhaps the greatest secret in Oz: that her young apprentice, a girl named Tip, is actually the presumed-dead heir to the Emerald City throne, Ozma. Through her magical abilities and cleverness, Mistress West awakens Ozma to her true identity and imbues her with magic. While attempting to recruit an army of witches to Ozma's cause, West hits a snag: Tip actually identifies as male, and once West fills Tip with magic, the heir to the throne transforms his body into a boy's. Once the witches arrive to support Ozma, they balk and claim the young man in front of them can't be the daughter of their former royal family. Tip makes a powerful sacrifice and changes his body back to female in order to lead a political and military movement to overthrown the tyrant Wizard.

As a boy with magic, Tip challenges the long-standing nomenclature whereby only women can be witches. He takes the throne of Oz appearing as a girl, and, although more bloodthirsty than Tip, West guides him through figuring out his leadership style, mentoring a boy witch in a girl's body. When the series concludes, West, a far cry from her wicked progenitors, has done more to repair the violent rifts in Oz than anyone else, having crowned a just monarch and convinced her sister Glinda to serve Ozma. The premature ending of the series unfortunately leaves open the question of how Tip will inhabit his body going forward, but the show's representation of a trans witch provides a welcome twist to a narrative that has been so iconic for the queer community for almost a century.

Moral Grayness as the Contemporary Condition

By erasing the good/evil binary, recent adaptations of the Oz narrative explore the complex and shifting identities of witches—and by extension, women. Cashdan argues: "At the same time that the witch poses an external threat to the hero or heroine, she magnifies inner flaws and frailties in the reader" (1999: 17). With a performance like Hamilton's, which frames the witch as wholly evil, MGM's film relegates ambition and desire in a woman to the realm of the sinful and immoral. But recent adaptations of the narrative, which often put witches in the role of supporting or even lead character rather than villain, create space for multiple performances of femininity (and masculinity) and reward ambition as long as it is accompanied by altruism. Morally gray representations of the Witch of the West signal to viewers that the flaws which Cashdan refers to need not be confined in a figure signifying wickedness, but can instead be embraced as strengths or at least dimensionality in a variety of characters.

Cashdan tells us we "must not take the figure of the witch too literally. She is less an actual person than a representation of psychological forces operating in the child's psyche" (1999: 18). But many witches of Oz represent the tensions among power, gender, and community in adults as well. They signal a shift in cultural attitudes about female ambition and the value judgments society associates with powerful women. While none of the versions of the Witch of the West are wholly good, most of the newer incarnations exhibit altruistic and community-oriented behavior, and the other characters audiences associate as "good" forgive these witches' misdeeds.

Some of these storylines seem to be as much about the Witch of the West's redemption as about Dorothy's journey, indicating a contemporary preoccupation with reconciliation. Unlike pre-2000s Witches of the West, these women aren't ostracized from the community; they squarely belong, in every complex and messy interpretation of Oz—which is always, on some level, an interpretation of the U.S. They represent the best and worst of fantasies of U.S. individualism and demonstrate for an increasingly urban, globalized audience that "home" is found in relationships (with Dorothy), not a place (like Kansas). Rather than the aspirational and idyllic story Baum and MGM's original versions put forward, these contemporary adaptations seem to tell audiences that they might make mistakes, but those mistakes need not define them. Audiences of all genders, then, are granted opportunities to revel in the fluidity of identity and goodness through these representations of magical women.

References

Baum, L. Frank. 2011. *The Wizard of Oz*. Illustrated by Robert Ingpen. New York: Sterling.
Bettelheim, Bruno. 1975. *The Uses of Enchantment: The Meaning and Importance of Fairy Tales*. New York: Random House Vintage Books.
Bunch, Ryan. 2015. "Oz and the Musical: The American Art Form and the Reinvention of the American Fairy Tale," *Studies in Musical Theatre* 9.1: 53–69.
Burger, Alissa. 2010. "Wicked and Wonderful Witches: Narrative and Gender Negotiations from *The Wizard of Oz* to *Wicked*." In *Beyond Adaptation: Essays on Radical Transformations of Original Works*. Edited by Phyllis Frus and Christy Williams. Jefferson, NC: McFarland.
_____. 2011. *The Wizard of Oz as American Myth: A Critical Study of Six Versions of the Story, 1900–2007*. Jefferson, NC: McFarland.
Cashdan, Sheldon. 1999. *The Witch Must Die: How Fairy Tales Shape Our Lives*. New York: Basic Books.
Knapp, Raymond. 2005. *The American Musical and the Formation of National Identity*. Princeton: Princeton University Press.
Leon, Kenny, and Matthew Diamond. *The Wiz Live!* NBC, 3 Dec 2015.
Purkiss, Diane. 1996. *The Witch in History: Early Modern and Twentieth-Century Representations*. New York: Routledge.
Rogers, Fred. *Mister Rogers Neighborhood*. PBS, 14 May 1975. https://www.youtube.com/watch?v=W23FRsHnegE
Roman, Christopher. 2009. "The Wicked Witch of the West: Terrorist? Rewriting Evil in Gregory Maguire's *Wicked*." In *Fairy Tales Reimagined: Essays on New Retellings*, Edited by Susan Redington Bobby. Jefferson, NC: McFarland.
Wolf, Stacy. 2008. "Defying Gravity": Queer Conventions in the Musical "Wicked." *Theatre Journal* 60, 1: 1–21.
Zipes, Jack. 2006. *Fairy Tales and the Art of Subversion: The Classical Genre for Children and the Process of Civilization*, 2nd ed. New York: Routledge.

"When witches don't fight, we burn!"

Monstrosity and Violence in American Horror Story: Coven

Emily Brick

Through its multiple representations of witchcraft, *Coven* (2014), the third self-contained series of *American Horror Story* (2011–present), produces a series of discourses on the relationship between witches, monstrosity, and gender. *Coven*'s use of witchcraft provides a supernatural mise-en-scène that facilitates structural and symbolic shifts in power relations. Magic is a political tool that offers a process of demarcation in which to confront and destroy the structures of patriarchy, capitalism, white supremacy, and male violence. The witch is a shifting signifier, incorporating discourses on monstrosity, abjection, and fear, as well as sisterhood, empowerment, and liberation. Witchcraft has multiple functions in *Coven*: as a narrative device to allow fantastical events, to provide a historical and mythological context to the action, as a political tool and as a framework which enables new configurations of traditionally gendered positions. Witches are unusually generically fluid monsters and appear regularly across children's literature (*The Wizard of Oz, The Witches, Harry Potter*, the *Narnia* series); romance (*Practical Magic, The Love Witch,*); comedy (*Hocus Pocus, Bewitched*); fairytales (*Snow White, Sleeping Beauty, Maleficent*); teen film and television (*The Craft, Sabrina the Teenage Witch, Twitches, The Secret Circle*); historical drama (*The Crucible, Witchfinder General, Salem*); TV supernatural drama (*Charmed, True Blood, Supernatural, Buffy the Vampire Slayer, Grimm*); and most significantly, horror (*Suspiria, Rosemary's Baby, Black Sunday, The Witch*) where they are most commonly positioned as monsters. In horror, "there is one incontestably monstrous role ... that belongs to woman—that of the witch" (Creed,

1993: 73). *Coven* is firmly grounded in horror and uses a gothic aesthetic, black comedy, and explicit violence but draws on multiple generic types in its depiction of witchcraft. The witch is an unusual trope of monster that can occupy multiple textual positions and witches in *Coven* are positioned in multiple incarnations of hero, victim, and villain. In *Coven*, witchcraft itself is not a mark of monstrosity, instead it is layered with other archetypes to denote witches as either good or bad.

The scope and space of a 13-episode television series allow *Coven* to engage with a wider spectrum of witch tropes from popular culture than is generally found in cinema: teens learning magic—Zoe, Madison, Nan, and Queenie; Fiona, the Supreme leader of the coven who is losing her powers and seeking youth; Misty, a "swamp witch" aligned with nature; Cordelia, headmistress of the school; Myrtle who runs the witches' council; and Marie, a voodoo Queen. They are joined by Delphine, a serial killer, made immortal and buried alive by Marie in 1834, then dug up by Fiona in the present. There are assorted male supporting characters, who are positioned primarily as victims or predators: Kyle (Zoe's boyfriend); Spaulding (the butler); Hank (Cordelia's husband); Luke (Nan's boyfriend); and the Axeman (a serial killer). The opening narrative is framed by Zoe, who has just learned about her black widow powers when she accidently kills her boyfriend during sex. She is summoned to Miss Robichoux's Academy, a school that fronts a coven of witches in New Orleans. Witches are called to the school, when they show signs of magic, to learn how to develop and control their powers. Witches are born with magical ability and each witch has a special power (telekinesis, clairvoyance, pyrokinesis, regeneration, human voodoo doll, black widow, and second sight).

Witch texts, particularly those featuring covens rather than just lone witches, produce a female-centered space which has implications for the ways that female monstrosity is positioned. In Barbara Creed's model of the monstrous-feminine, female monsters are products of male imagination; the monstrous-feminine "speaks to us more about male fears than about female desire and female subjectivity" (1992: 7). The positioning of witch-as-subject within the all-female dynamics of *Coven* explores fear and desire *between* women and in doing so provides an understanding of the relationship between the monstrous-feminine and other women. The narrative arcs and internal politics of the coven are propelled by a series of feuds and alliances, mediated through feminine frameworks of witchcraft, matriarchy, and motherhood. This essay examines how witchcraft mediates relationships between gender, monstrosity, and power. In a universe where most of the women are witches and all are killers, witchcraft does not in itself not demote monstrosity. Witchcraft provides the backdrop and means to enact/enable other tropes and produces a range of violent sadists, fetishists, and bad mothers. There are multiple narrative arcs of intertwined conflict: Marie vs. the coven, the witches vs. each other, Delphine vs. the witches, and the external threat from men. The positioning of femininity as dominant impacts the way that masculinity is represented. *Coven* produces a series of male monsters who are positioned as a threat to the witches (and women in general) and whose monstrosity is aligned with their masculinity. As a female space with a feminine symbolic economy, *Coven* produces male monsters who are specifically threatening to women, and in doing so generates a form of monstrous-masculine that functions as a cogent inverse of the monstrous-feminine. Monstrous-masculine as a term has not taken on the same resonance as monstrous-feminine in horror studies, however there is a range of men in *Coven* who occupy this space.

The Monstrous-Feminine

The practice and depiction of witchcraft as being innately linked with being female both in historical accounts and on screen is also foregrounded in critical analysis of witches. The world of *Coven* is a female space and the presence of witchcraft creates a feminine mise-en-scène. The main characters are female, the point of view is carried by women, the narrative is propelled by female actions, and many of the episodes are written and produced by women. There are only a few scenes in the whole series that feature men without women (frat boys and witch hunters). The all-female space of the coven, combined with their magical powers, allows them to inhabit a universe in which femininity is the structuring norm and masculinity is positioned overall as lack/non-magical. It is witchcraft which enables this reconfiguration. The primary relationships, exchanges of looks, political struggles, and violence all take place primarily between women. Barbara Creed's monstrous-feminine is specifically a product of male fantasy/fears about women "for the concept of the monstrous-feminine, as constructed within/by a patriarchal and phallocentric ideology, is related intimately to the problem of sexual difference and castration" (1993: 2). Central to her reading is the witch's positioning as monstrous due to "fear of the witch/ woman as an agent of castration" as the "*Malleus Maleficarum* is permeated by an extreme hatred of women and fear of her imaginary powers of castration" (1993: 74). *Coven* however does not use the terminology, metaphors, or symbolism of this masculine phallic economy in its female space. There are brief references to castration in *Coven* (Spaulding's self-castration by cutting out his tongue, Cordelia's blinding then self-blinding which only makes her more powerful). The phallocentric system of meaning that positions femininity as lack is here replaced by magical/non-magical as the primary signifier of power. Power is magical rather than phallic and magic is gendered feminine. The masculine norm which shapes and governs images of the monstrous-feminine is absent here and this female space produces new and complex feminine monsters.

Maidens, Mothers and Monsters

Coven foregrounds the mother/daughter relation as one of its main structuring narratives and conflicts. Witchcraft uses a maternal dynamic in structuring relations between women and positions mothers as both heroines and monsters. Mother-as-monster is a staple of horror. Julia Kristeva discusses fear of the mother as "fear of her generative power" (1982: 77) and Creed (1992) identifies various tropes of monstrous motherhood in *The Monstrous-Feminine*: the archaic mother, the castrating mother, and the monstrous womb. The monstrous mother has a political as well as psychical significance. Adrienne Rich writes in *Of Woman Born* that "the relationship between mother and daughter has been profoundly threatening to men" because it excludes men (1986: 226). The hierarchy of the coven is matriarchal and also uses the good mother (Myrtle, Cordelia) and bad mother (Fiona) archetypes derived from fairytales. Most of the women in this text are mothers, either literal or social. The older witches protect, mentor, and guide the younger ones. The collective generational power of covens involves the passing on of knowledge, spells, grimoires, and enchanted heirlooms. In Fiona's absence, Myrtle takes the role of good mother to Cordelia. She sacrifices herself for the sake of the coven and forces Cordelia to burn her at the stake as she has murdered other witches. Cordelia as the headmistress and eventual Supreme is in a maternal role that is contrasted with her desire for motherhood and the quest to heal her infertility. She protects the teen witches, welcomes Misty into the coven for protection, and teaches her spell craft. Zoe, Madison, Fiona, and Misty all play a part in Kyle's resurrection—they regenerate him, perform healing spells, and care for him. Marie links her magical power with her generative power. In contrast to Fiona who says that pregnancy has drained her of power, Marie talks about the surge in her powers she felt when she was pregnant. Tracey E. Hucks discusses the relationship between motherhood and spiritual power in voodoo: the African priestesses were "sources of maternal energy and theologically as female manifestations of divine power and agency" (2014: 95). Marie also takes on a matriarchal role in her entourage. She teaches Queenie about voodoo spell craft and her magical and political history. Fiona, despite everything, returns to protect her coven when it is attacked by witch hunters. The relationship between motherhood and witchcraft in *Coven* is a primary source of the witches' collective power.

The matriarchal framework, common to many witch texts, which protects and nurtures the coven also has a dark mirror. From Medea to Maleficent, the villainy of witches in culture is tied up with their monstrous maternity. Although *Coven* foregrounds the collegiate nurturing practices of witchcraft, in the main, the mothers inside and outside the coven are monsters to their own children. Marie exchanges her baby for immortality and has stolen a baby every year as a sacrifice for Papa Legba. Delphine abuses her daughters and kills a baby to use its blood in a youth potion. Fiona abandons her daughter and represses her powers. The sons of non-witches do not escape either: Kyle's mother sexually abuses him and Luke's mother kills him. The matriarchal power dynamic is literalized in the mother-daughter relation of Fiona and Cordelia. Fiona has been an absent neglectful and abusive mother to both her daughter and the coven. Her powers are fading so she returns to kill her successor. In order to save the coven from Fiona, Cordelia tries to orchestrate her suicide and finally earns her mother's respect: "If I knew how easy it was to win your approval I would have made an attempt on your life way before now" (3x8 "The Sacred Talking"). Fiona's presence is so domineering that Cordelia is unable to realize the extent of her powers until her mother is dead. The power dynamic in their mother-daughter relationship is underscored by Fiona's supremacy and Cordelia always defers to Fiona's status within the coven. Fiona is positioned as monstrous because she is a threat to the other women. She is motivated by her desire for youth and immortality and power and will ruthlessly eliminate anyone who threatens her supremacy. She slits Madison's throat when she thinks she may be the next Supreme and drowns Nan to get Marie out of a diabolic pact. When she kills Madison, it mirrors the scene in which she killed her own Supreme to claim power. Fiona is also a desirable monster. Played by the iconic Jessica Lange, she is also consistently styled as a traditional *femme fatale* and her seductive power echoes the glamoring effect of witchcraft. She is witty, beautiful, stylish, clever, and powerful. For Madison who is very similar to Fiona, Fiona is a role model to emulate and Madison is attracted to and replicates her monstrous qualities. The relationship between Madison and Fiona highlights the potential of the monstrous-feminine to function as an object of desire for other women. Fiona is a figure of identification for Madison rather than a symbolic threat (even if she is a literal threat). Witches are effectively positioned as figures of identification, desire, and fear because of their dual hero/villain positioning.

There are moments of redemption. Fiona performs an out-of-character random maternal act of kindness by reviving a stillborn baby. Marie also saves a baby she is due to sacrifice to Papa Legba (by killing Nan instead). Kyle kills his mother, and Nan kills Luke's mother to avenge his death. Delphine is forced to kill her own daughter when she reappears as a zombie: "She had a monster for a mother, this last act was the only kindness I ever did for her" (3x5 "Burn, Witch, Burn!"). In each case, the bad mothers are punished. The mother-daughter relationships are a natural hierarchy in a female space and the duality of witches as both good and bad is echoed in the good/bad mother archetypes employed here.

Magical Violence

Coven is a universe where most of the women are killers. When Madison refers to the Axeman as "a psycho mass murderer," Myrtle responds with "is there anyone here of whom that could not be said?" (3x12 "Go to Hell!"). The narrative is propelled by a series of internal and external feuds between women and the presence of witchcraft allows for complex and creative ways of acting out conflicts through the ability to cause magical harm. The majority of violence, murder, and harmful magic is committed by women against other women. The series constructs multiple axes of conflict which result in violence between Marie and Delphine, Marie and Fiona, and numerous fights between witches within the coven as well as the external threat from witch hunters. Marie's relationship to both the witches and Delphine is tied up with a history of slavery and race politics. Marie has a centuries-old feud with Delphine who tortured and killed her lover, Bastien, and replaced his head with a bull to make a minotaur. Marie punishes her by torturing and killing her children in front of her, making her immortal, and then burying her alive. In the present Marie keeps Delphine in a cage and cuts bits off her until she exists as a severed head. At the end of the series, Delphine and Marie end up in Delphine's torture chamber in Hell where Marie is forced to torture Delphine and her children for all eternity. In the absence of sexual difference, *Coven* also uses the different historical origins of witchcraft—voodoo and the Western European practices imported to Salem—to create warring factions between the witches. Marie and Fiona also have a long-standing hatred of each other. Fiona escalates their feud by killing Marie's lover and in retaliation, Marie hires a witch hunter to kill the coven. They eventually become friends and allies after Marie is attacked by the same witch hunters. She seeks sanctuary in the coven and Fiona welcomes her and from sworn enemies, the women bond. Their main exchanges take place in traditionally feminine spaces—Marie's hair salon, Fiona's kitchen table, Fiona's bedroom. They respect each other's power: Marie says that after three hundred years "it's a relief to have found an equal" (3x10 "The Magical Delights of Stevie Nicks"). The women join forces to destroy the witch hunters and protect the coven. The narrative arc does not build towards a final battle between Fiona and Marie; instead they unite to destroy the common enemy of Delphi. Overall, although feudal narrative arcs are predicated on conflict between female characters, in the main they work towards resolution.

Coven locates witches as agents of violence. There are various motives for violence within the text: self-defense, power struggles, revenge, and pure sadism. Even Misty and Nan, who are fundamentally nice, are killers: Misty kills some crocodile hunters by proxy by reviving the dead crocodiles to attack them and Nan compels Luke's mother to drink bleach as revenge for murdering him. *Coven* depicts various forms of magical violence. There are displays of power (pyrokinesis), harmful magic (Fiona literally sucks the life out of her doctor), the removal of agency through glamoring (Fiona again) and the teenagers attack each other with magic when they argue. What is surprising for a text about witchcraft is the amount of non-magical literal violence which is performed, particularly between the witches. They cause more harm to each other as a result of physical violence than by magic. Madison hits Misty over the head with a brick and Misty beats her up in return. Zoe kills Spaulding with a knife and Fiona kills Hank's father with an axe. Even when the coven confronts and destroys the Axeman, they beat him to death with weapons rather than using magic. The most significant violence is physical rather than magical. Magic and witchcraft are not used primarily to cause harm in *Coven* but as an enabler of power.

Women and Sadism

Sadism, traditionally a quality labeled masculine (Krafft-Ebing 1886, Freud 1905), is here reproduced in a feminine mode. The most overtly monstrous woman in *Coven* is not a witch and her inclusion serves to further dislocate witchcraft itself from monstrosity. Even in horror, it is rare for women to be framed as outright sadists or for their violence to be an end in itself. Delphine is based on a real female serial killer and is the only major female character who has no magical abilities. She is made immortal by Marie's magic and her story is closely intertwined with Marie and the witches. The other violence committed by women in *Coven* has a clear motive even if that motive is the pursuit of power (Fiona killing the Supreme and Madison, Madison attacking Misty) or is framed as defensive/revenge (killing the Axeman, Madison killing her rapists). For Delphine, the violence is the point in itself. She has a torture chamber in her attic where she keeps her slaves and servants imprisoned. She performs human taxidermy, makes a minotaur out of Bastien, serves human body parts to guests at her parties, and makes a face mask from the blood of a baby. She is also an abusive mother to the point where her children plot to kill her to escape. Delphine's power—and with this the means to commit violence—comes with the status of her class and race. Her power is social and economic; her status allows her to enact violence on those below her (slaves, servants and her children) with no consequence. She sees herself both as a visionary artist and a disciplinary punisher of an inferior race and class, acting out what she sees as a natural order: "I developed a scientific fascination for their body parts and their organs and their cries of agony" (3x11 "Protect the Coven"). Delphine's power is transient and she is powerless when her social status is removed. Having been an agent of violence in the past, Delphine is also in receipt of the most violence in the present. Fiona enslaves her to the coven and Marie refuses to let her die so she can continue to torture her. She is eventually killed by Queenie for refusing to renounce her racist views. Delphine's relationship with the witches is mediated by their disciplining and punishment of her. None of the witches perform the level of violence and torture committed by Delphine, she functions here as a more extreme monstrous counterpoint to the witches.

Magical Fetishism

It is also rare for women to be coded on screen as outright fetishists or sexual abusers. *Coven* generates a particularly unusual model of dominant femininity via its use of witchcraft for the purposes of fetishism. Like woman as sadist, woman as fetishist is an uncommon trope on screen and commonly read within psychoanalytic frameworks which name these qualities as masculine while coding the opposite masochist/fetish object position as feminine. Lorraine Gamman and Merja Makinen argue in their study of female fetishism that that fetishism takes many forms—anthropological, commodity and sexual—which allow space for specifically feminine modes and that a phallocentric model "is unable to explain how women would be able to fetishise, nor is it able to adequately conceptualise the female libido as active" (1994: 171). Both Kyle and Bastien are produced from within a particular type of fetishism that is linked to magical power and detached from a phallic / lack system of meaning. It is the process of their formation that places the women as fetishists. Both are formed from body parts, brought back to life through ritualistic practice, and now serve as sexual objects of exchange between the women. Bastien is a literal monster, a minotaur with a man's body and bull's head. Originally Marie's lover, the father of the child she sacrifices and a slave who is tortured and murdered by Delphine, he is seduced by her daughter and then framed as a rapist. He is resurrected by Marie and is implied to still be her lover in the present. Marie sends him to attack Delphine and Queenie defends her by seducing him. Fiona sends his head back to Marie in a box reigniting their feud and returning him to body parts. Kyle follows a similar trajectory. Zoe and Madison first meet him at a frat party where his friends gang rape Madison. In revenge she makes their coach crash and Kyle dies along with his friends. Feeling guilty, they go to the morgue and perform a resurrection spell and replace his missing limbs with other body parts from the crash. Madison plans to "take the best boy parts, we attach them to Kyle's head and we make the perfect boyfriend" (3x2). As Kyle is already dead, Zoe the black widow can have sex with him without killing him. Kyle structures the rivalry between Zoe and Madison, they compete over him: Zoe and Kyle love each other while Madison uses him for sex. In the Seven Wonders test, they demonstrate their mind control on him and Madison forces him to kiss her against his will. Kyle lacks agency, he goes on a traumatic journey from being sexually abused by his mother, killed in a crash, rebuilt from the body parts of his friends and used as a sexual object, and finally as a bodyguard to the coven. Both men function as monsters, victims, weapons, and fetish objects. None of this would be possible without witchcraft, both to realize the spells and to place women in these dominant positions. It is not witchcraft itself that marks women as monstrous in *Coven*, rather their magical power facilitates other forms of sadistic and fetishistic behavior. *Coven* is particularly unusual in its inclusion of female sadists, fetishists and sexual abusers although they are constructed very differently to the masculine norms of these tropes.

The Monstrous-Masculine

The ways in which monstrosity is constructed are distinctly gendered. In *Phallic Panic*, Barbara Creed argues that male monsters exist "outside the realm of what constitutes proper phallic masculinity" (2005: xvi). Kirk Combe and Brenda Boyle argue that "concepts of monstrosity and masculinity are two essential ingredients in any recipe of power relations formulating a predominant world-view" (2015: 6). In *Coven*, which uses femininity as its structuring norm, men represent patriarchy and phallic masculinity *in extremis* rather than existing outside it, nor are they feminized. The men are marked as monstrous primarily because of the oppressive structures, violence, and sexual abuse they enact on women. *Coven* uses witchcraft and magic to invert this dynamic and situates masculinity as both lack and a threat to the feminine symbolic order. The male monsters are split between Delphi, the modern incarnation of an "ancient order whose sole purpose is to rid the world of witches" (3x10) and a series of lone threats. *Coven* presents a series of male characters whose monstrosity is grounded in their masculinity: the rapist, the patriarch, the pedophile, the stalker, and a satanic figure.

Delphi is the corporate face of patriarchy. In contrast to the witches' spaces—the school and Marie's salon—the decor of Delphi HQ is distinctly corporate and masculine with wood paneled walls, leather chairs, and a gentleman's club aesthetic. They make reference to their friends in Washington, lawyers, and cops; they control the institutions by which patriarchy reproduces itself. Cordelia's husband Hank is revealed to be a spy for Delphi and "part of a sacred order. A soldier in a shadow war a war that has been raging since before the time of Salem. We are a brotherhood pledged in blood dedicated to stamping out the pestilence of witchery in the north American continent" (3x8 "The Sacred Taking"). Delphi is an active and ongoing threat to the coven and there is a sadistic, predatory edge to their quest. A flashback shows Hank and his father hunting witches like animals. In the present, they blind Cordelia and then attack the house. Fiona and Marie join forces and perform a joint spell to destroy their profits. The company HQ is raided, and their stock value drops fifty percent in ten minutes and they are powerless to stop it. The witches here exemplify Creed's positioning of the witch as "represented within patriarchal discourses as an implacable enemy of the symbolic order" (Creed,1993: 76). It is another distinctly political use of witchcraft, this time as a direct attack on patriarchal and capitalist power.

The rapist, as part of a spectrum of predatory men, is the logical paradigm of monstrous masculinity in a female-centered text. The first episode features a rape-revenge trajectory and both Spaulding and the Axeman are positioned as predatory voyeurs. Spaulding, the butler, comes from a family of "watchers" who have served the coven for ten generations. Even after death his spirit watches them. He is devoted to Fiona and cuts out his own tongue to avoid testifying against her. When Madison is killed, he dresses her body up like a doll. He describes himself as "a man of uniquely developed appetites" (3x6 "The Axeman Cometh"), a fetishist who has tea parties with his collection of dolls and Madison's body. The Axeman is a spirit who is released during an ouija board session. In flashback, we learn that he is a serial killer, stalking and killing his victims with an axe. He is released into the present and seduces Fiona who weaponizes his violence against her enemies and overlooks the corpses of women in his bathroom. Like Spaulding, he has watched over her since childhood, trapped as a spirit in the house where he was murdered by the witches. The Axeman eventually kills Fiona with his axe as a punishment for leaving him, the most powerful witch is killed in an act of domestic violence. He is stabbed to death by Zoe, Misty, Madison, and Queenie. The Axeman, like Delphi, serves to unite the witches against a clearly defined common enemy. All of the men are killed by women and their violence is framed as justified and retaliatory. The rapists are killed by witchcraft, the other men are killed with traditional weapons. Unlike the other witches, Marie must defer to a higher male power. She is immortal via a pact with Papa Legba and is unable to break out of his service. Papa Legba survives but is outwitted by Queenie so she can kill Delphine. *Coven* offers a space in which these male threats of violence to a female order are confronted, contained and defeated through witchcraft.

Conclusion

The ending of *Coven* builds towards the handing over of power and a new order and the final episode focuses on the appointment of a new Supreme. By the end of the series, only Cordelia, Zoe, and Queenie survive. In a similar mode to vampires in *True Blood* or mutants in *X-Men*, the series ends with the outing of witches, collapsing the boundary between the magical and non-magical worlds. The witches are all rescued, resurrected, and reunited to reappear in *Apocalypse*, series eight of *AHS* as the only force capable of preventing a demonic/patriarchal/capitalist plot to end the world. *Apocalypse* also introduces male witches into the female-centered witch universe and in doing so further highlights the feminine qualities of the coven by introducing a "masculine" way to do witchcraft. They are governed by the same Council and Supreme as the female coven but have a stricter hierarchy and are graded according to their power. They are a "brotherhood" rather than a matriarchy, their motto celebrates macho values of "Wisdom, Perseverance, Strength and Courage" (8x5 "Boy Wonder"). The warlocks practice magic in the same way as the witches but they are less powerful. Cordelia explains that "no man has ever reached the level of Supreme; men are simply not equal to women when it comes to magical ability. Testosterone is a known inhibitor, it impedes access to the ethereal realm" (8x4 "Could It Be.... Satan?"). The warlocks are motivated primarily to dominate the witches and take what they see as their natural place at the top of the hierarchy. Their desire for male leadership, obsession with male hierarchy, and rage against female power in any form align them with the same tropes of monstrous masculinity produced by *Coven*.

Witchcraft performs multiple functions in *Coven* which have implications for the narrative, symbolic systems, and power dynamics. It is multi-layered in its use of witchcraft as a political and symbolic device. It incorporates the multiple cultural origins of witch mythology and the differences and conflicts between them on a narrative, aesthetic and political level. *Coven* presents a spectrum of different types of witches and witchcraft and in doing so it allows witches to occupy a wide range of textual positions. The transformative potential of witchcraft is never fully realized outside of the fantastical space, most of the witches die and the final outing is an act of desperation. The structure of witchcraft does however offer a framework within which to understand an alternative feminine system of meaning. *Coven* creates a textual space in which the symbolic economy is grounded in the feminine, power is female and executed through magic. This framework also opens up ways of thinking about femininity as being active and powerful. Witchcraft allows for the reversal of traditional power dynamics to locate women as agents of violence, sadists, fetishists, and produces alternate female tropes of established male monster archetypes. In this text, true narrative power and agency can only be held by women as only women can be witches. Monstrosity and violence are gendered in specific ways and the female power structure allows a space in which new and complex tropes of both monstrous femininity and masculinity emerge.

References

Ball, Alan (Producer). 2008–2014. *True Blood*. US: HBO.
Boyle, Brenda, and Combe, Kirk. 2015. *Masculinity and Monstrosity in Contemporary Hollywood Films*. New York: Palgrave Macmillan.
Creed, Barbara. 1993. *The Monstrous Feminine: Film, Feminism, Psychoanalysis*. London: Routledge.
_____. 2005. *Phallic Panic: Film, Horror and the Primal Uncanny*. Victoria: Melbourne University Press.
Freud, Sigmund. 1905. "Three Essays on the Theory of Sexuality." In *The Complete Works Vol. 7*, edited by Angela Richards. London: Penguin.
Gamman, Lorraine, and Makinen, Merja. 1994. *Female Fetishism: A New Look*. London: Lawrence and Wishart.
Hucks, Tracey E. 2014. *Yoroba Traditions and African American Religious Nationalism*. Albuquerque: New Mexico University Press.
Krafft-Ebing, Richard von. 1886. *Psychopathia Sexualis* (reprint) London: Forgotten Books.
Purkiss, Diane. 2008 [1996]. 'Modern Witches and their Past' in *The Witchcraft Reader 2nd Edition*, edited by Darren Oldridge. New York: Routledge.
Rich, Adrienne. 1986. *Of Woman Born: Motherhood, Experience and Institution*. New York: W.W. Norton and Co.
Singer, Bryan (dir.). 2000. *X-Men*. U.S.: Marvel Entertainment Group.

The Witchy Body
Sexualities and Disabilities

Condensing the Palate

Queer Representation and Heteronormativity in Charmed

Samuel Naimi

In the context of 21st-century media, many queer characters have been fed into a binary form of representation that articulates them as either assimilationist or the Other. From *Friends* (1994–2004) to *The Kids Are All Right* (2010) and *The New Normal* (2012–2013), queerness has been captured on-screen as aberrational or in a fashion that trivializes people's real-lived experiences with oppression. The CW's newest reboot of *Charmed* (2018–present) aligns with this positioning of the queer body as (hetero)normative. While the program injects ideological values of third-wave feminism into the mainstream, *Charmed* perpetuates a quixotic narrative of queer tolerance that renders invisible the consequences associated with both the closet and with coming out. A close analysis of protagonist Mel Vera and her relationship with Niko Hamada in the new *Charmed* pilot will prove how the series assimilates queer identities to heteronormative standards: by erasing systemic oppression from the show's narrative, Mel and Niko become a heteroacceptable couple whose queer identities have no depth beyond the physical. At the same time, *Charmed* positions the contemporary lesbian body as the simulacrum of the heterosexual body by rendering Mel and Niko as mimeses of heterosexual couples. The portrayal of queerness in *Charmed* highlights the need for popular culture to represent LGBTQ+ characters as separate yet equal to their cisgender, heterosexual counterparts.

This essay critically accesses how *Charmed* eradicates the transformative potential of queerness by erasing systemic oppression from the show's narrative in favor of a heteronormative model of lesbianism. I will support this claim with an application of Suzanna Walters' theory of assimilation and universalism to Mel and Niko's fluctuating relationship. In the same way Walters shows how the contemporary on-screen queer family is apolitical and bereft of an extended queer network, I argue that the new *Charmed* comparably treats lesbian desire as incompatible with political investment and radical social change. Furthermore, because the series intersects with a historical, intertextual archive of cisgender, heterosexual couples, viewers contextually read Mel and Niko as out-of-place and as lackluster. I will substantiate this conception with an application of Stuart Hall's theory of the Other (1997).

Prior to my critical engagement with *Charmed*, it is important to explain the state of contemporary queer oppression in American society, as the theoretical lens I will utilize throughout my analysis was adopted before the legalization of same-sex marriage in June 2015. Although marriage equality has been achieved in the United States, I still argue that oppression extends well beyond the scope of institutionalized partnerships. The following statistics support this claim: 40 percent of homeless youth in the United States identify as LGBTQ+ (Durso & Gates 2012), and 92 percent of transgender adults will have attempted suicide before the age of 25 (Haas, Rodgers, and Herman 2016). At the political level, too, queer people are second-class citizens: within the first seven months of 2019, 19 gay, lesbian, bisexual, and transgender people have been murdered in the United States (GLAAD 2019); even more, there have been 29 counts of violent, anti-gay hate crimes during this same period. LGBTQ+ people in the United States are also still not protected at the federal level from employment discrimination (Walker 2019): depending on geography, a queer person may be fired because of his, her, or their gender or sexual identity. In tandem with these alarming statistics, Walters' theory, although legally anachronistic, nonetheless attests to my claim that oppression faced by queer people is still a harmful reality in America. Along these lines, by erasing oppression from Mel and Niko's narrative *Charmed* does more harm than good in regard to queer representation in 21st-century television.

Publicity Perpetuates Assimilation

During the premiere of *Charmed*'s pilot, the series' cast and crew participated in a public relations campaign to increase viewership. The rhetoric the actors and producers utilized during their public appearances highlights the problematic representation of assimilated queerness which the show perpetuates throughout its run. On October 15, 2018, one day after *Charmed*'s pilot aired on the CW Network, cast member Melonie Diaz completed an interview with culture magazine *Nylon*. When prompted to discuss her character Mel's queer identity, as well as *Charmed*'s propagation of third-wave feminist intersectionality, Diaz responded with a seemingly rehearsed statement that foreshadowed how the series would position her character as an assimilated lesbian: "[We have] made the decision not to ever talk about [Mel] being gay. Ever. It shouldn't be a headline. It shouldn't be a topic. Who[m] she loves is who[m] she loves. It's as natural as day. You know? Her sexuality is a part of who she is, but it's not everything.... We're really trying to normalize it, because I think too often we make a thing out of it" (Song 2018). Diaz's response to this innocuous question, while well-intentioned, portended *Charmed*'s treatment of queer sexualities as somehow comparable to heterosexual desires.

The actress' words imply that queer people do not have disparate experiences with sexuality and gender than do heterosexual and cisgender people. In this vein, Diaz's conversation with *Nylon* suggests to audiences that the world in which the Vera sisters live is bereft of oppression toward the LGBTQ+ community: "a new glib tokenism and erasure of community seem to be the signs of the difficult present. Gayness is the motivation for these plots but is emptied of any specific (gay) meaning. Instead, these stories offer up a liberal universalism that acts as a cultural pat on the back for tolerant heterosexuals and an accepting hug for assimilated gays" (Walters 2014: 229). In relation to Walters' theory of assimilation, Diaz perpetuates the damaging message to viewers that the fight for queer tolerance has been accomplished, and therefore, representations of the closet and queer systemic oppression no longer merit attention in the media.

The PR campaign for *Charmed* has also harmed queer representation by implying that the Vera sisters, and therefore viewers as well, live in a "post-gay," "post-coming-out" society. At the 2018 San Diego Comic-Con, *Charmed* executive producer Jessica O'Toole suggested that America aligns with this category of "post-gay" while discussing the writers' decision to portray Mel as a queer woman: "It felt very natural.... It didn't even come out of a purpose, it was just like, 'Yeah, that's Mel, she's gay'" (Kupfer 2018). O'Toole's comments, like Diaz's, tacitly instructed audiences to read Mel's queerness as something that should be normalized from the show's get-go. Through the cast and creators' words, audiences come to believe that queerness in America has no social, legal, or political connotations. As such, Mel's character, from the very beginning of the show's run, became embedded in an overarching universalist discourse of "sisterhood" and "witchcraft," rather than homophobia and heteronormativity:

> *Brokeback Mountain* [was sold] and marketed and reviewed as the film about gay cowboys that wasn't really about gay cowboys because it was about "love," which is, inevitably if implicitly, heterosexual. In much the same way, *The Kids Are All Right* circulates as both a radically "new" representation of "gay families" while embedding this newness in an overarching universalist discourse

of "family." Audiences can tolerate both—the queer cowboys and the lesbian moms—because they are reassured that these stories are not *really* queer stories after all but straight tales in gay drag [Walters 2014, 225].

Charmed's publicity efforts signified to audiences that queerness does not drastically affect a person's lived experiences. Mel Vera's character can thus be read as a mimetic performance of idealized heterosexuality that lauds the value of universal love over difference. Much like the queer characters in *Brokeback Mountain* and *The Kids Are All Right*, Mel Vera is written as a protagonist who reproduces normative conceptions of (cis)gender expressions and (hetero)sexuality. This discourse becomes evident in the very first scenes of *Charmed*'s pilot.

Normalizing the Other

The manner through which *Charmed* outs Mel Vera as a lesbian in the pilot signifies how the series utilizes representational methods of assimilation when portraying queer people on-screen. The surreptitious outing conferred onto Mel's narrative intersects with an archive of other images and texts from popular culture, ones which work to reinforce the scripts of heterosexuality onto the queer body. In alignment with Stuart Hall's "The Spectacle of the Other," *Charmed* initially manipulates the audience into believing Mel is heterosexual because of the meanings associated with the myriad images floating throughout the show. Concomitantly, the blasé revelation of Mel's sexual interest in women epitomizes *Charmed*'s identification of the queer body as devoid of sociopolitical connotation, and therefore, as one completely exempt from social oppression. In this vein, *Charmed* assimilates Mel and Niko into heteronormativity vis-à-vis the characters' appropriation of cisgender, heterosexual ideals which they can never fully reproduce as lesbians.

The first scene during which *Charmed* interacts with a canon of heterosexual texts to position Mel as heterosexual transpires within the first four minutes of the pilot. After a loving conversation with their mother Marisol, Mel and her sister Maggie leave the Vera family manor located in Hilltowne, Michigan. Maggie walks to a local sorority party, and Mel walks to a nameless individual's home to engage in sex (1x1 "Pilot"). The idea that Mel will be having sex is evidenced by the text message she sends to an anonymous, genderless recipient: she nonchalantly writes to this person, "Get naked" (1x1). As Mel confidently leaves the manor in pursuit of her partner, Camila Cabello's song "She Loves Control" (2018) plays in the background, an anthem which contextually sets up the viewer to assume Mel's love object is of the male gender. In particular, the fact that Cabello's lyrics are associated with a cisgender, heterosexual coupling—as corroborated by the song's lyrics and music video (2018)—instills in viewers the belief that Mel, like Camila, is seeking sex with a man: "[Images] accumulate meanings, or play off their meanings across different texts, where one image refers to another, or has its meaning altered by being 'read' in the context of other images" (Hall 1997: 232). Aligning with Stuart Hall's "The Spectacle of the Other," the inclusion of "She Loves Control" provides audiences permission to logically assume Mel is a symbol of heterosexual female desire, like Cabello, because they both seek out sexual partners on-screen and in-song at the same time. Almost shockingly, it is only until Mel receives a separate text message from Marisol later that evening when we come to understand that Mel's unknown partner is a woman.

As Mel reads this message from her mother—"Girls. Come home. Right now. Both of you" (1x1)—she leaves the bed on which she was previously sleeping. While putting on her clothes, the unfocused camera stays in position, revealing to audiences the blurry face of the individual lying next to Mel, the recipient of her earlier text message: Detective Niko Hamada. This revelation of Niko's gender shatters the assumptions of Mel's heterosexuality that *Charmed* implicitly fed to viewers in the beginning of the episode. Although the writers of *Charmed* have publicly stated that Mel's sexual orientation does not merit explicit limelight attention, their deceptive introduction to the character's relationship with Niko through these two scenes says otherwise. On the contrary, these scenes digress from the message Diaz and O'Toole disseminated during the show's premiere, because they work to reinscribe Mel's queerness within the formula of palatable cis-heterosexuality: "We trot out our lesbian moms to display our tolerance even as we insist that they are no different from those 'normal' moms down the street. This is the tolerance trap hard at work, measuring gay kids and gay parents by their similarity to their heterosexual counterparts" (Walters 2014: 218). O'Toole and other producers, by "nonchalantly" representing same-sex desire as irrelevant on-screen, align with Walters' theory of assimilation. Contrasting Mel's queerness to the canon that is Camila Cabello's anthem, while at the same time obfuscating Niko's gender identity, misleadingly tells audiences that queer people should be portrayed in the vein of their similarities to heterosexual scripts and tropes.

Although the show's writers argue that representing queerness as everyday promotes tolerance in and of itself, this media practice limits the growth of social perceptions concerning non-normative sexualities and genders. Indeed, Mel and Niko are not introduced as a couple per se, but rather strictly as sexual partners. The distinction here lies in the emphasis on physicality within the pilot's first few minutes, rather than on emotional complexity. In this sense, viewers may assume that Mel is having a one-night stand at the beginning of the pilot; it is not until Mel and Niko meet several scenes later at a coffee shop, after they have broken up, when one comes to understand that they were, in fact, romantically involved with one another (1x1). Along these lines, this primitive ascription of physical sex to the queer female body, symbolically when *Charmed* first introduces Niko, trivializes the complexity of queer identity.

In Mel and Niko's case, their queer personhoods are initially reduced to their sexual capabilities because viewers only read their relationship through a sexualized perspective: "As has so often happened in the representation of women, their biology was their 'destiny.' Not only were blacks represented in terms of their essential characteristics. They were *reduced to their essence*" (emphasis original, Hall 1997: 245). Following Halls' theory, Mel and Niko's queer identities attach only to their essentialized physical desires, rather than *also* to the sociopolitical consequences of outness in contemporary American society. In the very first scene to depict queerness in *Charmed*, the queer body is problematically associated only with sex. And, importantly, this is sex the viewer does not even witness. In reductionist circumstances such as these, lesbian bodies and their "essence," female-female sexual activity, seemingly do not make the cut. As such, *Charmed*, while well-intentioned, unfortunately positions the queer female body in a trivialized fashion.

Furthermore, Niko's appearance as female love object throughout the pilot reveals how *Charmed* packages queerness under the wrappings of heterosexuality; queerness is fashioned as universally tolerant under the guise of binary gender comparability. This idea is epitomized when Niko and her detective partner, Trip Bailey, interrogate Mel after she punches an undergraduate student at Hilltowne University. The mise-en-scène of the scene physically bifurcates Mel and Niko as they speak to each other across the manor's living room, signifying that they represent two poles of the gender binary. As Mel defends herself during the interrogation, she appropriates the image of the hysterical female, and Detective Hamada the image of the masculine breadwinner:

> NIKO: You punched an undergraduate in broad daylight. Which is assault.
> MEL: And I regret that. Completely my bad, but, Niko.... Detective Hamada, if you heard him, the things he was saying about my mom, I just think he knows more than he's letting on. No, don't do that.
> TRIP: What?
> MEL: Look at each other like this is crazy. It's not [1x1].

Mel and Niko's disparate gender comportments during this dialogue evidence the binary roles into which they are shoved as queer people who cannot fulfill the ideals of cis-heterosexuality. While Niko pulls her hair back and slouches forward on the couch, legs spread open, she dons a dark suit and thick, black glasses. In this sense, she appropriates the role of the man in the relationship. Mel, on the other hand, wears her long hair down, sits in a feeble, defensive position, and dons jewelry with a white blouse, thereby taking on the feminine, domestic role.

According to Walters, scenes such as these, during which same-gender partners are quietly reconstructed in terms of a heterosexual binary, are nefarious by nature: "*The Kids Are All Right* regenders (normatively) what could by all accounts be a queerer (and more feminist) family form. Two women become ... mom and dad, worker and lover, fire and ice, recuperating normative gender roles in a veritable bonanza of binary oppositions.... the abhorrent politics of this film provide the vehicle for the equally abhorrent universalizing politics" (Walters 2014: 223–224). Like the mothers in *The Kids Are All Right*, the two lesbians in *Charmed* do not queer our conceptions of same-gender relationships; instead, their representation of binary masculinity/femininity constricts the radical possibilities queerness could have extended this television text.

Moreover, Mel and Niko's constantly fluctuating relationship status detracts from the ability of the queer couple in *Charmed* to comment critically on social oppression. The emphasis on Mel and Niko's on/off relationship, rather than on the disruptive radicalism which queerness could have afforded this text, detracts from viewers' ability to establish genuine rapport with the lesbian characters. This lack of rapport borders fetishizing and poking fun at the plausibility of two women having a healthy romantic relationship with one another. Instead, the lesbian narrative in *Charmed* suggests queer relationships can never fulfill normative expectations of healthy coupledoms.

The fragmented narrative of Mel and Niko's relationship hinders viewers from resonating with the lesbian characters and from learning about the transformative potential of queerness. As previously explained, audiences maintain an ambiguity concerning Mel and Niko's relationship status from the beginning of the show. It is not until the two women meet at a local coffee shop, significantly during their third scene together, when Niko makes clear she and Mel were a romantic couple prior to Marisol's death. As the two check in with one another in public, Niko puts her hand on Mel's in an effort to placate her ex-girlfriend:

> NIKO: Mel, you need to breathe.
> MEL: Oh, is it that kind of coffee date?
> NIKO: No, it's an "I'm worried about you" coffee date. You seem like you're unraveling.
> MEL: Well good thing I'm not your problem anymore.
> NIKO: I still care about you.
> MEL: Then dumping me after my mom died was an interesting choice [1x1].

The fact that *Charmed* does not clarify the two women's relationship status until their *third* encounter trivializes the veracity of the queer relationship. How can audiences take seriously a relationship that undergoes multiple changes over the course of a show's first episode? How can a same-gender couple possibly educate us about social oppression when they are not provided the same representational depth as are cisgender, heterosexual pairings? On the contrary, this sincerity stripped from Mel and Niko's relationship borders mocking the reality of two women loving one another. Even more, because Mel and Niko are either strictly together or strictly separated, viewers can never look past the disjointed trajectory of their relationship. *Charmed*'s queer couple therefore exists in a liminal space, one that problematizes queer relationships as anomalous and unfulfilling.

It is for these reasons that Mel and Niko constantly vacillate from broken-up to back-together-again, because they cannot fulfill the impositions of cis-heteronormativity constantly expected of them. The socially scripted norms of (cis)gender(ism) and (hetero)sexuality are forcefully carved onto the queer bodies in this series, inhibiting the lesbians from transgressing the framework of desire chosen for them by the *Charmed* writers. Paradoxically, although O'Toole and Diaz may believe *Charmed* is "post-gay," this consistently unfulfilled queer relationship attests to the fact that American media still does not know how to properly represent queerness as different yet equal to heteronormative practices.

Separate Yet Equal

Charmed's mishandling of queerness within Mel and Niko's narrative(s) holds several implications concerning the future of queer representation in America. The women's heteronormative story arc expresses that queer people have become liminal cultural subjects whose identities, while no longer invisible, are still not considered separate yet equal to their cisgender, heterosexual counterparts. At the same time, the pilot's misleadingly innocuous lesbian storyline falsely suggests to viewers that the fight for queer sociopolitical equality has been fully achieved in an era post-marriage-equality. This portrayal of queer complacency by means of unrealistic equality implies viewers and media creators alike no longer see upward progress for the queer community. Overall, the displacement of queer history and queer radicalism in *Charmed* implicates gender and sexual equality in America with erasure; this implication must be dismantled.

Charmed's pilot aligns with the idea that queer people now exist within a liminal cultural space, one which does not know how to veritably handle gender and sexual "difference" despite the existence of same-sex marriage in America. The same scene during which Niko interrogates Mel at the manor, for instance, epitomizes this unfortunate predicament. In particular, because Mel and Niko segregate into discrete male and female roles as they converse on the couch, despite the fact that they both identify as women, confirms that popular culture still perceives queer people as anomalies in need of realignment to cisgender-heterosexual scripts. The very essence of same-gender relationships pertains to the fact that both participants *are of the same gender;* thus, why can Mel and Niko not express similar gender comportments that signify their complex feelings? This misalignment derives from the ever-present motif in *Charmed*'s script that convinces audiences queer people merit visibility, yet one that is ancillary and unequal to the visibility of cis-heterosexuality. For this reason, Mel and Niko prove that *Charmed*'s production team, a microcosm of American society, perceive queer people as individuals who happen to be equal in the eyes of the law, yet are nonetheless flawed in nature; they can never exist naturally on their own terms.

Furthermore, Mel and Niko's thrust into cisgender, heterosexual tropes of marriage and kinship implies to viewers that *Charmed* conceives of the LGBTQ+ community as one that has no proper cultural space; rather, queer people are out-of-place in a world naturally created for the cisgender, heterosexual majority. The notion that Mel and Niko are paragons of liminality is evidenced when they facetiously rekindle their fire through yet another sexual encounter. Niko checks in on Mel again, this time at the Vera manor the same evening as their coffee "date." Once Niko explains she was concerned by how Mel suddenly fled from the coffee shop, Mel kisses Niko; the scene then concludes as Mel closes the door to the manor, implying to viewers that the women will be having sex once again. After engaging in the act, Mel speaks with Maggie in the manor's attic. Maggie's comments to Mel in this scene represent a key moment during which *Charmed*'s dialogue reinscribes heteronormative identity categories onto queer people:

MAGGIE: So, just to clarify, ex-sex, or are you and Niko back together?
MEL: Priorities. Shh [1x1].

Maggie suggests here that queer people experience sex and romance in the same way cisgender, heterosexual people do. Her words imply that sex must either lead to a monogamous relationship, which will ultimately lead to marriage and reproduction, or sex must be frivolous and insignificant, rendering a relationship inconclusive; there is never an in-between. Non-monogamy, a salient practice amongst queer women in America (Zane 2018), is never considered a realistic option for the lesbians to nourish their queer relationship, despite the fact that it abounds within the queer female community off-screen. In this fashion, *Charmed*'s pilot perpetuates the false image, yet again, of queerness as culturally liminal, a form of desire recognized under the eyes of the law yet consistently portrayed as lacking or unproductive in the cultural sphere.

Despite the proliferation of same-sex marriage across all 50 U.S. states, the state of queerness in America inextricably aligns with oppression and inequity. Along these lines, the surreptitious apoliticality entrenched in Mel and Niko's queer relationship consecrates an erasure of queer (liberationist) history that unfortunately becomes read as complacency. This erasure of historical context, a context aligning with a slow and painful growth promulgated by past queer forbearers, hinders the immediate future of queer equality now. Indeed, if viewers are to forget the past tribulations that propelled the queer community forward to its current (liminal) state, this erasure will ultimately translate into regression. *Charmed*'s misplaced representation of complacency vis-à-vis Mel and Niko's cis-heteronormative relationship renders queerness a trivial identity category that a person may appropriate and exercise without consequence whatsoever. This erasure of the grueling efforts queer activists and allies alike undertook, to simply have queerness culturally recognized as an identity beyond pathology and ridicule, poses a threat to the future of LGBTQ+ representation in America. This notion holds particularly true if Mel and Niko's queer narratives are to be replicated in other texts. Thus, it is now, more than ever, when popular culture merits a merging of history and the present-day to veritably represent the queer community on-screen. As critical audiences we cannot allow for this paradoxical mode of representation to permeate into other factions of the media landscape.

Conclusion

The newest iteration of *Charmed* on the CW Network quixotically positions the queer body as one that is both normative yet out-of-place. The queer characters as sexual and gendered anomalies in the series' pilot attests to the current practices of representation conferred onto the LGBTQ+ community in contemporary American society. Although Mel and Niko appear confident in their sexual orientation, a notion once foreign to queer television, their inevitable slide into heterosexual paradigms reinforces a binarized understanding of gender and sexuality in the public sphere. The CW Network has renewed *Charmed* for a second season and now asserts that the series will rely less on "the family dynamic" (Nemetz 2019); whether this reduction in the family unit will alter the mechanisms of queer representation remains a mystery. What remains overt, however, is the dire need for positive portrayals of the queer body, a body that is separate yet equal.

References

Butler, Judith. 1991. "Imitation and Gender Insubordination." In *The Lesbian and Gay Studies Reader*, edited by Henry Abelove et al., 307–20. New York: Routledge.

Cabello, Camila. 2018. *She Loves Control*. Skrillex, MP3.

Durso, Laura E., and Gary J. Gates. 2012. "Serving Our Youth: Findings from a National Survey of Service Providers Working with Lesbian, Gay, Bisexual, and Transgender Youth Who Are Homeless or at Risk of Becoming Homeless." Los Angeles: The Williams Institute with True Colors Fund and The Palette Fund.

GLAAD. 2019. "Incidents of Anti-LGBTQ Hate Violence in 2019." https://www.glaad.org/blog/ incidents-anti-lgbtq-hate-violence-2019.

Haas, Ann P., Philip L. Rodgers, and Jody L. Herman. 2014. "Suicide Attempts Among Transgender and Gender Non-Conforming Adults." Los Angeles: The Williams Institute.

Hall, Stuart. 1997. *Representation: Cultural Representations and Signifying Practices*. Thousand Oaks, CA: Sage.

James, Sandy E., et al. 2016. *The Report of the 2015 US Transgender Survey*. Washington, D.C.: National Center for Transgender Equality.

Kupfer, Lindsey. 2018. "Charmed Producer: Reboot Wouldn't Feel Real Without LGBTQ Representation." *Page Six*. https://pagesix.com/2018/07/19/charmed-producer-reboot-wouldnt-feel-real-without-lgbtq-representation/.

Nemetz, Dave. 2019. "*Charmed* Gets New Showrunners, Will Focus on the Supernatural in Season 2." *TVLine*, March 25. https://tvline.com/2019/03/25/charmed-season-2-new-showrunner-the-cw/.

"She Loves Control" [Music Video]. 2018. YouTube video, 3:17, blux.

Song, Sandra. 2019. "'Charmed' Star Melonie Diaz Weighs in on the POC Reboot Debate." *Nylon*, Feb 1. https://nylon.com/articles/melonie-diaz-charmed-interview.

Walker, Harron. 2019. "If You're LGBTQ and Don't Know About October 8th, Pay Attention." *OUT*. https://www.out.com/news/2019/if-youre-out-and-dont-know-about-october-8th-pay-attention.

Walters, Suzanna. 2014. *The Tolerance Trap: How God, Genes, and Good Intentions Are Sabotaging Gay Equality*. New York: NYU Press. https://www.jstor.org/stable/j.ctt9qg0c3.

Zane, Zachary. 2018. "Who Really Practices Polyamory?" *Rolling Stone*, Nov 12. https://www.rollingstone.com/culture/culture-features/polyamory-bisexual-study-pansexual-754696/.

Queerness and Historical Sadomasochism in *Salem*

Tanner Alan Sebastian

A particular subset of feminists has tried to disavow lesbian sadomasochists since the sex wars of the 1980s.[1] Lesbian sadomasochism (S/M), the act of two or more women engaging in sexual practices that include elements of domination/submission and pain/pleasure, has been accused of borrowing heteronormative sex practices and power dynamics, thus expanding masculine domination into queer feminine spaces (Cottingham 1983: 23). Lynda Hart explains that certain 1980s feminists disavowed lesbian S/M because "lesbian s/m represents a strategy of resistance that is at odds not just with the 'morality' of mainstream feminism but in discordance with the notion of a separation of morality and power altogether" (1998: 47). Because lesbian S/M is rooted in women playing with power dynamics in a way that is associated with both heterosexual and gay masculinity (Hart 1998: 43), some feminists have viewed lesbian S/M as going against the values of feminism. My purpose here is not to erase or marginalize actual practitioners of lesbian S/M, but to explore the representation of lesbian S/M in two vastly different but linked media: the court manuscripts from the Salem Witch Trials of 1692 and the 2014–2017 television series *Salem* that is loosely based on the Trials. These two media depict often eroticized power dynamics between women, dynamics that resemble but are not fully representative of lesbian S/M; through these depictions, we can observe a middle ground in the sex war's conversation on S/M in which lesbian S/M simultaneously resists and reinforces patriarchal power.

Although we cannot be sure if any of the Puritan girls and women who accused others of witchcraft (or the women who were accused) were queer, the accusations against the "witches" depict a homosocial relationship of power and control, not entirely unlike lesbian S/M as I shall explain later. In examining both the fictional and real relationship between the accusers and "witches," I explore the potential and limitations of lesbian S/M as a patriarchal tool. In the first section, I read the Salem Witch Trials as a series of performances that resembles homosocial sadomasochistic interactions. I say "resemble" because the accusers' performances rely on the powerful/powerless dynamic of S/M, but without the masochistic pleasure of being powerless. Bill Thompson asserts in *Sadomasochism* that sadomasochists "[draw] a clear distinction between people who enjoyed what is now called SM sex and those who maliciously sought to harm others" (1994: 14). I want to make it clear that the traditional definition of S/M would not be applicable to the narratives of the Salem Witch Trials because of the lack of pleasure for the "masochists" involved. However, Margi Kaplinsky and Shulamit Geller have argued that sadomasochism structures identities in relation to other people even without a sexual component, that S/M as an analytical tool functions in unveiling power dynamics through pain, suffering, and submission, but not necessarily pleasure (2015: 246). My definition of S/M relies more heavily on Kaplinsky and Geller's definition. For this reason, I refer to pleasure-less performances that resemble S/M as peri-sadomasochistic[2] in order to separate when I am referring to S/M as a power structure rather than as an act of sexual pleasure (i.e., Thompson's definition). In analyzing both the narratives created through the accusers' testimonies and performances within the court as well as the reality of the relationship between the accusers and the accused, I reveal how the Puritan patriarchy rewarded the accusers for misappropriating the structure of lesbian S/M in order to condemn "witches."

In the second section, I look at the television melodrama *Salem* (2014–2017), a fictional, hypersexualized reimagining of the Salem Witch Trials. *Salem* engages in the current revival of the subgenre of erotic horror that can be traced to the release of Stephanie Meyers' novel *Twilight* and has become especially popular with the Ryan Murphy series *American Horror Story*. Erotic horror is not a new genre as horror and sexuality often co-exist in media, such as in slasher films of the '70s and '80s. But *Salem*'s participation in the reemergence of this genre becomes particularly interesting in that its subject matter has more direct historical roots than many of its contemporaries. I also focus on *Salem* in order to explore our current understanding of lesbian S/M and its relationship to patriarchal violence. *Salem* uses lesbian S/M between its witches to critique patriarchal domination. By empowering its witches who participate in S/M, *Salem* demonstrates the freedom that queerness and specifically lesbian S/M offers women that heterosexuality seemingly cannot. However, *Salem* contradicts itself by paralleling lesbian S/M and patriarchal domination too closely with one another, connecting its sadistic witches to male entities. *Salem*, then, views lesbian S/M in a liminal space between feminism and anti-feminism.

The Salem Witch Trials and the Performance of Peri-Sadomasochism

In order to understand the sexual power dynamics *Salem* engages with, some contextualization of the historical events *Salem* co-opts and (melo)dramatizes will be explored. The events which befell Salem, Massachusetts (originally called Danvers) in 1692 have been well-documented. To briefly summarize, during the winter of 1691 through the winter of 1692, 150 women, men, and children were accused of witchcraft, with 19 hanged and one crushed to death for denying the charges or refusing to plea either way (*Unsolved History* 2008). As suddenly as the fever for accusations began, it petered out. Alison Tracy provides an excellent summary of the critical approaches to the Salem Witch Trials, including "economic pressures," "Puritan theocratic culture," and, most importantly, "the emotional and hormonal fluctuations of adolescence and their effects on suggestible young women in a repressive and restrictive society" (2004: 18).

Linking some of these explanations for the events at Salem is teenage sexual repression. Boyer and Nissenbaum briefly argue this theory in *Salem Possessed*, noting that "the girls' behavior seem[ed] more exhilarated than tormented, more liberating than oppressive" (1974: 24). Boyer and Nissenbaum refer to the convulsions of Abigail Williams and Betty Parris before doctors diagnosed them with bewitchment. Still, the potential pleasure these fits may have given the girls could indicate their budding sexuality. Despite suggesting sexual desire as an explanation for the girls' behavior, Boyer and Nissenbaum do not explore this topic in depth. In addition to the potential role of sexuality in the Salem Witch Trials, homosociality may also play a part. Lyndal Roper, in exploring German witch trials of the 1500s and early 1600s, notes that most accusations are based around "deep antagonisms between women," (1994: 202), and certainly this can describe the case of the Salem Witch Trials because the majority of both accusers and "witches" were female.[3] I argue that the homosocial relationship of the accusers and "witches" offers the potential for queerness, or rather, the performance of queerness.

The constructed identity of a "witch" in Salem involves both marginalization and (alleged) sadism. Peter Charles Hoffer notes the connection between "progressively marginalized" women in Salem and the label of witch (1997: 39). The three earliest accused women were Sarah Good, Sarah Osborn, and Tituba, each having marginal social status due to poverty, rude or unaccommodating disposition,[4] or race/slave status. It is no surprise, then, that this marginalized status made these women easy targets for accusations of witchcraft. The well-documented accusations against these and other "witches" offer a narrative of the figure of the "witch" as a peri-sadistic being. The accused women of Salem, as far as we know, did not commit actual acts of violence against the accusers. However, I am reading the narratives of the accusers to understand how the Puritan public would have understood the witch, which I will later compare to the accusers' actual actions. William J. Birnes and Joel Martin describe that the supposed "victims" often claimed that the "witches" would choke them and force "the bodies of their victims into torturous postures" (2009: 71). Hoffer adds that the teenage and young adult accusers often claimed that they were being bitten or pinched by the accused witch even while the witch was on the stand during the court proceedings, and would perform fits and seizures (1997: 58). These actions fall under peri-sadism because the "witch," as constructed by accusers' narratives, asserts her power over accusers through physical force.

Additional peri-sadism that the "witches" were thought to perform on their victims include forced mimicry, in which the "witch" caused her victim to copy her body movements a peri-sadistic act because the accuser submitted control of her body to the witch. Hoffer describes that, when Rebecca Nurse was on trial, she tilted her head to the side. Elizabeth Hubbard, one of the accusers, titled her head in the same way and accused Nurse of causing it to happen (1997: 97). Robin DeRosa notes an eerily similar moment in which Mercy Lewis, the accuser, copied the movement of Mary Easty (2009: 44). In the court's eyes, this mimicry demonstrated the "witch's" bodily connection to and influence over the accusers, a display of power and somatic control that, while not inherently sexual or pleasurable, still can be categorized as peri-sadistic, for the act of controlling the girls' heads shares a dynamic model with a definition of desire that situates power in the seducing figure who "forces" the desired object or victim to comply. In this way, the courtroom performances enacted the alleged loss of an individual's bodily agency to a witch, or peri-masochism, because there was no pleasure in this loss (at least in the eyes of the court). Through the lens of queer sexuality and sadomasochism, the accusers' stories and performances construct the witch/accuser relationship as peri-sadomasochistic, involving torture as a display of the powerful/powerless binary, with the witch as powerful.

Yet, when we use this same lens to read the reality of accusers' allegations, we find a flattening of difference between witch and accuser. Accusers' complicity entered into an economy of peri-sadism/dominance and peri-masochism/submission through a combination of performance and actual injuries; the girls' fits in court, the copying of the body movements of the accused, and one of the accusers caught pricking herself with pins during the trial of Rebecca Nurse (Hoffer 1997: 67) are all somatic expressions linking accuser and accused, victim and witch. Bernard Rosenthal details one of the most surprising and elaborate forms of masochistic performance from the girls, in which the Reverend Lawson found some girls with their hands bound, and one of them hanging on a hook (1994: 39). Rosenthal reaches the obvious conclusion that the girls were working together to create the illusion that they were being tortured by witches, for few in Salem believed that the girls could fake such physical torture. And yet, we might read the same situation as the girls performing peri-masochistic roles in front of the court to aid in indicting the "witch," using peri-masochistic performances as evidence of the peri-sadism of the "witch," creating a false narrative about the relationship between accuser and witch. Creating this narrative of submission to the "witch" was key for the girls to remain in power during the Witch Trials, in order to provide the "spectral evidence" the court was seeking to prove the guilt of witches on trial. Several scholars have also thrown this charge against accusers. William Birnes and Joel Martin have described the girls to be "pretending so as to maintain their newly found power, [they] burst into fits, grimaces, screams, and contortions" (2009: 89), connecting the performance of pain to assertion of power. Birnes and Martin further this claim by exploring the celebrity status of Ann Putnam, Jr., and Mary Walcott, who were brought to Andover, Massachusetts, to seek out witches, demonstrating how the accusers, through their performance of torture that were considered "evidence" of witches, gained prestige and power ordinarily denied to them due to their gender and age (2009: 90).

Rosenthal, as noted early, describes that the girls by binding one another's hands and helping each other onto hooks created the spectacle of endangered bodies the trials relied upon. We cannot know if those assisting in the binding enjoyed their roles, but the necessary link between the inflictor of pain and the victim echoes and evokes S/M. Even without the knowledge of whether sexual pleasure factored into the accusers' actions, S/M and peri–S/M enable us to trace pain and power in the accusers' relationships. Pain was part of life for Puritan females: children, including girls, received beatings from their fathers or employers, and some might have endured sexual abuse as well (Hoffer 1997: 40, 49). Most girls were only taught domestic skills, and many were denied the chance to learn to read (Birnes and Martin 2009: 67), and they were thus kept from knowledge and power. Before the trials, young women were marginalized from the public sphere because of their age and gender. Robin DeRosa, describing the accused who confessed to the crime of witchcraft, argues that these women were trying to win power within the system, "to be part of the rule-making structure ... part of Salem's status quo" (2009: 49–50). In a similar vein, the accusers, discovering that male authority figures listened to them, found access to power within the Puritan patriarchy through hurting not only each other but also the "witches" who would hang through false accusations. The accusers forcibly broke away from their marginalized status as women to become a terrifying force of sexual duality, goaded on by the patriarchal court seeking to punish the "witches" that threatened society/patriarchy. Since powerful women primarily threaten patriarchal control, and as women were less powerful in Puritan society, the majority of accused "witches" were women. Although some men were accused of witchcraft when they threatened the girls' power (in the case of John Proctor), the girls would have found it easier to target other women with less objections from Puritan society. In other words, the accusers became their own "witches."

Visibility, however, had limits in its utility to moving these young women into a sustainable position of power. During the Witch Trials, some of the most fervent accusers would eventually be accused of witchcraft themselves. One of the most famous cases is Mary Warren, the servant of John and Elizabeth Proctor. Mary confessed to the court that the girls were acting (Birnes and Martin 2009: 84). In response, the girls turned on Mary and accused her of bewitching them, showing the thin line between accuser and witch in terms of identity. Mary's response to the accusation further shows the permeable boundary between "witch" and "accuser," for she confessed to being a witch alongside her employers John and Elizabeth. After this confession, Mary became "bewitched" again and rejoined the other accusers (Birnes and Martin 2009: 84). This episode demonstrates the central argument to this essay: the identity of "witch" and "accuser" was nearly permeable and both "witches" (after they were accused) and accusers were outside of traditional positions of power. On April 18, 1692, the court found it just as easy to believe Mary was a witch as it was to believe she was also bewitched again. This perceived fungibility of identity in a society of strict roles and rules makes paradoxical sense when the two identities are not opposites at all. The figure of the "witch," according to the narratives of the accusations, is a sadistic creature torturing the accusers for power and possibly pleasure; in reality, the accusers were actually enacting this sadistic narrative for control in Puritan society. Though certainly not an explanation for the cause of the Witch Trials or the mania which ensued, this similarity of identity with only arbitrary labeling of "witch" and "accuser" reveals the power of (peri-)sadomasochistic performances and the extreme acts of violence and self-harm Puritan women would endure for a brief moment of power and status.

Queer S/M as Critique of Heteronormative Power

When compared to the real Salem Witch Trials, *Salem* exaggerates and hypersexualizes the duality of witch/accuser created from peri-sadomasochistic homosocial relationships in order both to queer the women and expose oppression for a contemporary audience. The scene that details the origin of Mary Sibley's powers offers the first glimpse into how homosociality and sadomasochism intersect in *Salem*'s presentation of witches. *Salem*'s first episode, which debuted on 20 April 2014, works primarily as an origin story for the character of Mary, one of the leading witches working to destroy the mortal Puritans and claim colonial America for her kind. After a romantic tryst with Captain John Alden, who leaves Salem to fight in the French and Indian War, Mary becomes pregnant and uses her unborn fetus as an offering to Satan who, in exchange for the fetus, grants Mary her sorcery (1x1 "The Vow"). Years later, John returns to Salem to find the town abuzz with rumors of witchcraft and his love married to George Sibley, the wealthiest man in Salem (1x1). A pregnant Mary is led into the woods by Tituba, who, in this series, acts as a servant to Mary by day. However, Tituba asserts her true power and demonstrates her control over Mary, encouraging her to complete the ritual that will rid Mary of the fetus in exchange for an earthly power with supernatural force. In the middle of the woods near an old, mangled tree, Tituba has Mary lie face up on the ground. Tituba begins rubbing Mary's face and lips with her fingertips, with Mary submitting and seemingly enjoying the caresses (1x1). However, once Tituba's fingers drift down to Mary's stomach, Mary recoils from the touch. Tituba soothes Mary and returns her to her prone position. Mary spreads her legs apart as Tituba chants. Bugs begin to crawl over Mary's skin. Mary turns her head and sees a dark monstrous figure beside her. She screams for help, and on doing so, Tituba demands that Mary agrees to the ritual. Mary screams, "Yes, yes, yes!" and the ritual suddenly ends (1x1). Mary is now childless. Tituba holds her as Mary cries, reminding Mary that she now is a witch.

Homoerotic caresses are the site of the overturning of mistress/servant roles. Mary not only accepts but perhaps enjoys the ritual that will ultimately damn her soul. Mary takes the role of the submissive, enjoying that her body is being used by Tituba. Although the abortion scene does not depict penetration or any particular sexual act, certainly the subtext of the scene is sadomasochistic. In order to receive her powers (or rather, in order to become powerful herself), Mary must be submissive to a woman, accepting that she is powerless (masochism) to another woman who is powerful (sadism), fulfilling the qualifications for sadomasochism according to Kaplinsky and Geller. Queer sadomasochism is not only connected to witchcraft in this moment, but also to eternal damnation, as both go against Puritanical beliefs. The act of queer witchcraft becomes doubly subversive to the Puritanical heteronormativity of Salem. Note as well how this construction of the witch as a sadistic woman preying on a female victim parallels that of the "witch" in the real-life accusers' narratives.

The series' depiction of power relations, pleasure, and desire is complex. As her initiation scene demonstrates, Mary must partake in masochism to earn her magic. Mary's consent is ambivalent at best and non-existent at worst in this scene. Several times, Mary cries out for help or flinches from Tituba's touch, and Mary's sobs after the ritual has been completed may be a result from the trauma of the experience as well as losing her fetus to a pact with Satan (1x1). We are encouraged to find the abortion horrifying due to its supernatural method. Connecting the removal of the fetus and its subsequent corruption in the Devil's possession to queer intimacy reads as a conservative warning against homosocial intimacy, no matter how pleasurable it may be. Mary's sexual, romantic, and heterosexual attraction to John Alden stands in contrast to the illicit homosociality as the appropriate relationship for Mary.

Paradoxically, *Salem*, in warning against queer sexuality, also demonstrates how Mary's queerness empowers her. Sacrificing her body to another woman grants Mary the supernatural abilities used to silence and immobilize George Sibley after they are wed. Queerness offers Mary an escape from the patriarchal Puritan society by giving her agency through status and speech. During a town meeting regarding witchcraft, Mary suggests that Salem takes the threat of witches seriously to throw the town off her scent, claiming that her silenced husband would agree (1x1). Her heterosexual marriage grants her money and status in Salem, but her queerness frees her from the bonds of duty that marriage would normally impose. *Salem* keeps heterosexuality and homosexuality/homosociality in tension, as Mary relies on both to stay in power, similar to the ways in which the real-life accusers constructed and performed narratives of peri–S/M to gain power within Puritan society.

This tension between heterosexuality and homosexuality/homosociality continues throughout the series. In the second episode of season 2, "Blood Kiss," wealthy Salem resident Wendell Hawthorne threatens Anne Hale, a teenage orphan with newly discovered witch heritage, with marriage, forcing a kiss onto her hand. In her distress, Anne puts on her father's death mask and is transported to the Boston home of the exiled Cotton Mather, with whom she shares longing glances (2x2). Anne eventually marries Cotton later in the season (2x10). During this season, Anne confronts heterosexuality but, unlike Mary Sibley, rejects the advantageous match to Wendell and instead marries Cotton for love. Although clearly choosing heteronormativity, Anne still faces homosocial tension while in Boston due to the arrival of Countess von Marburg, a European witch who drags Anne within Anne's own soul on their first meeting. Anne awakes naked in a bathtub in the middle of a forest, with the Countess interrogating her for information on the Salem coven. When Anne asks who she is, the Countess replies "She who flowers from her own wounds" (2x2). The imagery of thriving, growing from "wounds" recalls S/M, in which the Countess has gained power after submitting to others who cause her pain. The Countess directly establishes an S/M relationship with Anne, kissing and biting Anne on the lips to draw blood. Much as Tituba establishes dominance over Mary, the Countess repeats the process on Anne, swearing Anne to secrecy about their conversation. The Countess relishes in her power over Anne with her son in the episode's final moments, but also savors how Anne's kiss tastes like "lemon and honey and innocence" (2x2). Like Mary, Anne faces a pull between the queerness of her witch alter ego and the heteronormativity of her Puritan identity.

Though kept in tension, heteronormativity and homosociality collide and collapse in the character of Satan whom the witches serve. In the pilot episode, Satan personifies the alterity of Mary's desires for power. She sees a demonic entity understood to be Satan lying beside her while Tituba performs the ceremony. This figure also appears in flashbacks of Mary's memories that she falls into during the ritual. She remembers her sexual encounter with John Alden in the woods and the memory corresponds to her partial physical enjoyment of Tituba's touch during the ceremony (1x1). However, Satan intrudes upon Mary's visualizations of the previous encounter at this point and begins to chase her through the woods, and as a result Mary rejects Tituba's caresses. Tituba in turn responds to Mary's resistance by forcing Mary to continue with the ritual. Tituba's sadism connects her to two opposed models of masculine sexuality: John Alden and Satan. For Mary, John is the source of sexual pleasure, while Satan represents invasion, violence, and pain. Roland Weierstall and Gilda Giebel define masochism as "erotic appeal by pain, submission, and humiliation" (2016: 735). In this definition, John and Satan represent the erotic and pain, respectively, or the pleasure and submission aspects necessary for true masochism. Mary's vision of both males during the ceremony further cements her as masochistic, and Tituba's embodiment of them connects Tituba to sadism. Yet even as the scene depends on the frisson of lesbian S/M, it also disavows it. Tituba's body becomes a sadistic tool for Satan to use in order to claim Mary's fetus and ultimately Mary herself as she embraces witchcraft. Tituba's fingers replace Satan's phallus—Satan does not physically interact with Mary's body until her fetus vanishes from her body—and Tituba's gender is destabilized as she embodies at once a masculine spirit and a feminine body in her role as "the sadist."

Salem argues that sadomasochism is a critical, even structural part of the witch identity because it is present in the initiation ritual. Recall the similarities between Mary and Anne's initiation scenes. The new witch must experience a sexual encounter with Satan through the body of another witch, an encounter in which pain and pleasure occur simultaneously. The physical body as well as the soul of the new witch suffers and is invaded by a masculine force, Satan. Although the initiation of a witch may be a queer sexual act, the initiation recalls heterosexual violence, with a male violating a body. DeRosa, discussing witchcraft as a performance in 1692 Salem, describes the witch's "origins" in a similar manner: "First, the devil must invade the witch, then the newly invaded interior soul must reach outside of said witch" (2009: 37). DeRosa's use of "invade" connects historical discourses concerning witches to sexual violation, indicating that, for her, the Devil is constructed as the witch's sexual partner, whether she is a willing participant or not. In *Salem*, Satan does not physically violate Mary during her initiation and instead uses Tituba as a proxy. As a result, the witch Tituba not only acts within a sadomasochistic binary, but also has the potential for ambiguous gender identity while within said binary through the embodiment of Satan. Thus, a witch's gender and sexuality, following the logic of *Salem*, is less about the physical sex of the witch and more about their role in the sadomasochistic relationship. In a scene set seven years after the initiation, the dominant Tituba encourages Mary to follow through with their plan to take control of Salem by way of the witch trials and, implicitly, to stay with her. In this way, she asserts that their queer relationship gives them power in Salem, not the heteronormativity of Mary's desires for Alden. In this series of slippages, witchcraft is defined as a queer act of resistance in Puritan society.

This slippage creates tension in Mary. On the one hand, Mary fully realizes that her (sexual and not romantic) relationship with Tituba is one that literally and figuratively empowers her to fight against the Puritan men who control Salem. And yet, she cannot and does not resolve her sexual desires for John Alden. Throughout the series, Mary continues longing for John and daydreaming about the life they might have had if John had not left to fight in the war. This tension between belonging to a queer homosocial group and a desire for a return to heteronormativity complicates Mary as a figure of resistance. *Salem* understands the powerlessness of Puritan women who bear children out of wedlock and the entrapment of women in heteronormative marriages, making Mary's turn to queer sexuality her only option for power in Salem. At the same time, *Salem* presents queerness in sadomasochistic terms, connecting queer sexuality to violence against female bodies, even if such violence is potentially pleasurable. By exposing its audience to Mary's masochism, *Salem* encourages a reaction of horror and disgust as queer sexuality leads to an abortion, but *Salem*'s treatment of Mary's other option, heterosexuality, is equally undesirable, as Mary would permanently submit to and be silenced by her husband.

The tension between heterosexuality and homosociality in *Salem* can be resolved by understanding *Salem*'s queer S/M as a satire of power dynamics in heterosexual relationships. Tituba's male embodiment connects the role of sadist to the androgynous even as a woman performs it. The first episode continues to connect sadism with androgynous/partially masculine power by introducing a young female accuser, 16-year-old Mercy Lewis. Cotton Mather, the town's newest priest, asks for three men to help him subdue Mercy who screams about a hag tormenting her (1x1). Cotton orders that Mercy be tied down to the bed to subdue her. After the men leave, the androgynous hag, with a predominant brow bone and large nose (traditionally masculine) as well as soft female voice and dress, appears and throws itself onto Mercy's body. The hag gnaws on Mercy's neck as the scene ends (1x1). Later in the episode the hag reappears as Mary Sibley's reflection, indicating that she is indeed the hag and Mercy's tormentor. Mary as the hag embodies the masculine power of the sadist through her androgyny, an external reflection of the blending of gender that occurs when a witch performs sadism in *Salem*.

Witches are not the only sadists in Salem, however. Season 1, Episode 4, "Survivors" opens with Mercy's father performing an exorcism on his daughter, a forbidden Catholic ritual that, as Mary informs Cotton later in the episode, is just as blasphemous to Puritan society as witchcraft. Mercy's father cuts open her stomach while she is still bound to the bed, allowing a snake (one of Mary's familiars) to slither out of her body. This exorcism shares common traits with Mary's initiation scene. First, both work as subversive acts, rituals that force the characters into identities, in this case Catholic and witch, that are seemingly incompatible with Puritan identity. Second, both are scenes of abortion, with an infant or a familiar being removed from the submissive's womb. Finally, both scenes are structured similarly to S/M, with a dominant enacting pain onto the submissive in order to change the submissive's identity as Mercy returns to her traditional Puritan womanhood. The difference, however, is the pleasure of the submissive: Mary experiences sexual pleasure through Tituba's caresses, while Mercy screams in terror and pain over her father's actions. Mercy only performs peri–S/M, embodying the masochist without the pleasure, while the queer relationship between Mary and Tituba allows real S/M to occur. *Salem* further explores heterosexual peri–S/M in its pilot, which has Cotton leading Mercy through the town square attached to a harness and leash, with Mercy crawling on all fours (1x1). Cotton justifies this action by claiming Mercy will point out the witch, but both this scene and her exorcism in episode four demonstrate Mercy's powerlessness at the hands of men. As the religious leader in Salem and her father respectively, Cotton and the Reverend Lewis can sadistically dominate Mercy without criticism from the town, while Mary's attacks on Mercy threaten the Puritan society. *Salem* reveals the hypocrisy of patriarchal demonization against queer relationships and witchcraft since *Salem* roots both heterosexuality and homosexuality in S/M. A similar critique could be made of the actual Salem Witch Trials: men condemned women for allegedly overreaching their power by hurting and controlling female bodies, yet many of these same men allegedly abused their wives and daughters in identical ways to the "witches."

Beyond exposing hypocrisy and female oppression created by male sexual desire, *Salem* uses queer S/M to show the desperate lengths women may go to in order to empower themselves within the patriarchy. Mary's willingness to submit to Tituba/Satan earns her the right to witchcraft, and Mercy's submission to Mary in episode four, where Mary as the hag repossesses Mercy with the promises of bringing her power, leads to Mercy's own deal with the devil, which grants her magic of her own. In *Salem*'s third season, Mercy uses her power to take control of the town brothel, taking young girls off the street to become prostitutes for her (3x4 "Night's Black Agents"). And the Countess, to gain power and information, forces Anne to be naked in front of her in the scene described earlier. In other words, *Salem* argues that a woman must abuse other women in order to gain and maintain a position of power within the patriarchy. The sadistic woman cannot simply torture men (as Mary and Mercy torture their husbands) because she tries to claim power in a patriarchal system. Patriarchy, a force oppressive to women, rewards any instance of female oppression. Thus, the witch, according to *Salem*, has a protected position of power within the patriarchy because of sadism towards other women. At the same time, in order to become a witch and become a sadist, a woman must be masochistic and submit to Satan through another witch. In this way, queer S/M provides for women what heterosexual S/M cannot: status and power. While queer S/M resembles heterosexual S/M in order to critique male domination, it paradoxically empowers women to become oppressors themselves. Witches in *Salem* are powerful and terrifying to other women not only because of magic, but also because of their similarity to men in terms of power dynamics. Again, recall the ways in which the Salem Witch Trials' accusers empowered themselves in Puritan society through accusations primarily against other women. Patriarchal necessity for oppressed, powerless women connects the fictional *Salem* to the real Salem.

Salem's definition of witch identity is one based on defiance of categories. A witch is a person who embodies both male and female gender as well as sadism/domination and masochism/submission in a tension that empowers the witch. The witch is also depicted as a subversive figure in society, one that uses queer sexuality as a funhouse mirror to heterosexuality, exposing heterosexuality as being violent and oppressive towards women. It is, after all, the system that forces Mary to make a bargain with the Devil to rid her of her baby rather than face the shame of being labeled a fornicator. Mary is no Hester Prynne, a figure of resistance living in exile on the outskirts of town. She is, instead, a witch, a wealthy figure within the Puritan system who works to destroy Salem and its patriarchy from the inside.

Conclusion: Lesbian S/M's Sacrificial Lambs?

What sets *Salem* apart from other television series is not its conceit that witches are real, but its graphic and hypersexualized depictions of torture and queer S/M. In many ways, *Salem* is the reimagining of the Salem Witch Trials. Certainly, much of the source material is presented in exaggerated and oversexualized forms in keeping with the trend toward increased sensationalism and embrace of sexual horror on television in series such as *The Vampire Diaries* and *American Horror Story*. But through subtle connections between its witches and the accusers of the Salem Witch Trials, *Salem* offers a surprisingly thoughtful and provocative interpretation and representation of historical events and people.

Salem understands the Witch Trials to be about sexuality, desire, and power dynamics. In dramatizing these dynamics following a logic of sadomasochism, the series enables us to visualize the heteronormative violence against women the Puritan patriarchy caused. *Salem*, in its portrayal of witches, encourages viewers to look at the events of Salem, Massachusetts, through a queer theory lens. Oversexualizing the relationships between women draws attention to the subtler sexual components to the accusations between the girls and the accused. This oversexualization also reveals a duality between victim (masochism) and attacker (sadism), one that made the identities of witch and accuser permeable for several of the girls and reconciled as a pursuit for centrality in a system that marginalized women. By queering heterosexuality and connecting male dominance over women to satanic possession, *Salem* can additionally critique heteronormativity and patriarchy for the female-on-female violence it rewards. Staging women's struggle for power and visibility in strict Puritan society as an economy of physical pain and sexual pleasure that destabilizes identities and the social structures dependent on them reveals the system itself methodically or rationally to produce what it understands as a "perversion" (of morals, of sexuality) and *also* to require the sacrifice of the female body for women to inhabit a central position of power in a patriarchal society. Mary Sibley only has power as a witch in her duality as sadist/masochist, her sadism earned by her willingness to submit to the trauma of a sexual encounter with Satan through the conduit of Tituba.

This same dynamic may be traced back to the actions of accusers of the Salem Witch Trials. Mary Warren, according to Rosenthal, could make herself "bleed from the mouth" (1994: 48), locating her power of testimony when she subjected her body to physical pain. By forcing their bodies into bizarre contortions and pricking themselves with pins, girls such as Warren performed peri-masochism, pretending that a force such as the spiritual/demonic shape of the "witch" in question was violating and attacking their bodies. By working together to create networks of sadomasochistic relationships in which the girls would help to torture each other to keep the illusion of bewitchment alive, the girls found that they were heard in a society that did not want to hear them.

The marginalization of young women led to a critical divide on the witch as a revolutionary figure. Brian Levack, in his edited collection *Articles on Witchcraft, Magic and Demonology: Women and Society*, argues that many accusations of witchcraft in Europe stem from women "exercising female power" that "challenged the system of male control or excluded men from the female sphere" (1992: ix). In other words, the witch is a figure of power because she is able to challenge the patriarchy. But Carolyn Matalene in this same collection rejects Levack's optimistic take on the witch, claiming it was "equally wrong-headed" of "some feminists to romanticize the witches of the past and with no historical evidence whatsoever, turn them into social rebels. For whatever witches might have been, one thing is certain; they always lost" (1992: 63). Matalene agrees the witch did in fact challenge the patriarchy, but her interpretation focuses on the witch's failure to resist patriarchy. *Salem* offers an alternative reality in which the witch can both challenge and resist patriarchy, upheaving society for her own personal gain. The witch is both a sadistic agent bent on destroying the patriarchy as well as a masochistic victim confined to work within patriarchy and heteronormativity to fulfill her plans. She learns the S/M dynamic between powerful and powerless, and uses the latter to become the former. For the witch, whom we root for in *Salem*, queer S/M empowers her to resist male dominance, revealing S/M to be compatible with feminism. Simultaneously, however, queer S/M in both the court manuscripts and the television series encourages and demands female submission with the promise for potential power later on, creating a cycle of women oppressing women for power, an anti-feminist statement. The witch's ability to borrow from heterosexual power structures and apply them to homosocial relationships, sacrificing other female bodies like lambs to gain a foothold of power within the patriarchy, is the true horror of *Salem*'s witchcraft.

Notes

1. See Gayle Rubins, "Blood Under the Bridge: Reflections on 'Thinking Sex.'"
2. I use peri-sadism to refer to actions that resemble sadism, and peri-masochism to refer to actions that resemble masochism.
3. While there were male accusers and male accused, the primary actors in the trials were women, demonstrating that the "antagonism" that Roper identifies in the German trials can apply to the Salem Witch Trials. Women were in conflict with one another, for reasons I identify later in this essay.
4. By not complying with the typically submissive/passive/gentle female role, Sarah Osborn ostracized herself from the Puritan community, marginalizing herself in the process.

References

Boyer, Paul, and Stephen Nissenbaum. 1974. *Salem Possessed: The Social Origins of Witchcraft*. Cambridge, MA: Harvard University Press.
Birnes, William J., and Joel Martin. 2009. *The Haunting of America: From the Salem Witch Trials to Harry Houdini*. New York: Tor.
Cottingham, Laura. 1983. "Feminism and Lesbian S/M." *Off Our Backs* 13, 5: 23–4.
DeRosa, Robin. 2009. *The Making of Salem: The Witch Trials in History, Fiction and Tourism*. Jefferson, NC: McFarland.
Hart, Lynda. 1998. *Between the Body and the Flesh: Performing Sadomasochism*. New York: Columbia University Press.
Hoffer, Peter Charles. 1997. *The Salem Witchcraft Trials: A Legal History*. Lawrence: University Press of Kansas.
Kaplinsky, Margi, and Shulamit Geller. 2015. "The Sadomasochism of Everyday Life." *Psychoanalytic Inquiry* 35, 3: 245–256.
Levack, Brian P. "Introduction." In *Articles on Witchcraft, Magic and Demonology: Volume 10 Witchcraft, Women and Society*, edited by Brian P. Levack, ix–xi. Princeton: Garland Publishing.
Matalene, Carolyn. "Women as Witches" In *Articles on Witchcraft, Magic and Demonology: Volume 10 Witchcraft, Women and Society*, edited by Brian P. Levack, 51–63. Princeton: Garland Publishing.
Roper, Lyndal. 1994. *Oedipus and the Devil: Witchcraft, Sexuality, and Religion in Early Modern Europe*. London: Routledge.
Rosenthal, Bernard R. 1994. *Salem Story: Reading the Witch Trials of 1692*. Cambridge: Cambridge University Press.
Rubin, Gayle. 2011. "Blood Under the Bridge: Reflections on 'Thinking Sex.'" *GLQ: A Journal of Lesbian and Gay Studies* 17, 1: 15–48.
Thompson, Bill. 1994. *Sadomasochism: Painful Perversion or Pleasurable Play?* London: Cassell.
Tracy, Alison. 2004. "Uncanny Affliction: Spectral Evidence and the Puritan Crisis of Subjectivity." In *Spectral America: Phantoms and the National Imagination*, edited by Jeffrey Andrew Weinstock, 18–39. Madison: University of Wisconsin Press.
Unsolved History. 2003. "Salem Witch Trials." 2x3. Directed by James Younger. *Discovery*, 22 October.
Weierstall, Roland, and Gilda Giebel. 2017. "The Sadomasochism Checklist: A Tool for the Assessment of Sadomasochistic Behavior." *Archives of Sexual Behavior* 46: 735–745.

Teenage Furies
The Rape-Revenge Genre
in American Horror Story: Coven

Christine R. Payson

In 2013 when Ryan Murphy and Brad Falchuck's third season of the miniseries *American Horror Story* aired, Tim Stack of *Entertainment Weekly* observed that "magical maidens" had become the "go-to supernatural trend in movies, TV, and books." As this volume itself demonstrates, interest in the trend and its meanings continues to flourish. While witches are not newcomers to the entertainment industry, Stack noted that in the twenty-first century the focus on them "seems to coincide with a desire to highlight strong, active female characters." *American Horror Story: Coven*'s primary setting, a New Orleans boarding school for young witches disguised as Miss Robichaux's Academy for Exceptional Young Ladies, creates rich opportunities to explore the dynamics of relationships between and among powerful girls and women. Much of the drama within the coven itself revolves around determining who among them will be the next Supreme—the coven leader and most powerful witch. Despite this extended power struggle, the final episode features an unexpected Supreme with two teenage apprentices at her side, welcoming a crowd of talented girls to the academy with the implication that a new, diverse generation of witches is emerging.

The inherent empowerment of discovering magical talent enables the young witches of Miss Robichaux's Academy to respond to sexual violence in ways that forcefully challenge patriarchal rape culture. The world-building of the series is partly anchored by young witches' decisions about how to use their supernatural abilities to take revenge for acts of rape. This revenge establishes a connection between their sexual trauma and their growing power to reshape a world that subjects them to sexual and other forms of violence. In her study of television dramas led by teenage girl characters, Susan Berridge finds that "sexual violence narratives across the teen genre [often] contain rather than enlarge discussions about the relationship between gender, sexuality, and power" (2013: 480). *Coven*, however, uses models from the horror and rape-revenge film genres to expand conversations about sexual violence rather than to foreclose them. Murphy and Falchuck integrate components of familiar coming-of-age narratives about young women (natural and supernatural) with horror and rape-revenge elements in ways that ultimately empower young women.

As Sarah Projansky (2001) explains, rape plotlines are versatile in American film and television and used to support both feminist and post-feminist or antifeminist ideologies. *Coven* interprets the rape-revenge genre to argue for the necessity of women's solidarity and collective action against the threat of violence, sexual and otherwise, posed by groups of men. The necessity of this solidarity resonates with the recent efforts of the #MeToo movement, women's march, and the surge in women seeking political office in the United States. While it features no shortage of unsympathetic women characters, *Coven* depicts women as capable of protecting themselves and one another against the patriarchal society that surrounds them. In particular, Madison Montgomery (Emma Roberts) and Zoe Benson (Taissa Farmiga) exact retribution against rapists in ways that ask audiences to imagine the potential of powerful women acting together for their individual and collective benefit.

The genre of rape-revenge has a complicated relationship to feminism, as many critics have addressed.[1] Within American film it is generally agreed to originate from *Last House on the Left (1972)*, a horror film inspired by Ingmar Bergman's *The Virgin Spring* (1960). David Maguire (2018) argues that despite the fact that it was released six years later, the 1978 film *I Spit on Your Grave* "has effectively become ground zero for the genre" (67).[2] While some viewers read these films take-down of misogynist men and the ideology they represent, others challenge their extensive, graphic depiction of sexual assault. For example, the noted film critic Roger Ebert called the 2010 version of *I Spit on Your Grave* "a despicable remake of the despicable 1978 film," observing that in the newer version "less time is devoted to the revenge and more time to verbal, psychological and physical violence against [Jennifer]. Thus it works even better as vicarious cruelty against women." Ebert's concerns about audience enjoyment of and identification with the perpetrators of sexual violence against women cannot be dismissed as prudishness. As Projansky (2001) explains in *Watching Rape*, representing and discussing acts of violence, while not equivalent to the violence itself, can potentially habituate the audience and effectively normalize sexual violence rather than challenging it. *Coven* does include graphic depictions of sexual violence. The rape scenes in *Coven* are short compared to those in *I Spit on Your Grave* and *The Last House on the Left*, and do not relish sexual violence in the mode of torture porn, though other scenes in the series do (LeBlanc 2018).[3] The witches' supernatural power shifts the focus from the violence against them to the violence of which they are capable. Their status as revenging furies emerges from their experiences as survivors of rape and trauma but is not limited by typical human abilities; their wounds are human, but their potential for response is superhuman.

The first dramatic act of supernatural rape-revenge occurs when Madison Montgomery uses her telekinetic powers to overturn a bus carrying rapist fraternity brothers away from a party. In this scene Madison resembles the figure Carole J. Clover (2015) describes when she states that "female self-sufficiency, both physical and mental, is the hallmark of the rape-revenge genre" (143). At the moment when Madison uses her magic to kill her attackers the act seems almost effortless, as though with a simple gesture she can complete her revenge and then return to her normal life with neither help nor sympathy from anyone. Although she struggles to cope with the trauma of her gang rape afterward, she creates a façade of self-containment, independence, and even indifference. She appears to other characters to be strong because of her telekinetic power and mental self-sufficiency in that she displays almost no emotional response to having been attacked beyond taking immediate revenge. Her response to the attack is immediate, lethal, and literally explosive. In retaliating so dramatically, Madison shows her own strength and fortitude both as a woman and as a witch. She is self-avenging, not dependent on others for protection and even dismissive of the violence against her, aligning her with the self-sufficient figure Clover describes as essential to rape-revenge film. Viewers, however, know that she is masking her feelings with pithy dismissals of any suggestion that she needs someone else's help.

Aired between Tarana Burke's coining of the phrase #MeToo in 2006 and its rise to viral popularity in 2017, *Coven* asks viewers to reconsider how an individual, and more importantly a community, can respond to the widespread reality of sexual violence against women. The party setting in which the rape occurs relies on familiar narratives about rape including that of the rapists' motivations of disempowering a woman they perceive as haughty and overconfident.[4] After drugging her, fraternity brothers "take turns"[5] raping Madison as she grunts in pain, clearly indicating her distress but apparently unable to act on it. The initiator of the attack, Brener, embodies the cliché of entitled, misogynist masculinity. Projansky argues that "[t]he figure of the white fraternity brother or sports star rapist is so common" that, in her estimation, "he is the normative rapist in contemporary popular culture" (2001: 113).[6] In his review of *Coven* for *The Atlantic*,

Spencer Kornhaber (2014) wrote of Madison that her "violent, magical revenge was shocking, but not as shocking as her lack of surprise about what had happened." The cliché rapist character and Madison's lack of surprise reinforce the familiarity of the sequence of events that include Madison's rape. These scenes ask viewers to confront the prevalence of sexual violence in American society.

The scene's emphasis on video—Brener instructs one of his fraternity brothers to move Madison's hair so that her (famous) face will be clear in the recording—draws on another element of the norm Projanksy identifies. She writes: "If the typical rapist is a young clean-cut white man, quite often a sports star, fraternity brother, or soldier, the most *vile* villain in many of these texts is not the rapist but the man who *watches* the rape" (2001: 116, emphasis original). The members of the fraternity cooperate to execute the attack and document it, making it possible to watch the rape over and over. Distributing the video through the internet would add another layer of humiliation to Madison's experience. Kornhaber describes Madison's character as a "Lindsay Lohan sendup," likening the fictional character to the real-life actor whose career has been dominated by scandal. Just as Lohan has suffered public humiliation, including leaked nude photographs, so too might Madison Montgomery experience the personal and professional ramifications should her attackers share the video of the assault.[7] Creators, distributors, and viewers of that content would participate in continuing to victimize Madison.

Coven deploys the revenge portion of the rape-revenge sequence immediately after this act of rape, truncating the usual timeline of the sequence by showing Madison striking back at her attackers before they have even escaped the scene. Rape-revenge films often rely on portraying the revenger's anticipation of their retributive action, including trapping its subject(s). In the case of both *I Spit on Your Grave* and *Last House on the Left*, a revenger lures her victim by offering sex and then, at a moment of highly anticipated reversal, she maims or kills the rapist instead of providing the promised sexual gratification. Madison's magical powers, on the other hand, ensure that she achieves her revenge within moments of being attacked with no planning and no need to offer sex as bait.

By drawing attention to the medium through the fraternity brothers' video recording, the scene entangles the viewer as another witness to Madison's suffering. While Ebert saw *I Spit on Your Grave* (1978) as encouraging viewers to sympathize with the rapists, Clover and other critics argue that it asks its audience to sympathize with the rape survivor, and to confront the brutality of the action against her. Despite Madison's apparent self-sufficiency, she has been meaningfully harmed by her experience of rape. In the scene when she flips the bus, a close-up on Madison's face, visible to viewers but not to Zoe, reveals her fighting back tears, an expression that Madison quickly masks with her usual self-assuredness. A later scene shows her crying in the shower, an image very common to rape narratives in film and television (Projanksy 2001: 109). In one light, these expressions of emotion show that despite her fame Madison is "just like us" but the significance of her efforts to appear self-sufficient also contributes to *Coven*'s larger assertion that solidarity, rather than individualism, will preserve the witches (and young women). Madison's desire for individual power at the expense of her sister witches ultimately costs her not only a place in the coven, but her life, while her more cooperative sister witches survive to remake the coven and, as their emergence from secrecy suggests, American society.

When Madison attacks the entire group of fraternity brothers, she reinforces the assumption that sexual violence against women is the fault of men collectively rather than individually. The next day, when Zoe points out that one of the fraternity brothers, Kyle Spencer, intervened to stop the attack, Madison spits back that he would "have happily taken a turn on [her] if he had the chance" (3x2 "Boy Parts"). She is unmoved by Zoe's objections, stating: "Those guys were his frat brothers. It's guilt by association" (3x2). Clover's analysis on *I Spit on Your Grave* (1978) may help to elucidate questions of male responsibility. In the film, when Jennifer seeks her revenge on Matthew, the mentally disabled member of the group who rapes Jennifer, he apologizes and tries to defend himself by reminding her that the rape is his friends' idea, not his. Clover (2015) reads his pleas as part of the film's argument that "the dynamic of male groups is greater than the sum of its parts" (123) but does not allow such dynamics to absolve any individual of responsibility. Within the film, the rapists are not personally but instead "corporately liable; any of them—in this case all—are proper targets for retribution, regardless of their own degree of participation" (123). In some ways the obvious villainy of Madison's attackers and the comparative decency of the one member of the fraternity who tries to stop them align with a pattern Berridge notes in teen drama series led by female characters: she observes that in these shows "sexual violence frequently becomes the domain for the display of ideal masculinity, as central male teens heroically protect and comfort female victims against these individual 'bad' men" (2013: 483). The collusion of Madison's multiple rapists refuses the idea of sexual violence against women as a character flaw of one individual and instead attributes it to a collective misogyny one man cannot unmake. Kyle does intervene to stop the rape, but he appears to remain part of the fraternity, getting on the bus with his brothers when they flee even if his purpose is to persuade them to delete the recording.

Kyle can be read as restoring a kind of "ideal masculinity," but that masculinity is itself a source of horror. Beginning in Episode 2, Kyle becomes not only corporately connected to his fraternity brothers, but corporeally united with them when Madison and Zoe piece together their own Frankenstein's monster using Kyle's head and a patchwork of his brothers' body parts. In one sense Kyle's return allows for the recuperation of masculinity in the way Berridge (2013) describes as common to female-led teen dramas: Zoe learns that Kyle volunteered for the United Way during his breaks from college, and the audience witnesses Kyle's memory of stating his intention to become an engineer in order to better protect his home of the lower 9th ward (3x3 "The Replacements"). Madison wants to return him to life as a gesture of gratitude to Zoe for Zoe's counterattack on Madison's rapist. This thank-you gift is, however, literally the sum of his dead fraternity brothers' parts.[8] His mind and will struggle to control this pieced-together body, continually reiterating the violent danger posed by groups of men and Kyle's insufficiency to counteract it. Almost paradoxically, however, Kyle's lack of self-control later enables him to complete his own rape-revenge sequence when he kills the person who has sexually abused him throughout his childhood.

Coven uses the rape-revenge genre to develop Zoe's character by making Madison's experience of rape part of Zoe's decision to embrace her magical abilities. In his book on *I Spit on Your Grave*, Maguire notes that in film "[p]rior to the late 1970s … the inclusion of sexual assault was typically a catalyst to spur a male character into action, i.e., it was a crime against *him* when the victim was his wife/girlfriend/sister/daughter" and this formulation positions women as props rather than subjects (2018: 68). However distasteful critics found *I Spit on Your Grave*, it does insist on the survivor of sexual assault as a subject, not an object. In *Coven*, sexual assault catalyzes Zoe's actions and launches her development into a powerful young woman who can act in defense of others. Zoe's transition from being seeming helplessness to taking action insists that victims are not the only ones responsible for correcting rape culture and misogyny. She exerts the (admittedly violent) power she possesses in an effort to right an individual wrong against Madison and a larger social injustice[9] and this choice is the first significant decision viewers see her make.

Zoe, the most deliberate of *Coven*'s rape revengers, discovers her magic in a sex scene designed to contrast with Madison's experience of rape. Zoe's talent manifests when her first attempt at sexual intercourse reduces her partner, a boy named Charlie, to a bloody corpse. The daylight setting, the absence of intoxicants, and the images of Zoe pulling Charlie toward her bedroom by the shirt collar ensure viewers' understanding of Zoe's clear, enthusiastic consent. The dialogue reinforces her decision-making when she verbally reassures Charlie that she wants to continue. The scene's framing foregrounds sincere voiced consent as a feature of the encounter, establishing it as a component of the "normal" teenage love story portion of Zoe's life before she discovers her magic. The scene turns horrific when, mid-copulation, Charlie begins to bleed from his nose and then from his ears, mouth, and eyes. Zoe screams in terror as he collapses onto the bed and seizes. Her voiceover in the next scene explains that the doctors attribute the boy's death to an aneurism, but her mother explains to her that the real cause is "an affliction" that runs in her family[10] (3x1 "Bitchcraft").

Zoe's discovery of her magic is a profoundly traumatic reinterpretation what Barbara Creed (1986) calls the "monstrous-feminine" in conventional horror film. Based on Kristeva's conception of the abject, the monstrous-feminine creates horror by forcing the viewer into contact with abject objects of blood, gore, and, especially "the ultimate in abjection," the corpse.[11] In the scene, the first drop of blood falls from Charlie's nose onto Zoe's lip before it is followed by more blood gushing from every orifice. The camera zooms out from a close-up on Charlie's face as streams of blood pour from his eyes onto the bedding behind his head.[12] This involuntary power to kill men through sex builds on and reinterprets horror's association of women and blood by keeping Zoe's body intact and showing Charlie's body bleeding spectacularly as a result of contact with it. Using a psychoanalytic framework, Creed argues that the "obsession with blood, particularly the bleeding body of woman, where her body is transformed into the 'gaping wound,' suggests that castration anxiety is a central concern of the horror film" (1986: 46). *Coven* weaves this obsession into what looks like a normal instance of tentative but excited teenage sexual exploration. Zoe's sexuality does not render her abject but does empower her to transform men from living subjects to abject horrors and in this way *Coven* builds on the existing horror trope of the monstrous feminine while playing with its gender dynamics.

Teen girls' sexuality is a frequent subject of American prurient fascination and moral panic, often pitting "good" girls against budding seductresses. For example, in the 2009 film *Jennifer's Body*, a plain girl-next-door character must stop her demon-possessed and very attractive friend (played by Megan Fox) from feeding on young men. *The Craft* (1996) relies on one character (Nancy) to represents destructive sexual desire as contrast for the protagonist's tamer ambitions. *Coven* unites the characteristics of shy sexual innocence and voracious, destructive female sexuality in the same character, Zoe. Her long, straight hair worn in pigtails, her family's middle-class home, and sister-witch Madison's jibe that Zoe's entire wardrobe came from the Gap (3x1) all signify her typicality, and yet her sexuality is rooted in an ability to kill. The integration of these qualities and the direct connection between Zoe's sexuality and her magic suggest that power, including the power to inflict violence, belongs even to the "girl next door," once she discovers it. At first Zoe's access to her own monstrous qualities expels her from her family of birth and her home community, but ultimately her conscious awareness of those qualities makes her a founding member of a new coven that breaks through assumptions about who young women can be and what they can do. Through the loss of her sexual innocence she gains access to talent, power, and sisterhood.

Maguire (2018) describes how in pre–1970s rape-revenge horror films the rape of a woman often motivates the action of a man connected to her who feels himself wronged by the attack on *his* "wife/girlfriend/sister/daughter." Films including *Last House on the Left* (1974) and *I Spit on Your Grave* (1978) pioneer the female character propelled into action by rape, and Zoe combines the earlier model of a man "protecting his own" and this more recent female revenger model. Her actions are motivated by her sister witch Madison's rape.[13] At first Zoe seems helpless, but in the days following the rape she finds a way to "put [her] curse to some use" (3x1). Upon learning that two of the bus passengers have survived the crash Madison caused, Zoe goes to the hospital hoping to find that Kyle has not been killed. Instead she discovers Brener, who led the attack on Madison. "It should have been you, asshole," she declares to the unconscious Brener before closing the hospital room curtains and raping him to death (3x1). He bleeds out just as horrifically as Charlie does, but this time Zoe is determined rather than surprised. Zoe could also have killed Brener by unplugging his ventilator, contaminating his IV or otherwise sabotaging the medical interventions keeping him alive after the crash, but she chooses rape as a murder method in order to degrade as well as kill him. Maguire (2018) explains that rape as an instrument of justice against a rapist is central to the 2010 remake of *I Spit on Your Grave* and its sequels, noting that in the 2013 sequel the protagonist's "methods of retaliation mimic her assailants' deviances" (96). Claire Henry's analysis in *Revisionist Rape Revenge* indicates this mimicry is a pattern in contemporary rape revenge film. She observes that films including *Hard Candy* (2005), *Descent* (2007), *Straightheads* (2007), and *The Girl with the Dragon Tattoo* (2009) feature "victim-avengers" who, with the exception of Haley Stark in *Hard Candy*, "rape their rapists, making the rapists (and to a lesser degree the spectator) not only understand but actually feel the pain, humiliation, and degradation of rape feels like" (2014: 75). It is not clear that Brener feels this pain or humiliation at the moment of his death, but Zoe's attack does mimic his on Madison, who has been drugged to the point of incapacitation when Brener and his fraternity brothers rape her. From a postfeminist perspective Zoe's act should balance the scales, but *Coven* does not allow the situation to be resolved that simply.

Zoe is not herself the victim of the rape she seeks to revenge but she is a member of a marginalized group with Madison in the coven, as women with supernatural powers. Because of her supernatural powers, Zoe can inflict a punishment mirroring the crime and achieve a kind of justice common to rape-revenge films, but the scene offers less catharsis than Madison flipping the bus. Murdering Brener this way requires Zoe to accept rather than resist a broader culture of rape. Henry describes similar dynamics in rape-revenge films in which the pubescent girl as the "new generation heroine ... does not expect a world free of sexual violence, instead adapting (or even mutating) to the sexual culture she finds herself in" (2014: 57). The distress visible on Zoe's face in the act of raping Brener indicates the cost of taking revenge through the existing sexual culture and makes it clear that she endures yet more sexual trauma in her effort to defend another woman.

Raping Brener is Zoe's first deliberate use of her magical power. Her magic as it initially manifests seems to preclude the possibility of sexual relationships, limiting her experience of her own sexuality to Charlie's traumatic death and then to her use of her body as a weapon. In the words of the voiceover during the hospital rape scene: "since [she'll] never be able to experience real love, [she] might as well put this curse to some use" (3x1). The scene separates the act of rape from sexual desire, reinforcing a definition of rape as an act of power and violence against a person incapable of self-defense.

Episode 3 reveals that Zoe and Madison's supernatural power enables Kyle, himself a victim of childhood sexual abuse, to fight back against his abuser at the cost of more violence and trauma. After resurrecting him from the dead into a new, patched-together body she and Madison created, Zoe returns an undead Kyle to his mother's home, hoping to help restore his mind and comfort his grieving parent. The cinematography of the episode emphasizes the ways in which Kyle's experiences of sexual violation resonate with Madison's. When he showers, the audience sees flashes of his mind realizing the bodily trauma of being constructed from pieces of his former friends. The visual elements of the scene, including the white clawfoot bathtub encircled by a curtain, recall images of Madison privately crying in the shower at Miss Robichaux's. While his fraternity brothers use their comparative physical strength and teamwork to attack their victim, Kyle finds that his new physical power and impulsivity enable him to protect himself against assault in ways he could not when he was a child. At the moment Kyle's mother initiates sexual contact by sliding a hand down his abdomen toward his trousers, the camera focuses on Kyle's face as it contorts with tears—his only apparent response to his mother's actions. Just as when Madison flips the bus, this scene uses the close-up shot to reveal a victim's emotions in response to sexual assault immediately before they take retributive action.

The Rape-Revenge Genre (Payson) 135

Like Madison's revenge, Kyle's violence against his attacker depends on his new-found supernatural power. When Zoe arrives to join Kyle and his mother for dinner, she finds Kyle bashing at his mother's bloodied head with a sports trophy, repeating angry cries of "No!" The camera focuses on his face as more and more blood spatters onto it and he continues screaming the single word—the first he has spoken since his return from the dead. Rendered uninhibited and almost nonverbal by his resurrection, he is finally able to tell his rapist "no." Zoe and Madison's magic empowers him to defend himself and justice, however bloody, becomes possible because of their intervention. They do not recognize this consequence of their actions, but it suggests a solidarity of survivors that is not limited by gender.

After her own death and resurrection, Madison initiates a sexual relationship with Kyle based on their shared experience of returning from the dead. Kyle's undead nature also makes him immune to Zoe's lethal sexuality. The witches resolve to "share" him which, given his reduction to childlike verbal abilities and emotional self-regulation, introduces another problematic power dynamic. Madison soon grows jealous of Kyle's emotional attachment to Zoe, a conflict which culminates in Kyle refusing Madison's attentions and declaring his love for Zoe. While Zoe seems to respect Kyle's autonomy to a greater degree than Madison does, his desires are clearly subordinate to Madison and Zoe's fight for power within the coven. This power struggle prompts each witch to violate Kyle's consent in order to establish ownership of him, a dynamic uncomfortably like his abusive mother's possessiveness. Near the series' conclusion both Zoe and Madison must demonstrate their capacity to manipulate another person's mind. Rather than attack Zoe directly, Madison applies her power to Kyle, forcing him to come to her, kiss her, and then to lick her shoe (3x13 "The Seven Wonders"). Though Zoe claims, "[h]e's not a part of this!" (3X13) she then demonstrates her power by manipulating Kyle herself, and the two fight one another through him until Cordelia stops the test. From a postfeminist perspective, Zoe and Madison's ability to overpower a man with their magic should mean the work of feminism is complete because they can now embody the same position of control and objectification.[14] In using Kyle as an object Madison reinforces an existing sexual culture that sees sexual partners as conquests and as accessories to power struggles between rivals. Zoe takes the bait, showing that while she may objectify Kyle less than Madison does, she has not unlearned the assumptions of American culture that encourage sexual objectification.

The rape-revenge elements of *Coven* allow showrunners Falchuck and Murphy to imagine a future where girls and women are both individually powerful and unified in mutual protection. While hardly utopic, this vision harnesses horror conventions to challenge American society as it currently exists. Despite the show's limitations and blind spots, showing a collective of women who fight misogyny and marginalization recognizes and encourages feminist efforts in the present and also asks its viewers to wonder what powers they, and the women around them, may be able to unleash. For all her flaws, perhaps Cordelia's mother and predecessor is right when she says to the girls under her power and instruction: "When we don't fight, we burn" (3x1).

Notes

1. Maguire's book chapter "Only Women Bleed: Filth or Feminist?" in his recent book on *I Spit on Your Grave* provides an excellent explanation of existing criticism and its relationship to this controversial and influential film.

2. Maguire likens *I Spit on Your Grave*'s impact on rape-revenge films to the influence of Hitchcock's *Psycho* in the horror genre and *Halloween* for slasher films. Despite not being the first of their kind, these films became models for subsequent work. Maguire argues that that *I Spit on Your Grave* continues to influence its genre "with almost every rape-revenge film since lifting its narrative structure, motifs, tropes and archetypal characters" (67).

3. According to Henry (2014), "[c]ontemporary rape-revenge films are often hybridized with torture porn ... and similarly present spectacles of violence that are connected to—and perhaps help to process—sociopolitical conflicts and their media representation, particularly around issues of violence, retribution, torture, and trauma" (9). See also LeBlanc's (2018) analysis of depictions of the torture of enslaved people in *AHS: Coven*.

4. At the party Madison asks Brener if he "want[s] to be her slave tonight" and orders him to bring her a drink (3x1 "Bitchcraft"). This display of power seems to incite the rapists, though no attitude of Madison's would justify their next actions. From this perspective, her strident independence and even power over them are undercut by their attack on her. Projansky (2001) explains that "[w]omen are often vulnerable in rape films, but the relationship between rape and women's vulnerability is complex. Specifically, two seemingly antithetical types of narratives are common: those that depict women's vulnerability as leading to rape and those depict the rape of an independent woman as making her vulnerable... Paradoxically, the first set of texts suggests that women should be more self-sufficient and independent in order to avoid rape, while the second set of texts suggests that the independent behavior and sometimes independent sexuality can lead to rape" (30). Madison's story can be read through both paradigms and *Coven* implicitly relies on each set of assumptions as the character develops.

5. *I Spit on Your Grave*'s rapists lack the privilege of these fraternity brothers, but show a similar effort to "one-up" each other and demonstrate their virility not to their victim, but to their collaborators. Clover (2015) describes the rapes in that film as, for the perpetrators, "a sporting game" (122) that reinforces the existing power dynamics within their group.

6. The high-profile dissolution of fraternities at Swarthmore College in 2019 indicates the degree to which fraternities specifically are held responsible (appropriately, in my view) for sexual assault on college campuses. See Zipporah Osei's May 10 article for *The Chronicle of Higher Education*, E.J. Dickson's piece for *Rolling Stone*, Callen Rain's letter "I was a member of Phi Psi—Swarthmore's Fraternities Must Go," and David F. Hill IV's "I Was in D.U.—Swarthmore's Fraternities Must Go" in Swarthmore's campus newspaper, *The Phoenix*.

7. Given the American appetite for scandals about young women and especially young actors, the video could affect both Madison's personal and professional life. Without Madison's magic, this event could resemble the scandal around the release of nude photographs of actors including Jennifer Lawrence in 2014 and Emma Watson, Amanda Seyfried, and Miley Cyrus in 2017, among many others. The passage of laws prohibiting revenge porn in 46 American states indicates the degree to which non-famous women cope with a similar threat.

8. According to Clover (2015), "The Frankenstein scheme of killing women for their parts... is in the best tradition of low horror, from the 1963 *Blood Feast* (in which an Egyptian caterer collects female bodily parts, one female per part, for sacrifice to the goddess Ishtar) to the 1990 *Frankenhooker* (in which a bereaved boyfriend collects bodily parts from other women in an effort to rebuild his mangled girlfriend)" (232–233). *Coven* also plays with this trope by reversing the gender positions and showing young women constructing a sexual companion from the bodily parts of his dead fraternity brothers.

9. When she first meets Kyle at the college party she says "I think frats are full of fascists" (3x1). The scene does not necessarily suggest that Zoe is entirely sincere in this remark, but it does indicate that she shares negative cultural assumptions about members of fraternities, which have long been associated with sexual violence, racism, and homophobia among other social problems.

10. Zoe's mother tries to comfort her daughter by claiming responsibility for Charlie's death. Her parents fail to tell Zoe that this could happen in hopes that the power would not manifest in her. Her great grandmother had what her mother euphemistically calls "the same affliction" (3x1).

11. Extending this importance of the corpse to producing horror, Creed explains, "Within the biblical context, the corpse is also utterly abject. It signifies one of the most basic forms of pollution—the body without a soul... In relation to the horror film, it is relevant to note that several of the most popular horrific figures are "bodies without souls" (the vampire), the "living corpse" (the zombie), and the corpse-eater (the ghoul)" (1986: 41).

12. See Henry's (2014) analysis of *Teeth* and *Hard Candy* in "The Postfeminist Trap of Vagina Dentata for the American Teen *Castrice*" in *Revisionist Rape Revenge*.

13. Zoe also blames Brener for Kyle's death, reasoning that if he had not raped Madison, Madison would not have flipped the bus and killed most of the fraternity. Zoe is offended by the attack on her friend and by her loss of a romantic interest, even though her magic would have prevented a sexual relationship with Kyle.

14. As Projansky explains, when describing their central figure of the empowered woman, "postfeminist discourses define the feminism that made her choices possible as focused entirely on a deracialized (but implicitly white) desire for 'sameness' with men, particularly in terms of economic success and (hetero)sexual freedom" (12). Madison knows what she wants and has the power to take it if she chooses—she has conquered the position of the successful heterosexual man in an American capitalist culture that views sexual partners as possessions, the value of which increases when they are desired by others. This ability to achieve the same position qualifies as victory from a postfeminist perspective, and Madison's eventual death and defeat indicate *Coven*'s preference for the new, more inclusive and communal ideal to which Zoe and Cordelia aspire.

References

Berridge, Susan. 2011. "Personal Problems and Women's Issues: Episodic Sexual Violence Narratives in US Teen Drama Series." *Feminist Media Studies* 11, 4: 467–81. https://doi.org/10.1080/14680777.2011.555967.

_____. 2013. "Teen Heroine TV: Narrative Complexity and Sexual Violence in Female-Fronted Teen Drama Series." *New Review of Film and Television Studies* 11, 4: 477–96. DOI.org (Crossref), doi:10.1080/17400309.2013.809565.

Cerny, Cathleen, Susan Hatters Friedman, and Delaney Smith. 2014. "Television's 'Crazy Lady' Trope: Female Psychopathic Traits, Teaching, and Influence of Popular Culture." *Academic Psychiatry* 38, 2: 233–41. https://doi.org/10.1007/s40596-014-0035-9.

Chusna, Aidatul, and Shofi Mahmudah. 2018. "Female Monsters: Figuring Female Transgression in *Jennifer's Body* (2009) and *The Witch* (2013)." *Jurnal Humaniora* 30, 1: 10–16. https://doi.org/10.22146/jh.v30i1.31499.

Clover, Carole J. 2015. *Men, Women, and Chainsaws: Gender in the Modern Horror Film—Updated Edition.* Princeton, NJ: Princeton University Press.

Creed, Barbara. 1986. "Horror and the Monstrous-Feminine: An Imaginary Abjection." *Screen* 27, 1: 44–71. https://doi.org/10.1093/screen/27.1.44.

Cuklanz, Lisa M., and Sujata Moorti. 2006. "Television's 'New' Feminism: Prime-Time Representations of Women and Victimization." *Critical Studies in Media Communication* 23, 4: 302–21. https://doi.org/10.1080/07393180600933121.

Dickson, E.J. 2019. "Swarthmore Frats Disband After 4-Day Student Sit-In" *Rolling Stone* (blog) April 30. https://www.rollingstone.com/culture/culture-news/swarthmore-students-protesting-campus-fraternities-829170/.

Downey, Dara. 2019. "Tracing Tituba Through American Horror Story: Coven." *European Journal of American Culture* 38, 1: 15–27. https://doi.org/10.1386/ejac.38.1.15_1.

Earle, Harriet, and Jessica Clark. 2019. "Telling National Stories in American Horror Story." *European Journal of American Culture* 38, 1: 5–13. https://doi.org/10.1386 /ejac.38.1.5_7.

Ebert, Roger. 1980. "Review of *I Spit on Your Grave*. Directed by Meir Zarchi." July 16. https://www.rogerebert.com/reviews/i-spit-on-your-grave-1980.

———. 2010. "Review of *I Spit on Your Grave*. Directed by Steven R. Monroe." Oct 6. https://www.rogerebert.com/reviews/i-spit-on-your-grave-2010.

Fleming, Andrew (dir.). 1996. *The Craft*. Columbia Pictures.

Gibson, Marion. 2006. "Retelling Salem Stories: Gender Politics and Witches in American Culture." *European Journal of American Culture* 25, 2: 85–107. https://doi.org/10.1386/ejac.25.2.85/1.

Goldberg, Lesley. 2013. "Hollywood's New Season of the Witch." *Hollywood Reporter*, Nov 8. General OneFile.

Henry, Claire. 2014. *Revisionist Rape-Revenge: Redefining a Film Genre*. New York: Palgrave Macmillan.

Hill, David F. 2019. "'I Was in D.U.—Swarthmore's Fraternities Must Go" *The Phoenix*. Apr 23. https://swarthmorephoenix.com/2019/04/23/i-was-in-d-u-swarthmores-fraternities-must-go/.

Hutchison, Phillip J. 2018. "When TV Became a Target: Ritual and Burlesque in Television Creature Features." *Journal of Popular Film and Television* 46, 2: 95–107. https://doi.org/10.1080/01956051.2018.1458020.

Jermyn, Deborah. 1996. "Rereading the Bitches from Hell: A Feminist Appropriation of the Female Psychopath." *Screen* 37, 3: 251–67. https://doi.org/10.1093/screen/37.3.251.

King, Amy K. 2017. "A Monstrous(Ly-Feminine) Whiteness: Gender, Genre, and the Abject Horror of the Past in American Horror Story: Coven." *Women's Studies* 46, 6: 557–73. https://doi.org/10.1080/00497878.2017.1356302.

Kusama, Karyn (dir.). 2009. *Jennifer's Body*. Atomic Fox in association with Dune Entertainment.

LeBlanc, Amanda Kay. 2018. "'There's Nothing I Hate More Than a Racist': (Re)Centering Whiteness in American Horror Story: Coven." *Critical Studies in Media Communication* 35, 3: 273–85. https://doi.org/10.1080/15295036.2017.1416418.

Maguire, David. 2018. *I Spit on Your Grave (Cultographies)*. New York: Wallflower Press, Columbia University Press.

Monroe, Steven R. (dir.). 2010. *I Spit on Your Grave*. CineTel.

Moseley, Rachel. 2002. "Glamorous Witchcraft: Gender and Magic in Teen Film and Television." *Screen* 43, 4: 403–22. https://doi.org/10.1093/screen/43.4.403.

Osei, Zipporah. 2019. "After Protests, Swarthmore Will End All Greek Life on Campus." *The Chronicle of Higher Education*. May 10. https://www.chronicle.com/article/After-Protests-Swarthmore/246279.

Projansky, Sarah. 2001. *Watching Rape: Film and Television in Postfeminist Culture*. New York: New York University Press.

Rain, Callen. 2019. "I Was a Member of Phi Psi—Swarthmore's Fraternities Must Go." *The Phoenix*. Apr 21. https://swarthmorephoenix.com/2019/04/21/i-was-a-member-of-phi-psi-swarthmores-fraternities-must-go/.

Stack, Tim. 2013. "The Witching Hour" *Entertainment Weekly EW.com*. Apr 12. https://ew.com/article/2013/04/12/witching-hour-4/.

Zarchi, Meir (dir.). 1978. *I Spit on Your Grave*. Barquel Creations.

Witches with Disabilities on 21st-Century Television Programs

Aaron K.H. Ho

Why doesn't Harry Potter magic his myopia away? In a fantasy world, limbs can regenerate just as Deadpool regrows them each time they are severed. Prosthetic eyes become real eyes as Thor pops one into his socket. Like Superman, with his impressive immune system, witches don't fall ill and become disabled, as attested and declared by Sabrina (Kiernan Shipka) in the Netflix production (2018–2020) and Cassandra Nightingale (Catherine Bell) in *Good Witch* (2015–present). A witch's magic cures and protects her and her premonitory powers prevent accidents that may lead to disabilities. A witch's innate, protective magical powers may be the reason that few witches with disabilities are portrayed onscreen but lest we forget, magic is not real. Harry Potter wears glasses because J.K. Rowling, the creator of the Potter universe, dictates rules of what magic can and cannot achieve, restricting boundaries for her creation. Likewise, in any television series which constructs a make-believe world, to excuse showrunners for not including actors with disabilities or not depicting disabilities in narratives about witches because they possess power to protect themselves is to quixotically and foolishly believe that magic is real. Showrunners can follow Rowling's example and stipulate rules of magic in fictitious settings, allowing for narratives to discuss and represent disabilities onscreen.

Although 25 percent of American adults are disabled (CDC 2018), only 2.1 percent of televisual characters have disabilities (GLAAD 2019). The GLAAD report does not state if the characters are played by actors with disabilities but evidently, people with disabilities are severely underrepresented on television. And when they are represented, disability theorists have pointed out that people with disabilities onscreen are often dehumanized stereotypes comprising sadcrips (pitiful victims), supercrips (who "overcome" their disabilities to gain success), murderous villains, circus freaks, and useless burdens who are better off dead (Barnes 1992; Darke 2004; Ellis 2008; Gray 2000; Longmore 2003; Luther, Ringer Lepre, and Clark 2012; Mitchell and Synder 2001; Nelson 2000; and Riley 2005). These negative, systemic representations not only affect the lived experiences of people with disabilities but also shape how society views them, which in turn restricts their access to power, agency, and status (Barns 1992; Cumberbatch and Negrine 1992; Hadley and McDonald 2019; Nelson 2000; Quayson 2013; and Ross 1997).

However, as I have suggested in the introduction of this collection, a new, "woke" consciousness entered television programs in the 2010s with the rise of international streaming services catering to a broad spectrum of audiences, calling for diversity in casting, characters, and narratives. This essay, then, sets out to test the relevancy of the above-mentioned assumptions about media stereotypes of people with disabilities: are current representations still depicting them to be threats or to be pitied, with little or no "evolution in their public image … over the past four decades" (Riley 2005: 1)? Furthermore and specifically, an examination into programs on which witches can achieve a fission other programs may not: as a fantasy, why and when is magic used to heal or not heal disabilities? What happens to programs on witches as fantasies of women's empowerment when witches themselves have disabilities? How do women with power *and* disabilities confound and redefine our understanding of subjectivity? This essay begins with a brief discussion on the definitions and theories of disabilities, helpful in our reading of *American Horror Story: Coven* (2013–4) and *Apocalypse* (2018), *Chilling Adventures of Sabrina*, and *The Magicians* (2015–2020). I argue that while it may take a complete ideological shift to separate some clichés regarding people with disabilities from the horror genre, people with disabilities are depicted fairly in some cases. Furthermore, issues of disabilities often imbricate with gender and race such that they together challenge systemic inequalities.

Definitions of Disabilities

As Barbara M. Altman observes, "Part of the difficulty of defining disability has to do with the fact that disability is a complicated, multidimensional concept" (2001: 97). She means that while there is only a single way to define an abled body, disabilities occur and can manifest in myriad, variegated ways. Among the many definitions of disabilities—medical, economic, sociopolitical, and administrative (for a detailed explication of these definitions, see Altman 2001 and Williams 2001)—this essay adopts the sociopolitical perspective defined by the Americans with Disabilities Act (ADA): "To be protected by the ADA, one must have a disability, which is defined by the ADA as a physical or mental impairment that substantially limits one or more major life activities, a person who has a history or record of such an impairment, or a person who is perceived by others as having such an impairment" (ADA 1990). This definition spans widely from physical to mental disabilities such as alcoholism and post-traumatic stress disorder (PTSD).

There are several reasons why I chose this definition above others. Firstly, ADA's definition is situational and reveals the social construction of disabilities; a person who is viewed as disabled in some social situations may not be disabled in others. For example, in Bengkala, a small Balinese village, 44 out of the 3,000 people living there are hearing impaired due to a recessive gene passed down for seven generations. As a result, 80 percent of the population choose to learn Kata Kolok, a unique local sign language (*Great Big Story* 2018). In this society, people with hearing impairment are not disabled, they function perfectly well without any assistance; on the contrary, those 20 percent who cannot sign are the ones who are disabled regardless of their hearing ability. This situational definition is sometimes hypostasized in television programs. In *The Magicians*, Quentin, who is a depressive, manages to hold on to a magical artifact that drives most people to suicide precisely because he is inured to having morbid thoughts and can ward off the evil magic (3x6 "Do You Like Teeth?"). In this case, Quentin is the abled one and his triumph in not succumbing to the artifact's influence positions his disability as something worth celebrating.

ADA's definition also eradicates the binary bias found in the medical model which states disability to be a clear-cut medical condition. As first propounded by Irving Kenneth Zola (1989), disabilities should be seen as a spectrum of abilities such as degrees of walking, visual, and hearing impairment; autism; Down syndrome; diabetes; and HIV infection. The spectrum of abilities avoids the academic fallacy of simplification due to dichotomous thinking; allows new and complex ways of defining abilities and disabilities; reminds us the contingency that anyone could be disabled and people with disabilities can achieve abilities that abled bodies can; and, since anyone can be disabled at any time, interrogates the social construction of stereotypes shown on television and other forms of media. Instead of the medical binary model of disabled/abled, the ADA's sociopolitical definition engenders a dialectic conversation between cultural assumptions and bodies of people with disabilities; Disabled bodies become a battlefield where subliminal social stereotypes threaten to tear them asunder but, at the same time, they generate new meanings and significances in the discourse on subjectivity and agency.

Disabilities and Witch Programs as Horror Genre

Currently, the genre of horror finds it hard to divorce itself from depictions of disabilities since images of disabilities induce an eerie atmosphere, not because disabilities are unfamiliar and defamiliarized, but because audience has been conditioned to associate disabilities with evil; the use of disabilities to create a preternatural atmosphere is more telling of the social construction around disabilities than disabilities themselves. Barbara Maria Stafford (1994) traces the association of physiognomy to innate qualities since the eighteenth century; physical features were correlated to traits such as sanity and immorality. The horror genre thus often profits from this social association by presenting disabled people as evil and vile (Bogdan, Biklen, Shapiro, and Spelkoman 1982). Paul Longman remarks, "[A]mong the most persistent [stereotypes] is the association of disability with malevolence. Deformity of body symbolizes deformity of soul. Physical handicaps are made the emblems of evil" (2003: 133). He goes on to identify three stereotypes of this association: "Disability is a punishment for evil; disabled people are embittered by their 'fate'; disabled people resent the nondisabled and would, if they could, destroy them" (2003: 134). In *Apocalypse*, Wilhelmina Venable, who suffers from severe scoliosis and walks with a cane, reveals her condition in a scene designed to terrify viewers with its mise-en-scène of a darkened, shadowy, cavernous space lit by a flickering fire, the ominous music, the close-up on her spine, and the creepy caressing of her spine by the son of Satan, Michael Langdon (8x2 "The Morning After"). While her condition is meant to frighten the audience, perhaps scarier is Michael's perverse need to humiliate her by forcing her to strip. He requires a physical examination and when she tells him that he can read it from her file, he insists on her stripping because he needs to see her shame. If we read the voyeuristic Langdon as a stand-in for voyeuristic viewers, then this scene exposes the hypocrisy of viewers who are both fascinated with and unnerved by Wilhelmina's scoliosis. Still, she is cruel and evil, and as the leader of an underground bunker, she creates her own rules about celibacy and those who violate it face capital punishment. In the end, she murders almost all the residents of the bunker. Although *Apocalypse* adheres to the stereotypes of disabled villain and sadcrip, the scene also exposes the societal voyeurism on disabilities.

A particular feature of witch programs in the 2010s situated in the genre of horror is that the constructed universe usually approaches an apocalypse, which occurs in *Salem* (2014–2017), *The Magicians*, *Sabrina*, *Charmed* (2018–present), and *Apocalypse*. En route to, during, or after the apocalypse, destruction and ruin demand the spectacle of disabled bodies—limbs torn apart, eyes gorged out, skin charred—as visual images of negative symbolism. While this link between world destruction and disabilities is negative, it is perhaps not possible to imagine a world on the brink of apocalypse on a visual medium without showing people with disabilities, quite similar to the implausibility of not depicting disabilities in war movies. Yet in many of these television series, most characters, while saving the world, are killed in preference to being maimed. Among the reasons involved in this narrative decision are to trigger audience's emotional catharsis; to provide a visual spectacle when characters are resurrected with magic or rescued using time-travel via magic; and, for practicality, the main cast of normate-actors, who are and will be on the show for seasons, could not sustain playing characters with disabilities nor should they attempt to crip drag. Showrunners and scriptwriters are caught in a double bind: the normate-actors, who are cast right at the beginning of the season up till the scene of apocalypse, shouldn't be made disabled because such roles should be reserved for actors with disabilities, yet if they cast actors with disabilities right from the start of the season, their disabilities have no visual effect on the scene of apocalypse. I suggest that showrunners include actors with disabilities when and after, not before, apocalypse occurs in a narrative that showcases their subjectivities so that there exists a sense of devastation that apocalypse brings but also a well-rounded narrative allowing agency on the part of characters to prevent stereotypes of sadcrip.

Sabrina *and the Lack of Representations*

A random Google search on "diversity and *Sabrina*" would reveal that the streaming program is heralded as horror with a focus on diversity, featuring people of color, a transgender character (played by a nonbinary actor Lachlan Watson), and queer characters. Yet few characters with disabilities exist in the show. This is not to say that *all* media productions should portray people with disabilities, but for a show that champions a diverse cast and characters, the glaring dearth demonstrates the exigency of disability representations on television.

There are, however, two depictions of disabilities, blindness and PTSD. Roz Walker, Sabrina's best friend, suffers from myopic atrophy, slowly going blind. She finds out from her blind grandmother that the Walker women were cursed by witches generations ago, but in return for the loss of sight, they gain what the grandmother calls "the cunning," enabling them to have visions about the past and the future. Roz's blindness is associated with having no faith in Christianity—her father is a minister—and her sexuality (1x6 "An Exorcism in Greendale"); she goes blind after passionately kissing a boy as if she is punished (by god?) for her sexual transgression (2x3 "Lupercalia"). The characterization of blindness in *Sabrina* falls into the stereotypes of the wise disabled and disability as punishment.

Furthermore, Roz's struggle with the acceptance of her disability merits only 3.5 minutes of onscreen time (2x6 "The Missionaries"). Worse still, the scene is shown from Sabrina's perspective, neglecting Roz's subjectivity as a person with disability. In this scene, Sabrina offers to use magic to cure Roz's eyes but she rejects the offer, which may appear to be a celebration and embracing of her disability, but in effect the scene serves to convey Sabrina's isolation and ostracism, just as all but one disciple abandoned Jesus. Like Jesus, Sabrina is later killed in the episode and resurrected, fulfilling part of the prophecy that she performs Satanic perversions of Jesus's miracles. In the next episode, Roz changes her mind because she is scared that if she goes to a school for the blind, she "will never come back" (2x7 "The Miracles of Sabrina Spellman"). While it should be noted that leaving her posse and entering a school for blind people is so terrifying that Roz, a Christian who knows about Sabrina's history of a blotched spell which has brought about much grief, rather risks her soul and eyes, perhaps the more offensive and subtler point is that Roz's blindness is used to further Sabrina's trajectory. In healing Roz's eyes, Sabrina performs another Christ-like miracle, allowing Sabrina to bring about the apocalypse. David Mitchell and Sharon Snyder (2013) term this exploitation of characters with disabilities to extend other characters' arcs "narrative prosthesis." The portrayal of blindness in *Sabrina* acts as a plot device that allows Sabrina to fulfill her destiny and Roz to possess "the cunning" without losing her sight, enabling Roz to assist Sabrina in her future chilling adventures.

Unlike Roz who suffers from a matrilineal curse, the other character with disability, Nick Scratch (Gavin Leatherwood), suffers PTSD from trapping Satan within his body and being imprisoned in hell, topless, chained at the foot of Madam Satan (Michelle Gomez), similar to the iconic scene of Princess Leia in a golden bikini by the side of Jabba the Hutt in *Star Wars: Return of the Jedi*. PTSD is often coded as a masculine disability because, as Charles A. Riley notes, it is the masculine violence of 9/11 that brought PTSD to prominence as a disability (2005: 79), with numerous post 9/11 television series depicting veterans with PTSD. Like veterans who suffer from PTSD, Nick has fought a war (against Satan) and has been tortured like a prisoner of war. Even as PTSD is coded masculine, Lenore Manderson and Susan Peake argue that "since masculinity is defined as able-bodied and active, the disabled man is an oxymoron. Being disabled for a man means to 'cross the fence' and take on the stigmatizing constructs of the masculine body made feminine and soft" (2005: 233). Nick's disability emasculates him in several ways, some of which are marked on his body: he is bullied by two of the Weird Sisters for the first time in the series for having Satan "in" him; he cannot or does not want to sleep with Sabrina when he has been characterized as promiscuous, but he hires sex demons for sadomasochistic acts; he drinks to severe intoxication and abuses substances; and as an outward sign of his disability, he develops a clubfoot of mangled, excessive toes which evolves to an indestructible hoof that he attempts but fails to amputate. The scene when the clubfoot is first revealed shocks and terrifies the audience, much like Wilhelmina's severe scoliosis in *Apocalypse*. As a narrative prosthesis, Nick releases Satan in exchange for drugs so that eventually, Sabrina can triumph over and wrestle control of hell from Satan. Nick's disability turns the usually active, resourceful, powerful witch into an effete, languishing, whiny boy for the whole of the third season.

After Nick releases Satan, Sabrina, with the help of her cousin Ambrose, restrains and coerces Nick into a magical cold turkey and rehab. This is not the first time Sabrina bulldozes her way to cure someone's addiction: she gifts a magical rum eggnog to the father of her ex-boyfriend Harvey Kinkle (Ross Lynch) to cure his alcoholism, unbeknown to the father and son. Even though she uses magic on men without their consent—and this is contentious—she seems to cure their toxic masculinity along with their addictions and the men turn out for the better. Harvey's father no longer abuses him, no longer compels him to take over the mining family business and accepts Harvey's artistic ambitions. Nick, who has been verbally abusing Sabrina during his PTSD, cheating on her, castigating her for his own failures, arrives at an epiphany after he is cured that he has wronged Sabrina, realized how awesome she is, and is full of regret for missing out on a golden opportunity to remain her boyfriend. In *Sabrina*, the fantasy of performing magic to heal disabilities prioritizes the abled body over the disabled, which is problematic, but at the same time, disabilities reveal the gender disparity in an attempt to balance the power by allowing Roz to retain "the cunning" while removing toxic masculinity from the men.

Diversity and Desiring Disabilities in American Horror Story: Coven *and* Apocalypse

Brad Falchuk and Ryan Murphy, the showrunners of *American Horror Story*, created one of the most popular and endearing characters with disabilities on early 21st-century television: Artie Abrams (Kevin McHale), a student in a wheelchair from *Glee* (2009–2015). Like *Glee*, *Coven* immediately announces its interest in diverse representations by including a mute butler in service of the witches, Spalding (Denis O'Hare); and casting Jamie Brewer, an actor with Down syndrome, in the role of Nan, a student-witch, a role she reprises in *Apocalypse*. Later, Cordelia Goode (Sarah Paulson), the headmistress for the school for witches, becomes blind—twice.

The young witches in *Coven* take on primary powers apposite to their situation and/or heritage: Zoe Benson (Taissa Farmiga), a virgin, kills every man she copulates with; the angsty and somewhat heartless movie star Madison Montgomery (Emma Roberts) possesses the active power of telekinesis; Queenie (Gabourey Sidibe), a black witch, is a human voodoo doll, transferring her self-mutilated injuries to her target; and Nan, who has Down syndrome and is clairvoyant, is said to be "smarter than all of you [new witches] put together" (3x1 "Bitchcraft"). In this case, even though Nan is portrayed to be the wise disabled, a stereotype, and even though she is sometimes used as a narrative prosthesis (such as when she discovers Delphine LaLaurie [Kathy Bates], forwarding Fiona's [Jessica Lange] search for immortality and extending Queenie's racial storyline), her character subverts societal notions of how a person with Down syndrome behaves. She possesses agency; has a sexual history; competes with Madison for Luke, the boy-next-door who looks like an Abercrombie & Fitch model and who reciprocates Nan's affections; plays a pivotal role in solving Madison's murder by reading Spalding's mind; and revenges Luke's murder by mind-controlling his killer to drink bleach. However, in the end, she is sacrificed to Papa Legba, a loa in Haitian voodoo, as an innocent, negating the things she has done previously, things that are not that innocent. The narrative makes it so that although she is killed, she is contented to be Papa Legba's helper. In *Apocalypse*, when Cordelia gathers her "girls" to fight Satan's son, Nan chooses to stay with Papa Legba in hell, leaving Nan out of most of the series. Although I personally view this directorial decision to omit a person of Down syndrome in the series to be problematic because of the narrative inconsistency that Nan, who has been portrayed as kind-hearted throughout the series, is forthwith cruel after she is murdered, therefore choosing to remain in hell to torture souls, it is without doubt that the character possesses agency.

Like Nan, Spalding's disability has been mocked by the cruel Madison: "Did you use your tongue for something wicked? Or maybe you just suck at going down. Oh, come on, Jeeves. Show us your stub. Maybe we can put it to use" (1x1). Madison abuses Spalding and Nan verbally over their disabilities because she is an equal-opportunity termagant, offending everyone, abled or disabled; however, such abusive dialogue directed at anyone in her way does not excuse her atrocious behavior and reveals the discrimination people with disabilities face. Although Madison sexualizes Spalding, it is apparent that she bullies him for his effeteness. Like Nick in *Sabrina*, Spalding is evirated but in this case, it is even clearer that he is symbolically castrated through the tongue mutilation: in an act of love, told from his perspective, he chooses to cut off his tongue rather than betray Fiona. But he does not play the stereotype of a self-sacrificial person with disability; he demonstrates his own tastes and preferences. After Fiona murders Madison, Spalding, dressed in a nightgown and bonnet, plays tea with her corpse as if she were a doll (3x4 "Fearful Pranks Ensue"). Spalding's tongue is finally recovered and magically sutured after being severed for forty years, allowing him to tell his story, but he is killed immediately after he finishes his narrative. Although, like Nan, he is eventually murdered, he returns as a ghost to save Fiona and to create trouble. His disability, like Nick's, puts him in an emasculated position but where Nick is cured of his disability/toxic masculinity, Spalding being "whole" is killed off, signaling perhaps that he has more worth as a person with disability than one without. As a consequence, he and Nan own their agency and show their subjectivities, unlike the characters with disabilities in *Sabrina*.

Cordelia the headmistress, who occupies center stage of the narrative, goes blind mid-series when she is attacked by a witch hunter who is a part of a group disguised under a male supremacist financial corporation called the Delphi Trust. But her blindness gifts her an inner sight like Roz in *Sabrina*. Although on the surface Cordelia's blindness plays into the stereotype of the wised disabled, her blindness empowers her, unlike Roz who remains much or less Sabrina's sidekick. Before her incident, she is consumed with the desire to have a child with her husband, but with the new power, she glimpses his affair and chases him out of her life. She begins to regard the young witches as her family, her daughters, devoting her life to the good of the coven. At the same time, unlike Roz's three-minute tantrum over the loss of sight, Cordelia displays genuine anger and fear and helplessness throughout the series when she is blind. She is frustrated when people move furniture, causing her to trip (3x9 "Head"). She cowers in fear under a hall table when she hears but is unable to see a serial killer in the same room (3x6 "The Axeman Cometh"). When she first returns home from the hospital with her husband and mother, Fiona, her room is decorated with roses, which bring love and romance (3x6). She gets angry and rejects the roses: "I need chrysanthemums. All kinds of them, for strength and protection." The scene underscores her fear and vexation, but also her independence as a strong woman to symbolically reject love (with her husband standing beside her) and protect the young witches, embracing her role as a mother to them. She regains her sight but loses her inner sight (3x9). Deciding that the second sight is important to protect the coven of young witches, she stabs her own eyes in a gruesome scene (3x11 "Protect the Coven"). Although the scene demonstrates the stereotype of disability to be ennobling, her disabled body, like Spalding's, is placed in circumstances where it is valued more than the abled. Empowered by her blindness, she emerges from the shadows of her mother, the most powerful witch in the coven, and becomes the leader. Passed from leader to leader for generations, her mother's powers are transferred to her body, allowing her to recover her sight like Roz. However, unlike Roz who desires to regain her sight, Cordelia becoming sighted again is just part of the benefits she reaps with her increased powers; that is to say, Cordelia (and by extension *Coven*) does not hierarchize her abled body over the disabled. In *Coven*, the body is often tortured, suffered, and pained to the point of disability but the disabled body is more than a functioning one, and perhaps better adapted to situations than its original state.

White Men Without Disabilities in The Magicians

Although white men in *The Magicians* do suffer from mental disabilities—Quentin Coldwater (Jason Ralph) and Eliot Waugh (Hale Appleman) suffer from depression—their disabilities are not explored nor do the disabilities affect them greatly. And so it is problematic that characters with physical disabilities in *The Magicians* are minorities, women and/or people who are not white: people who are already disenfranchised. Kira (guest actor Yanni King) hits the multiaxial quota of affirmative action by being lesbian, woman, hedge witch, black, mute, and completely paralyzed (1x9 "The Writing Room"). As a narrative prosthesis, Kira, the stereotype of the wise disabled, points Julia Wicker (Stella Maeve) the way to growing her powers when Julia enters Kira's mind. In exchange for the information, Kira wants Julia to euthanize her. In a dilemma, Julia consults Richard (Mackenzie Astin), a priest and a hedge witch, asking, "What if a magician finds a cure tomorrow? What if there really is a hell and this takes me there?" He replies, "You're already in hell. So is she." At first blush, the scene appears to be derogatory, yet disabilities are depicted kindly in the series in sophisticated ways that cannot simplistically be called discriminatory. Even in the scene, Kira sets a test for Julia before Julia can access to her mind, that is, Kira grants her consent unlike how Sabrina bends men with disabilities to her will even if she has their best interests at heart. The scene is played out in Kira's mind, giving her subjectivity, and the decision to be euthanized is hers, empowering her.

Such sensitive handling of disabilities continues throughout the series. In the very first episode, an evil magician attacks Brakebills University, a school for young magicians, plucks out the eyes of the African American dean, Henry Fogg (Rick Worthy), and chops his hands off to prevent him from casting spells. (The appearance of the evil magician is noteworthy—he is *not* physically disabled but shrouded in butterflies, much scarier than any disabled character.) Magic heals Fogg to a small extent: he can make out shadowy outlines and his hands require physiotherapy, rendering him a poor and inaccurate spell caster (1x8 "The Strangled Heart"; 2x4 "The Flying Forest"). To others, he insists that he is fine, but he undergoes a period of private anguish, denial, and adjustment before coming to terms with his disabilities. He is partially blind for three seasons—an admirably long time to sustain this trajectory—and develops into a high-functioning alcoholic (3x6 "Do You Like Teeth?"). However, Julia, hedge witch-turned-god, senses a "desperation" in Fogg and volunteers to heal his eyes (3x12 "The Fillorian Candidate"). He rejects her offer twice: "[F]ixing them [his eyes] with magic risks changing the very core of who I am." She reasons that she is a god and hears prayers and is "supposed to do something about them," otherwise there is no reason she's gifted with the powers. While her reasoning appears contrived because Fogg hasn't prayed to cure his eyes, *The Magicians* proves sensitive to issues of disabilities by showing the daily struggles of Fogg and his cherished subjectivity as a person with visual impairment. Furthermore, his abilities are hardly affected in that he competently carries out his duties as a dean, no matter blind or sighted.

However, it becomes problematic when another man of color loses his hands in the same season: Fogg in the first episode and Indian American Penny Adiyodi (Arjun Gupta) in the last (1x1 "Unauthorized Magic"; 1x13 "Have You Brought Me Little Cakes?"). The magicians use elaborate hand gestures to do magic, and chopping off the hands of male minorities, symbolic of castration, leaves them powerless and emasculated. This white male fantasy of emasculating men of color is so much desired that Penny has his hands chopped off twice by white men (1x13; 2x4 "The Flying Forest"). (Fogg's hands are also sliced by a white man.) Even when Penny's hands are cured, he requires physiotherapy like Fogg. His reattached hands, being cursed by yet another white man, remain unruly and have a life of their own (2x1 "Knight of Crowns"): they swing and hit people in unpredictable situations; they cast teleportation spells that put him in dangerous places, such as in a volcano, putting his life in peril; they are unable to cast the right spell when Penny wants them to. In order to prevent mishaps, a spell is cast to restrict his hands: his hands are fettered in chains for a night and, after that night, have to be weighed down by a pair of bracelets, symbolic of shackles, reminiscent of American slavery. Still, the bracelets aren't the solution. He has to sign over his life *and* his afterlife for *one million years* to be an employee at the Library, an organization in an alternate universe, Neitherlands, that holds the world's knowledge, so that he can research a cure for his hands. As an Asian American, Penny is so dangerous and threatening that he has to be maimed (twice!), shackled, and relegated to an alternate world. His danger emanates from his sexuality as a virile, attractive man. Standing at 6'1", the well-built handsome Arjun Gupta, who plays Penny, is often shown topless or displaying much skin. His hirsute chocolate body signals sexual maturity and oozes sex appeal. From the first episode of the series, Kady (Jade Tailor) and Penny engage in coitus with them levitating off the bed. Penny, along with his alter-ego, Penny-23, is involved with two female lead characters, one of whom, Julia, is the unattainable childhood crush of Quentin, the "mediocre" and "unimpressive" (as he is often described by other characters) white man, the lead of the series, who perhaps inadvertently is one of the men who chops off Penny's hands (2x4). Disability, in Penny's case, highlights the taming of dangerous sexuality a non-white man can possess.

It is strange that people of color share similar disabilities: While Fogg loses his sight, Margo (played by Summer Bishil with Mexican, Caucasian, Indian descent) loses one eye as a toll for transgressing into the fairy world. What should be a traumatizing event turns out to an opportunity for dry-humor banter with her best friend, Eliot:

> MARGO: I look like Jack Sparrow if he were played by a man.
> ELIOT: I was actually thinking more like a Fembot Nick Fury.
> [...]
> ELIOT: Wait, is your good eye crying right now?
> MARGO: No. Yes. And it's not my good eye, it's my only fucking eye.
> [ELIOT CHUCKLES]
> MARGO: It's not funny, you dick, I'm a Cyclops!
> ELIOT: A mythological monster at last. Box checked [2x13 "We Have Brought You Little Cakes"].

While the conversation appears to be flippant, Margo and Eliot communicate in this strain of dry humor throughout the series. As a form of therapy, Margo's self-deprecating humor is at once funny and poignant, although she does not continue to struggle with her disability like Fogg and Penny. Her missing eyeball is employed by the Fairy Queen to spy on Margo—a narrative prosthesis (3x1 "The Tale of the Seven Keys"). But when she steals her eyeball from the Queen, and the Queen demands it back, she squashes her eye rather than giving it to the Queen. Similar to Cordelia who stabs her own eyes in *Coven*, Margo chooses (what seems to be) an irreversible disability at the moment, but their disabilities empower them. In Margo's case, she refuses to be subjugated under the Queen, and in destroying her eye, she gains dignity and self-respect—a little triumph amidst her oppression by the Queen. In *The Magicians*, unlike the men whose disabilities emasculate them, Margo and other women thrive because of their disabilities.

Another woman character, Harriet Schiff, played by Marlee Matlin, the only performer with hearing impairment to win an Oscar for Best Actress in *Children of a Lesser God* (1986), one of the few disability-affirming movies, thrives as a resistance leader amongst hedge witches against the tyranny of the Library's selfish hoarding and gatekeeping of magical knowledge. She works at FuzzBeat—a simulacrum of BuzzFeed—to encode information on casting spells in viral listicles to open up knowledge to magicians and hedge witches who have no access to the Library. Seen in this light, the Library and FuzzBeat are allegories of authoritarian and democratic regimes respectively, and she heads the resistance against authoritarianism. Her disability thus affords her a different ability to help others: "This is my magic," she says, pointing to a listicle (2x10 "The Girl Who Told Time"). Her disability also allows her to bond with women, a way of empowering them. Penny, now a Librarian, and Kady visit Harriet at the FuzzBeat office to collect an overdue library book. When Harriet begins to sign, Penny ducks, misconstruing that she is casting a spell. Even though Penny is disabled, he cannot recognize her disability and they cannot reach a mutual understanding of each other. By the end of the scene, Penny is so frustrated that when she wishes him, "Have a nice day," he says, "Fuck off" (2x10). He treats everyone in a brash manner, but unlike Madison in *Coven*, he does not attack people based on their personal, physical traits, and thus his no-kids-gloves treatment of Harriet paradoxically signifies his respect for her. On the other hand, Kady, who understands sign language, banters jocularly with Harriet, and it is through this mentor-student bond that Harriet guides and helps Kady several times. This mentor-student bond circumvents the stereotype of the wise and kind disabled: Harriet is a hedge witch who believes in a democratic world of sharing information (and so she helps Kady), and whose knowledge comes from experience in the school of hard knocks, not mysteriously from her disability. Her disability empowers her in two ways: providing her with an ability, a different type of magic, to help others; and creating strong bonds with other women. In addition, it is empowering for audiences with disabilities to witness two characters with disabilities holding the highest authority in their respective organizations: Fogg as the dean of the university and Harriet as the leader of the resistance fighters.

Harriet also differs from most characters with disabilities in never searching for a magical cure for her disability. In a powerful flashback scene detailing three periods of her life—as a girl, a teenager, and an adult—with her mother, Head Librarian Zelda Schiff (Mageina Tovah), they altercate over the functions of books and the Library (3x8 "Six Short Stories About

Magic"). The overly protective mother demands that Harriet remain in the safety of the Library and read about the millions of worlds offered in the books, but Harriet wants to be written about, she wants a life outside the enclosed space of the Library. When Zelda wants Harriet to withdraw from Brakebills and finish her education in the Library, Harriet counters, "You don't go to school just for the books, you go to make friends, try new things, drink shitty beer" (3x8). When Zelda requests she be a librarian, Harriet agrees on the condition that the Library opens up to more people. Neither relents. Not only do viewers witness Harriet's development of subjectivity—she is a headstrong, idealistic, independent, adventurous, strong, trusting, original thinker—the 9.5-minute long scene is almost silent. Throughout the scene, the muted sound is similar to the whirring of a large industrial ventilation fan heard through ear plugs, punctuated with occasional sharp sounds of heels clacking or mirrors shattering. Viewers are put in Harriet's mind and world, and to a hearing viewer, this perspective is vertiginous and disorienting. This brilliant scene, an exemplar of portrayal of disabilities onscreen, highlights her agency and subjectivity and elucidates to the audience her struggles and perspective without resorting to the sadcrip stereotype.

Unfortunately, the episode ends with what the audience assumes to be her end. Killing a character with disability is not disallowed; Spalding and Nan in *Coven*, for instance, are murdered without falling into the helpless sadcrip stereotype. But for an experienced, knowledgeable hedge witch, the way Harriet dies—being pushed into the Mirror Realm that is then destroyed with her in it—is ignominious; helpless, she doesn't even retaliate. Moreover, when she is later discovered to be alive, trapped in the Mirror Realm, she pleads with her mother, with whom she has a terrible relationship, to rescue her, replicating the stereotype of the dependent disabled child (4x7 "The Side Effect"). When Zelda moves into the Mirror Realm to find her, she discovers that Harriet is split into three fragments: herself, a doppelgänger with no eyes, and another with her mouth sliced like Batman's Joker (4x7). It seems particularly vulgar and humiliating to depict her blind (no eyes) and with a distorted mouth (perhaps representing a difficulty in speech or even muteness). During the magical spell to rescue Harriet, Alice (Olivia Dudley), the most talented magician, blotches the process, only one fragment of Harriet escapes and Alice is split into two persons with Jekyll and Hyde personalities (4x9 "The Serpent"). In contrast to Harriet's disfigured triplets, Alice's double images are whole and utterly similar. This discrepancy between the treatment of Harriet and Alice signals the work to be done in disability advocacy in media. The escaped Harriet frantically signs to Alice to advise her on the spell, but Alice repeats several times that she doesn't understand sign language.

Unlike other scenes when Harriet signs, there are no subtitles here. While absent subtitles at this point emphasize the desperation of Alice, it also silences Harriet, not giving her a voice. Sensitive as *The Magicians* generally is in the portrayal of characters with disabilities, certain scenes with Harriet empower viewers with disabilities but other scenes require reworking and more consideration.

Conclusion: A Different Kind of Magic

Across the board in the three series examined here, men with disabilities are emasculated whereas women are empowered by disabilities, perhaps attesting to the success of gender advocacy. Women played by normate-actors in the three series often have to "overcome" their disabilities to acquire new powers, but looking into the context, this narrative trajectory isn't as derogatory and stereotypical as it appears in summary (see Cordelia in *Coven* and Margo in *The Magicians*). Women played by actors with disabilities use their disabilities to their advantage, creating a different kind of magic (Nan in *Coven* and Harriet in *The Magicians*). Out of the ten characters with disabilities analyzed in this essay, only one-fifth are played by actors with disabilities, and half are actors of color (mostly due to *The Magicians* where most of the characters with disabilities are people of color). The association of people with color and disabilities perhaps reflects a fear of the increasing social status of non-white people, almost to the same level as white people. This is not to say that disabilities diminish them, but it is a symptom of the visual representations, which tend to hegemony and normativity, to think so, as David Hevey (2013) unveils how normative culture commodifies imageries on disabilities.

Normality, as Lennard J. Davis (2013) argues in his seminal essay on disabilities, defines representations of disabilities. But from 2010s, advocacy from different groups (women, queer, black, etc.) demand diversity of bodies in media, bodies that are found in everyday life, and not "perfect" bodies that were the norm on television, movies, and print; Lizzo, Lena Dunham, and Peter Dinklage, all of whom are talented, benefited from this movement. This demand for diversity also extends to representations of disabilities. Examining disabilities through television series with witches necessitates a reconsideration of curing disabilities. In *Coven* and *The Magicians*, audiences are confronted with powerful female witches who can heal their disabilities but refuse to do so or who have healed themselves but actively seek to return to their disabled states. In witches' refusal to be healed or desire to revert, audiences then are confronted with disabled lives that offer a different kind of value to society and are worth living.

References

ADA. 1990. "Information and Technical Assistance on the Americans with Disabilities Act." Accessed on Feb 20, 2020. https://www.ada.gov/ada_intro.htm.

Altman, Barbara M. 2001. "Disability Definitions, Models, Classification Schemes, and Applications." In *Handbook of Disability Studies*, edited by Gary L. Albrecht, Katherine Seelman, and Michael Bury, 97–122. Thousand Oaks, CA: Sage.

Barnes, Colin. 1992. *Disabling Imagery and the Media: An Exploration of the Principles for Media Representations of Disabled People*. Report for the British Council of Organisations of Disabled People. http://www.leeds.ac.uk/disability-studies/archiveuk/Barnes/disabling%20imagery.pdf.

Bogdan, Robert, Douglas Biklen, Arthur Shapiro, and David Spelkoman. 1982. "The Disabled: Media's Monster." *Social Policy* 13, 2: 32–5.

Centers for Disease Control and Prevention (CDC). 2018. "Morbidity and Mortality Weekly Report." Aug 17. Accessed Feb 20, 2020. https://www.cdc.gov/mmwr/volumes/67/wr/mm6732a3.htm?s_cid=mm6732a3_w.

Cumberbatch, Guy, and Ralph M. Negrine. 1992. *Images of Disability on Television*. London: Routledge.

Darke, Paul. 2004. "The Changing Face of Representations of Disabilities in the Media." In *Disabling Barriers—Enabling Environments*, edited by John Swain, Sally French, Colin Barnes, and Carol Thomas, 100–5. Thousand Oaks, CA: Sage.

Davis, Lennard J. 2013. "Introduction: Disability, Normality, and Power." In *The Disability Studies Reader 4th Edition*, edited by Lennard J. Davis, 1–16. New York: Routledge.

Ellis, Katie. 2008. *Disabling Diversity: The Social Construction of Disability in 1990s Australia National Cinema*. Saarbrücken, Germany: Verlag Dr Müller.

GLAAD. 2019. "2018–2019. Where We Are on TV." Accessed Feb 20, 2020. https://glaad.org/files/WWAT/WWAT_GLAAD_2018-2019.pdf.

Gray, Jonathan. 2008. *Television Entertainment*. New York: Routledge.

Great Big Story. "Everyone in This Village Can Speak Sign Language." Accessed Feb 20, 2020. https://www.youtube.com/watch?v=PwXBwV1YJ-s.

Hadley, Bree, and Donna McDonald. 2019. "Introduction: Disability Arts, Culture, and Media Studies—Mapping a Maturing Field." In *The Routledge Handbook of Disability Arts, Culture, and Media*, edited by Bree Hadley and Donna McDonald, 1–18. London: Routledge.

Hevey, David. 2013. "The Enfreakment of Photography." In *The Disability Studies Reader 4th Edition*, edited by Lennard J. Davis, 432–446. New York: Routledge.

Longmore, Paul. 2003. *Why I Burned My Book: And Other Essays on Disability*. Philadelphia, PA: Temple University Press.

Luther, Catherine A., Carolyn Ringer Lepre, Naeemah Clark. 2012. *Diversity in U.S. Mass Media*. Chichester, UK: Wiley-Blackwell.

Manderson, Lenore, and Susan Peake. 2005. "Men in Motion: Disability and the Performance of Masculinity." In *Bodies in Commotion: Disability and Performance*, edited by Carrie Sandahl and Philip Auslander, 230–42. Ann Arbor: University of Michigan Press.

Mitchell, David T., and Sharon L. Snyder. 2001. "Representation and Its Discontents: The Uneasy Home of Disability in Literature and Film." In *Handbook of Disability Studies*, edited by Gary L. Albrecht, Katherine Seelman, and Michael Bury, 195–218. Thousand Oaks, CA: Sage.

———. 2013. "Narrative Prosthesis." In *The Disability Studies Reader 4th Edition*, edited by Lennard J. Davis, 222–35. New York: Routledge.

Nelson, Jack. 2000. "The Media Role in Building the Disability Community." *Journal of Mass Media Ethics* 15, 3: 180–93.

Quayson, Ato. 2013. "Aesthetic Nervousness." In *The Disability Studies Reader 4th Edition*, edited by Lennard J. Davis, 202–13. New York: Routledge.

Riley, Charles A. 2005. *Disability and the Media: Prescriptions for Change*. Hanover: University Press of New England.

Ross, Karen. 1997. "But Where's Me in It? Disability, Broadcasting and the Audience." *Media, Culture & Society* 19, 4: 669–677.
Stafford, Barbara Marie. 1994. *Body Criticism: Imaging the Unseen in Enlightenment Art and Medicine*. Cambridge, MA: MIT Press.
Williams, Gareth. 2001. "Theorizing Disability." In *Handbook of Disability Studies*, edited by Gary L. Albrecht, Katherine Seelman, and Michael Bury, 123–44. Thousand Oaks, CA: Sage.
Zola, Irving Kenneth. "Towards the Necessary Universalizing of a Disability Policy." *The Milbank Quarterly* 67: 401–26.

Disembodiment of the Witch
Ecofeminism, Digital Humanities and Beyond Blood

The Literal and the Metaphorical

Othered Voices in Salem

Fernando Gabriel Pagnoni Berns

Close shots of female lips. Words performing magic. References to silence. Tongues torn apart. Bleeding mouths. Mute men. Animality occupying the place of the male voice. Mouths as intimate spaces to experience witchcraft. Many incidents in the TV series *Salem* (2014–2017) refer to the word, to language, to silence and rhetoric. The series revolves around a time where words and speaking were killer instruments; just accusing someone of witchcraft might seal the fate of an innocent soul. Mary Sibley (Janet Montgomery) is a young woman living in the puritan community of Salem in the seventeenth century. Lost and without a man to protect her, Mary marries George Sibley (Michael Mulheren), the wealthiest, most powerful man in the village, as a way to ensure some kind of personal safety. As Mary says, "We women are utterly defenseless without a man" (2x5 "Lies"). Mary also embraces the practices of witchcraft as another path to enhance her power within the community. After becoming a powerful witch, she steals her husband's voice, pushing a toad down his throat. Soon, she is speaking for him, thus becoming a leader within Salem. The toad and the throat unite together in an imagery that transforms male rhetoric into animality, language into a form of bestial communication that highlights what has been historically obscured: the voice of women and animals.

Femininity and nature are inextricably linked through the series. After a superficial examination, *Salem* presents this link as a form of monstrosity and evil: most of the main female characters are evil witches and their characterization as embodiments of nature codes the natural world as monstrous and evil as well. Through this reading, the series is a reactionary text that legitimates the linkage between women, nature and evil. Conservative ideas about an antagonistic wilderness, the objectification of animals, and the "essential" evilness of women do not facilitate the critical discussion of images that sustain patriarchal dominion over the sphere of nature. It can be argued, however, that this link between the natural and female spheres provides a kind of "dead metaphor," a linguistic play that has lost the power to trigger complex mental images in the minds of readers and spectators (Lakoff and Johnson 1980). A metaphor which loses its power becomes part of the conventional language and female-as-nature has become a worn-out cliché. The union of femininity with the natural world as "sisters in distress" is an image that, rather than subverts, sustains culturally valued patriarchal paradigms. *Salem*, however, pushes the phallocentric to the margins, replacing it with animality, while downplaying any clear-cut form of binary thinking. Language, the first and most important social and cultural construction, is demolished to give voice to the animal, to a new voice that blends gender and the nonhuman. Rather than favor the dead metaphor, *Salem* successfully brings new forms of rhetoric and engagement with nature that privilege internal tensions within the text.

The magical cosmology of women as depicted in *Salem* involves an ecocritical approach: animals such as toads, pigeons, rats and pigs are predominant through the narrative. Animals replace male voices and male sexual organs. Meanwhile, the woods are the place for female agency through acts of witchcraft and abortion. The TV series employs fantasies of witchcraft and gender inscribing the female figure as an allegory of nature, a characteristic of witch feminist narrative (Sempruch 2008: 33), but avoiding the oversimplification that aligns the female and nature in an uncritical relationship of similitude and/or equality. Rather than being one and the same, the female and nature unite in a (sometimes uneasy) relationship to make their voices heard.

The Toad and the Throat

The first episode of the series (1x1 "The Vow") begins with Mary and the rest of the townsfolk of Salem gathering together to salute the men of the village that leave to fight the French and the Indians. Among the men is Mary's secret lover, John Alden (Shane West), who is disheartened to leave her behind. John vows he will return for her within a year. Later, Mary finds out that she is pregnant with his son. In consequence, Mary and her servant and friend Tituba (Ashley Madekwe) sneak into the woods at night. Once deep in the darkest part of the woods, Tituba begins a ritual where Mary has visions of creepy creatures crawling to her. With no place in the village for an unwed pregnant woman, Mary gives the life of her unborn child to the dark forces and sells her soul to Satan, thus becoming a witch. John returns seven years later to find the town in the midst of a paranoiac witch hunt and his beloved Mary married to George Sibley, the man who sent him to war (and to an almost certain death).

This first episode establishes the strong relationship between femininity and nature as opposed to culture. As a woman fleeing from patriarchal structures that build misogynistic paradigms, Mary is obliged to hide and, later, dispose of her pregnancy. She does so in the space that most heavily contrasts with that of her society's culture: the wild woods. The wilderness is the place for Mary to give her son to the forces of Hell, and this image allegorizes an abortion. Mary and nature are complicit in illicit actions. This image is further enhanced in later episodes. In "Lies" (1x5), a group of young girls fooling around posing as witches make their own version of the Sabbath in the darkest part of the forest, knowing that they are playing with dangerous things that they must hide from men, daylight, and the village. Again, the woods are the privileged space for both criminal activities and femininity. Even if women practice witchcraft in the village, too, the privileged and preferred site for the feminine seems to be the woods, producing two separate places: culture as represented by the little village of settlers (dominated by a council of men), and the dark woods, a site where women can be free from the ever-watchful patriarchal gaze.

To Timothy Morton (2016), the great divide between culture and nature is delimited historically through an "agrilogistic" moment: the first settlements, which shaped a set of oppositions regarding culture/nature, and out of which models of humanity emerged. What Morton calls "agrilogistics" refers to a combination of effects such as colonial settlement, civilization, economy, and technology, and for Morton this form of logistic—the human versus nature divide—is responsible for the anthropocene. The settlement of Puritans in *Salem* replicates the historical gendered differentiation of spaces, as culture is coded male while nature symbolizes femininity. Further, Salem's geographical center, the main square, is occupied with the gallows where people declared guilty of witchcraft are hanged. Visible from every point of view, the gallows is a rhetorical device that codes the community as a site for religious fanaticism and punishment.

The first episode enthrones the imagery that links femininity with wilderness, and does so through a scene of abortion, Satanism, and witchcraft. In this scenario, it seems that femininity and nature are coded as "evil," thus sustaining the stereotypical imagery denounced by ecofeminists: "feminine biology has been considered culturally coextensive with nature (e.g., 'Mother Nature') and both have been portrayed as wild, irrational, and in need of being mastered" by men (Sander-Staudt 2006: 122). This link between femininity and Mother Nature can be taken to monstrous levels (Freeland 2018), as *Salem* seemingly does in the abortion scene. Thus, while women in the series strongly stand for untamed nature and criminality (witchcraft), men embody cultural values and "good" religion (Puritanism). In brief, the series may be read as a text that calls for the imprisonment and surveillance of both the feminine and natural landscapes.

Arguably, the linkage between women and nature follows a logical pragmatism. "Women are advised to trust nature, because births have always happened in nature (a quantitative reason)" and because nature "is the mother which can take care of her own children—the environmentalist reason, which capitalizes on the traditional mother-nature metaphor" (Teodorescu 2018: 81). It seems, then, that the feminine and nature can be regarded, certainly, as "sisters." This relationship has been investigated and analyzed in ecocriticism, especially the branch known as ecofeminism,[1] which claims a place for the subjectivity of both women and nature. Human ideology is inscribed within our relationship and understanding of nature, a comprehension especially biased to masculine characteristics while downplaying the weight of both womanhood and nature as less important. Linking nature with femininity has been a useful tool to unpack the many ways in which patriarchal powers devastate the natural through politics of oppression in the same way hegemonic powers do with women. In brief, the patriarchal domination of women and the natural are related (Bile 2011: 7), transforming the relationship of women with nature to one that is dominated by witchcraft (as evil) and irrational lust (Nhanehge 2011: 178).

This connection between the feminine and nature, however, is a double-edged sword. It serves, on the one hand, to denounce institutional practices of patriarchal oppression and exploitation. Women and landscapes alike are used and abused. On the other hand, paralleling women with nature can lead to new ways to essentializing gender. Ecofeminist Chaia Heller warns us about dead metaphors that may legitimate the status quo, rather than subvert it. Even the most well-intended ecological collective or animal rights activist can fall into the trap of using "good" metaphors to save the ecosystem. "Mother Nature" is an essentialist metaphor that obscures machismo and misogyny when offering an image of the environment as maternal, a princess waiting for her knight in shining armor to rescue her from the claws of evil men (Heller 1993: 219–20). "We must be critical in our use of metaphors and nature images, making sure that they do not reflect racist, sexist, or ableist beliefs about society" (Heller 1993: 231). In other words, the ecologist metaphor that unites in simplistic ways women with nature does not necessarily lead us to a critical point of view, but to stereotypes that are centuries old:

> Within the current patriarchal society, female metaphors and images of nature cannot be abstracted from the patriarchal values, desires, and definitions of women that saturate our media, religion, and education from the day we are born. The metaphor of "Mother Nature" is crafted within a patriarchal ideology that "justifies" women's compulsory heterosexuality, motherhood, and submissiveness [Heller 1993: 232].

Catriona Sandilands admits that the union practiced by many ecofeminists between the ecosphere and womanhood may lead to rooting gender within the natural world, thus closing down potential subversive images due the construction of new essences (1999: 120). The natural sphere should be neither completely empty of the human nor fully habited by humanity; there should be a tension between the two poles. "The production of an accessible, feminine nature ... bespeaks a desire to render nature knowable in democratic and nondominating ways (creating a new language to speak nature), but this desire is always underpinned by a strangeness that permeates even this supposedly immediate and comfortable (and domesticating) representation" (Sandilands 1999: 181). Sandilands argues that scholars should avoid imbuing metaphor with essence (such as saying that nature is like African Americans, women, gays, etc.). The idea of the earth as female (Mother Earth, Sister Volcano, etc.), "bears traces of a desire to melt feminist politics with natural experience" but these images "tend to lose their metaphorical qualities in the conflation of representation with essence" (Sandilands 1999: 196). Further, "the emphasis on nature as intimately knowable in both of these representations ... tends to obscure the Otherness of nature, the moment where nature is not female, is not human mother or sister" (Sandilands 1999: 197). If nature is our Mother, then we should first discuss how patriarchy understands motherhood, because this is the prevalent image in our society (O'Loughlin 1993: 153). Mother Nature, as a gentle giver of fruits, romanticizes and obscures the relationships of exploitation shared by animals, the ecosphere, and women while sustaining an uncritical imagery that associates the feminine with the natural (Gaard 1993: 9). If it is true that women and the ecosphere share a history of exploitation, said abuse is based in a patriarchal discourse which in turn supports material practices rather than the fact that both nature and womanhood are, *essentially*, alike.

Jacques Derrida's and Akira Lippit's theories can subvert the femininity-equals-nature (dead) metaphor. New metaphorical forms such as the *animot* (Derrida) or the negative metaphor (Lippit) may be the most adequate rhetorical solutions to fragment all metaphorical solidifications. Derrida underlines the linguistic, symbolic, and material violence that humans have historically enacted upon animal species. Derrida tells a simple anecdote: the author steps out of the shower to find his own little cat looking at him. He knows that his cat cannot comprehend his nakedness, but he feels embarrassment nevertheless. "I have trouble repressing a reflex of shame. Trouble keeping silent within me a protest against the indecency. Against the impropriety that can come of finding oneself naked, one's sex exposed, stark naked before a cat" (Derrida 2008: 4). Humans construct the animal, which remains passive, as a cultural artifact. We know how to express the animal through art, social and cultural discourses, etc. The biological animal, meanwhile, remains mute. It is an asymmetrical relationship of power. The cat, however, looks at the human without further differentiation of his (supposedly) unique *humanhood*. For the cat, there may be no or little difference between a human and a nonhuman animal. Still, the animal has no language to express itself. Derrida tries to access a way of thinking that could conceptualize the mute animal as something else deprived of words. "How to welcome or liberate so many animal-words?" (Derrida 2008: 37). Derrida offers his own interpretation: the *animot*, a verbal body that reunites three heterogeneous elements. First, the term inserts the French plural *animoux* into the singular, thus avoiding the homogenization of all animal species under the word "animal," which may be construed as linguistic violence. Second, "the suffix *mot* in *l'animot* should bring us back to the word, namely, to the word named a noun [nomme' nom]" (Derrida 2008: 48). Thus, the author combines the homonym of the French plural "animals" and the word for "word." Lastly, it is not a question of "giving speech back" to animals, for this would simply be another instance of enthroning the anthropocentric. The *animot*, as a multivocal concept, denotes a being that cannot be subsumed by any species. The concept represents the animal and something more. It carries an alien element to human language which is now invaded by animality. As such, this tension between human language and animality affects the text as the tension evokes ambiguity. Like Derrida, Lippit coins the term *animetaphor* to replace "metaphor." According to the author, the animal is already a metaphor, a social construct built upon the literal, biological animal. Together, the animal and the metaphor "transport to language, breathe into language, the vitality of another life, another expression: animal and metaphor, a metaphor made flesh, a living metaphor that is by definition not a metaphor" but anti-metaphor, or *animetaphor* (2000: 162). Both the *animot* and the *animetaphor* recuperate the lost ambiguity of metaphors.

This linguistic tension between the word and animality is enacted in *Salem*. Each powerful witch in the series has a "familiar," a supernatural animal (a demonic creature) employed as a witch's domestic companion and servant. Mary's familiar is a toad, which she uses to keep George subjugated to her will. The familiar is forced down George's throat, taking control of his body, forcing him to a paralysis, and to remain speechless. Thus, and thanks to the animal, it is Mary who speaks for him. As George is the head of the selectmen board and one of the founders of Salem, his authority is unquestionable. Since he remains mute and paralyzed, this power is shifted to Mary. This way, a woman gains control and the male voice is replaced with another language, one that fuses together the animal and the female *without being either*. Is it the animal or the woman who really holds control of George's voice? The patriarchal power has been stolen by those previously silenced, women and animals. Like the *animot* or the *animetaphor*, the familiar spirit is a being which accesses human language to destabilize its foundations, to paralyze it. Amidst the ruins of the male rhetoric, animality and femininity rise.

Further, animals are able to make their voices heard in the series. In "Children Be Afraid" (1x9), Tituba mentions that familiars choose their human hosts, rather than vice versa. This way, the image of animals as pets is severely disrupted when animals show agency of their own. The animal voice, thus, holds some degree of privilege within the world of witchcraft.

George's voice is turned animal-like in the episode "Cat and Mouse" (1x11). In the episode, John Alden is unjustly accused of witchcraft and brought to trial. A new, severe witch hunter, Increase Mather (Stephen Lang), is adamant in leaving Mary at the margins, since he knows she wants to protect him. As Mary is technically not able to vote for her husband, Increase invites George to vote in the trial by spitting. George has recuperated to some extent, but his voice is that of a beast, an animal. He can communicate through spitting and grunts, a bestial-like language that codes him as less than human or, better said, less than man. Further, Mary calls George "a beast" (1x3 "In Vain"). In "The Wine Dark Sea" (2x5), George calls himself, in a croaky voice, "a worm."

The mixing of the animal with the human is not bounded solely to George. In "The Stone Child" (1x2), Magistrate John Hale (Xander Berkerley), also a witch, asks for the help of Petrus (Christopher Berry), a blind Seer who lives deep in the forest. On Mary's behalf, Hale tasks the Seer with the job of identifying the person who spied on them the night before during their Sabbath. The blind Seer grabs a lizard that has its eyes stitched closed. He does a little ritual involving fire and starts to watch the past event through the eyes of the animal. Thus, animality replaces human (male) senses. The Seer literality adopts an animal's point of view, becoming himself a complex image that blends the human and the bestial. Even stuffed animals in the cabin serve as the Seer's eyes to watch and spy those who invade his space. In "Cry Havoc" (2x1), female witches castrate men and later replace their genitalia with crows as a way of magically controlling them. Here, the metaphorical gives way to the literal: the phallocentric has been replaced by animality.

Ambiguity remains, however: is it the animal or the feminine that has stolen the patriarchal power? Mary herself rejects any simplistic semiotic binaries. Neither an evil character (even if she is cruel to those who challenge her) nor a good woman, she navigates between opposite poles. She is a creature of both culture and nature who lives at the fringe of civilization. Polished and prudish in her "civil" role within the community, she lets her feral nature come out in the deepest parts of the forest, where she practices acts of witchcraft with people wearing pig heads as headpieces. She blends the animal with the human, goodness with evilness, civility with savagery, thus blurring any clear boundary. Mary's usual dress is a black velvet cape with a feathered lining at the neck that she keeps close tightly; the clothes make her look like a crow, another creature associated with witchcraft. Still, hers are rich, expensive clothes, which place her firmly within the privileged class and, by extension, within culture. She is able to easily shift from one point to another, from culture (rich upper class) to nature (witchcraft in the woods).

Mary's power is recurrently questioned in the forest by the council of elder witches, while her position in the city remains mostly unchallenged, a situation that complicates the uncritical linkage between femininity and nature. Furthermore, it is not only humans opposing witches who run the risk of being harmed, animals such as doves, rabbits, or mice are killed by female witches to concoct magical potions. Animals are both companions *and* victims of witchcraft. In this scenario, nature is neither completely a shelter for the witches nor free from human oppression at the hands of those who follow witchcraft. This way, the series avoids an uncomplicated, dead metaphorical relationship between women and nature. Like the familiar spirits, which are demons in animal form, the witches of *Salem* are *animots*, images that carry tension to the text. They are equivalents to animals and, at the same time, different. As negative metaphors, they are in constant flux, avoiding fixity. Humans and culture over-impose upon animals and nature and vice versa, both cohabiting in uneasiness.

Speaking in Oblique Ways: The Literal and the Allegorical

Salem deals in metaphors as well as many allegorical forms. Metaphors and allegories are enemies of the literal. Both poetic figures are forms of speaking obliquely about something. Following Adam Lowenstein, "allegory" is derived from the Greek *allos* ("other") and *agorein* ("to speak publicly") (2005: 5). The European allegory from which the American tradition developed was transported to the New World with the first Puritan settlers

(Madsen 1996: 6). Their comprehension of the allegory, however, was sustained by the literality of their reading of the Bible. The references to the oral scattered through *Salem* are not circumstantial but an important part of the ethos of the Puritan/witchcraft mind. Deborah Madsen retraces the uses of the allegory in America beginning with the particular use that Puritans made of it. According to Madsen, because the allegorical narrative developed historically from biblical models of interpretation, the American narrative genre is characterized by the thematization of allegorical hermeneutics. This allegorical hermeneutics "is the quest for spiritual meaning which is sought through the correct interpretation of material signs: the signs of temporal history, corporeal nature and human reason" (Madsen 1996: 6). The Bible is allegorical, speaking in parables, but there are interpreters who can testify what the sacred book is really saying: "When spiritual meanings are manifest in secular signs they no longer remain purely spiritual and yet they are not purely secular" (Madsen 1996: 8). In other words, Puritans downplayed the Biblical allegorical indeterminacy through the searching of secular signs and hints that could lead to divine intervention found in nature, history, and/or the individual's psyches and spiritual life. Thus, the allegorical (the Bible) and the literal (human common life) are reconciled; there are reflections of the oblique nature of the sacred Christian Scriptures in the real world. Puritans, indeed, made a concrete use of allegory. "They interpreted their experience of migration and the hardships they endured in typological terms as significant repetitions of biblical models and as signs of God's special interest in his new chosen people" (Madsen 1996: 9). Allegory in the case of the Puritans functions in a conservative way, passively reflecting in the Puritan world what was told by the Bible. The hardships of the life in the Puritans' community reflected the harsh reality suffered by those who followed Jesus in the sacred book. The allegorical, then, becomes literal, sustained in their view of the authority of the Bible and those who interpret it *correctly*.

This literal use of allegory is clearly visible in "The Dark Wine Sea" episode (2x5). Wendell Hathorne (Jeremy Crutchley) is one of the most prominent selectmen and a magistrate of Salem. He, as a true religious fanatic, is the embodiment of the quintessence of Puritanism. He cites all the prominent people of the community in the church, where he declares that the increase of witchcraft and the plague haunting the village must be interpreted literally as a divine sign that God is telling the people that all must leave Salem behind. A new exodus must start, one that will lead all them to the South (the Carolinas), where resides the Promised Land. Hathorne even names himself a new Moses leading his people out of the claws of Satan's influence. Life, in this rhetorical arena, should "recreate" events and the epic nature of the Bible the same way Hathorne wants to do with

Salem. Allegorical rhetoric is thus interrupted as the Holy Spirit guides those open to hear Him to correct readings. Further, on many occasions, Hathorne speaks using whole phrases lifted from the Bible, thus mixing his own discourse with Biblical rhetoric, right up to the point that it becomes confusing to differentiate if it is his voice or Scripture. The *animot*/animetaphor is thus interrupted when the oblique is turned crystal-clear by men who interpret in a literal way. If oblique discourse is especially important "during periods of uncertainty regarding the nature of communication," destroying the allegorical thus serves to guarantee "the reliability of language" while obscuring the "complexities and difficulties inherent in the activity of interpretation" (Madsen 1996: 4) is a move arguably characteristic of patriarchal rhetoric.

Still, there is a subversive use of the allegorical rhetoric that "provided the means by which voices that otherwise would remain silent could participate in important cultural debates" (Madsen 1996: 9). While Puritan men mostly interpret in literal ways, others use the allegorical mode as resistance and dissidence. It is the indeterminacy at the heart of interpretation that opens up the space between the literal and the oblique that enables those marginalized to alternative constructions of agency. As the first season progresses, Mercy Lewis (Elise Eberle) gains agency as both a witch and a victim. Mercy is a girl affected by witchcraft right up to the point that painful exorcisms are exerted upon her. Tortured, sick, and in constant pain, she prays for liberation. As some point, she is chosen by Mary as the host for her familiar and is forced to feed the evil creature. After learning that Mary, one of the most prominent citizens of Salem, is actually a witch, Mercy begins her vengeance. Triggered by bitterness and malice, Mercy starts to use her cultural role as "woman-touched-by-the-supernatural" to denounce anyone who crosses her path to be a witch. Mercy, together with a group of girlfriends, heads to the market, where she pretends to be under a supernatural influence. The townsfolk run away from her, as she starts to make accusations against those cross her. Soon, Mercy becomes a respected "witch hunter," a girl with the power of "seeing" those who communicate with Satan. This new "power," however, animalizes Mercy. When "possessed," the girl wears a steel contraption "made to torture witches" on her face and walks on all fours, spiting and growling like an animal. Her friend leads her, attached to a leash like a dog, a feral beast sniffing a prey. Mercy becomes a powerful woman within the community, someone whom everyone (including real witches) fears. Like the male magistrate of Salem, her voice is heard. Mercy's friends notice that "no woman in Salem has ever had that kind of power." She is "correctly" reading the Bible as she becomes a hunter of evilness. That voice, however, is animalistic, a mixture of grunts and growling. Women can steal male rhetoric but, to make it their own, they need to make it nonhuman first. Two oppressed groups, women and nature, unite to replace phallocentric rhetoric that pushes femininity and all things nature to the social periphery, incorporating them into the central religious discourse of the community. This new animal rhetoric, in turn, is neither "less" nor "better" than that of masculine subjects. It is the *Other*, a general disruption of the literal.

The disruption of the dead metaphors is enhanced even further when the series finally destroys the pastoral image of nature as a passive, lovely caregiver. In "Lies" (1x5), the main artifact capable of triggering the "Ritum Magni," the great ritual that prepares the land for the return of Satan, is shaped as an apple. It is the fruit of the earth that can bring evilness to the world. The apple has Biblical connections as the fruit evokes the myth of Adam and Eve and the Garden of Eden where animals and humans cohabited peacefully. The fruit also (re)connects nature with Satan and evil. This link is sustained when the village's priest Cotton Mather (Seth Gabel) mentions that the words apple and evil share the same Latin roots (1x12 "Ashes, Ashes"). Indeed, "in Latin, 'malum' means apple and, at the same time, 'sin, evil,' eating 'malum,' created 'malum'" (Brüssow 2007: 266). Eating the apple means the spreading of evilness and shaping a new connection between nature and evil. Since those who produce the apple-shaped Malum are witches, femininity is again anchored to the equation of nature-as-evil.

This equation of linking femininity as complicit with nature is shattered in the second season of the series. The completion of the Great Rite that prepares Earth for Satan triggers a plague. Season two tells about the pox spreading through Salem, killing those not aligned with the witches. Supernatural in nature, this "witch pox" strongly resembles natural diseases such as chickenpox or bubonic plague in which nature decimates humans. Large plagues are events that can turn the ecological into a necro-ecology that, in turn, could result in mass extinction and the end of life on earth. Thus, nature is neither sister nor mother as ecological and metaphoric rhetoric tells; nature is, in fact, *completely indifferent to the human*. The decimation of the human race is part of existence, and nature does nothing to protect humanity. Not even women are protected against nature's ugly face, disrupting the link of femininity-equals-nature. In "Cry Havoc" (2x1), the first victim of the pox is a woman, her face completely covered by oozing pustules. Camille Paglia argues that the ideal that nature is peaceful and beautiful is a human, Apollonian invention. For Paglia, *real* nature (not the pastoral one) is linked to lust, violence, filth; nature is daemonic, chaotic, and ugly (1991: 6). If one scratches the surface, the real natural world becomes an amorphous darkness and violence erupts. Any relationship between femininity and a romanticized version of nature is disrupted here, as nature is indifferent to notions of gender. Further, the victims of the plague are thrown into pools of steaming liquid that feed the soil. Nature, rather than a mother that protects her children, greedily feeds on them without the distinction of gender.

It can be argued that the witches are protected against this magic plague, thus uniting once again womanhood and evil nature. Two things disrupt this oversimplified argument. First, not all the witches are women. Powerful witches as Baron Sebastian Von Marburg (Joe Doyle) are (heterosexual) men.[2] Second, nature cannot so easily be aligned with evil. John Alden, after learning Mary's true nature in the season one finale, dedicates himself to the search and the killing of witches, both male and female. To protect himself, he has the help of the Mohawk Indians, who invest him with shamanic magic to protect him from the witches' powers. When Mary hires the Seer (a male evil witch) to search for John, the Seer's powers are thwarted by Mohawk magic—a giant dreamcatcher made with feathers and dead toads to foreclose any witch's intervention. Like the witches of Salem, the Mohawk Indians kill and use animals to battle those who oppose them.

Nature does not help or hinder according to a person's gender. Nature is not gendered, but an Other that is not even completely alien to culture. Still, ecological metaphors can be useful to unpack generations of patriarchal oppression. It is undeniable that womanhood and nature share oppression, but aligning one with the other simply produces new essentialisms. *Salem* rejects this oversimplification, producing a serialized story where nature and femininity replace men's speech but without the two being interchangeable. Both nature and femininity are companions, but not the same thing, and, when the two mix, they produce *animots*, alien forms of speech. *Salem* playfully displaces the male voice and allows female/nature rhetoric to take its place. As Mary says to Increase's specter in "The Beckoning Fair One" (2x7), "If you would speak, perhaps in death you must first learn what you never did in life ... to listen. Painful, I know, for a man who lived by the power of his speech being silenced. Or perhaps you weep for all those voices you silenced." Next, she cuts her own finger with a little knife; it is her blood, once ingested by Increase, which allows the resurrected man to speak. In an upturning of traditional gender politics, it is the female that allows, and only momentarily, men to speak.

Salem navigates between a sea of contradictions: nature and the female are always at the brink of becoming a cliché, but Mary Sibley's insistence in a world free of Manichean dichotomies keeps the series anchored in the rich possibilities offered by the metaphorical. Only the last scene of the last episode of *Salem* (3x10 "Black Sunday") concedes some space for stereotype, as Mary is resurrected to reunite with her beloved John in the middle of pastoral scene. Mary, wearing white, kisses John while the two are surrounded by green pastures, bird songs, and a lake. The last scene of the episode, however, shows Anne Hale (Tamzin Merchant), the new most powerful witch of Salem, taking the role of the town's most prominent citizen. Salem has survived but is now led by female rhetoric. The last shot of the series depicts Anne sitting alone in her home with a rat, her only companion for new times to come.

NOTES

1. Ecofeminism is a discipline that looks to dismantling the relationships shared between the natural world—including animals, the vegetal, landscapes, etc.—and the politics of gender.
2. Still, male witches are not depicted as engaging with nature throughout the show, preferring to pass their time in urbanity. Like men—bearers of power—they do not seem to need the protection of the natural world as female witches do.

REFERENCES

Bile, Jeffrey. 2011. "The Rhetorics of Critical Ecofeminism: Conceptual Connections and Reasoned Response." In *Ecofeminism and Rhetoric: Critical Perspectives on Sex, Technology, and Discourse*, edited by Douglas Vakoch, 1–38. Oxford: Berghahn Books.

Brüssow, Harald. 2007. *The Quest for Food: A Natural History of Eating*. New York: Springer.

Derrida, Jacques. 2008. *The Animal That Therefore I Am*, translated by David Wills. New York: Fordham University Press.

Freeland, Cynthia. 2018. *The Naked and the Undead: Evil and the Appeal of Horror*. New York: Routledge.

Gaard, Greta. 1993. "Living Interconnections with Animals and Nature." In *Ecofeminism: Women, Animals, Nature*, edited by Greta Gaard, 1–12. Philadelphia: Temple University Press.

Heller, Chaia. 1993. "For the Love of Nature: Ecology and the Cult of the Romantic." In *Ecofeminism: Women, Animals, Nature*, edited by Greta Gaard, 219–242. Philadelphia: Temple University Press.

Lakoff, George, and Mark Johnson. 1980. *Metaphors We Live By*. Chicago: University of Chicago Press.

Lippit, Akira. 2000. *Electric Animal: Toward a Rhetoric of Wildlife*. Minneapolis: University of Minnesota Press.

Lowenstein, Adam. 2005. *Shocking Representation: Historical Trauma, National Cinema, and the Modern Horror Film*. New York: Columbia University Press.

Madsen, Deborah. 1996. *Allegory in America: From Puritanism to Postmodernism*. New York: Palgrave Macmillan.

Morton, Timothy. 2016. *Dark Ecology: For a Logic of Future Coexistence*. New York: Columbia University Press.

Nhanehge, Jytte. *Ecofeminism: Towards Integrating the Concerns of Women, Poor People, and Nature Into Development*. Lanham, MD: University Press of America, 2011.

O'Loughlin, Ellen. 1993. "Questioning Sour Grapes: Ecofeminism and the United Farm Workers Grape Boycott." In *Ecofeminism: Women, Animals, Nature*, edited by Greta Gaard, 146–166. Philadelphia: Temple University Press.

Paglia, Camille. 1991. *Sexual Personae: Art and Decadence from Nefertiti to Emily Dickson*. New York: Vintage Books.

Sander-Staudt, Maureen. 2006. "Of Machine Born? a Feminist Assessment of Ectogenesis

and Artificial Wombs." In *Ectogenesis: Artificial Womb Technology and the Future of Human Reproduction*, edited by Scott Gelfandm and John Shook, 109–128. New York: Rodopi.
Sandilands, Catriona. 1999. *Ecofeminism and the Quest for Democracy*. Minneapolis: University of Minnesota Press.
Sempruch, Justyna. 2008. *Fantasies of Gender and the Witch in Feminist Theory and Literature*. Indiana: Purdue University Press.
Teodorescu, Adriana. 2018. "The Women-Nature Connection as a Key Element in the Social Construction of Western Contemporary Motherhood." In *Women and Nature?: Beyond Dualism in Gender, Body, and Environment*, edited by Douglas Vakoch and Sam Mickey, 77–95. New York: Routledge.

"The world never did help a smart girl"

Disembodied Digitalization, the Open Access Library and BuzzFeed in The Magicians

Natalie R. Sheppard

Based on Lev Grossman's 2009 book of the same name, Syfy's 2015 television adaptation *The Magicians* (2015–2020) follows a group of magical misfits as they defeat monsters, go on quests, and learn magic. Though this sounds like any number of fantasy adventures for young readers, *The Magicians* is also filled with adult themes like sexual assault, substance abuse, and brutal violence. Rather than a continuation of hope and wonder found in children's book series such as *Harry Potter* or *The Chronicles of Narnia* from which it draws inspiration, *The Magicians* is a powerful deconstruction of those themes, arguing that despite what readers were promised as children, magic does not solve all of life's problems and magical worlds are far from utopic. In *The Magicians*, the magic school is a source of isolation and elitism, patriarchal religion is a source of unspeakable abuse, and governmental bodies are ruled by nonsensical and misogynist traditions. But *The Magicians* doesn't simply tear down the fantasy many of its audience members grew up with, it also offers real alternative solutions to problems both magical and benign. Each of these institutions is established as a damaging force in the world, particularly towards society's most vulnerable members, before being rebuilt as disembodied digital educational spaces by female characters.

In *The Magicians*, established educational and informational institutions such as Brakebills University and the Library are deeply entrenched in a hierarchical tradition and dedicated to the enforcement of their own authority. Both Brakebills and the Library rely primarily on physical presence and material culture in order to disseminate information, and thus they severely limit access to knowledge in order to maintain control. These elite spaces are geographically isolated so that they might hoard knowledge and share only with those who prescribe to their own ideologies under the guise of paternal protection. Brakebills and the Library believe that they are protecting humankind by hoarding and hiding their vast stores of knowledge. Even the "heroic" male characters of the series only work to reinforce the established norms of their school or workplace, while the female characters break down the rigid structures of established institutions in favor of building new open societies[1] which eschew hierarchical authority. While establishments such as Brakebills and the Library seek to control through physical and material means, female characters of the show work to move educational spaces beyond the need for physical presence or material texts and into the disembodied and digital world. This move from the physical to the disembodied opens the educational space from one that is exclusive, elite, and hierarchical to one that is democratic, openly accessible, and egalitarian.

This essay will discuss three female characters in the context of digital and disembodied education within *The Magicians*' universe. After first establishing Brakebills and the Library as physically restraining and tyrannical educational environments, I'll then turn to Julia Wicker, and her continued quest for disembodiment while constantly being sexually objectified by male powers. This essay will then discuss liminal spaces and contrast Victoria Gradley, a very minor character with the ability to teleport anywhere in the world, with her more prominent male counterpart, Penny Adiyodi. Finally, Harriet Schiff and her clickbait website FuzzBeat will be analyzed through the lens of the open data library and the revolutionary ways clickbait acts in the show. Though other female characters on the show may form their own feminist resistance spaces, such as Margo Hanson and the first democratic election in the magical but monarchical kingdom of Fillory, I've chosen to focus on digitization and disembodiment, as well as the creation of new spaces rather than the reformation of the old.

Brakebills and the Material School

Though there exist many schools for young magic users in literature and pop culture,[2] Brakebills University for Magical Pedagogy is clearly modeled after J.K. Rowling's Hogwarts School of Witchcraft and Wizardry. Both are institutions which train young witches, wizards, and magicians in the magical arts while students are isolated from the outside, non-magical world. However, where Hogwarts is almost always described as a whimsical safe place where children feel at home in an otherwise dangerous world, Brakebills is established in the first episode as a highly exclusive, dangerous, and starkly unromanticized environment. Though Brakebills University is not a political institution, it is the audience's introduction to the magical world of *The Magicians* and therefore the establisher of magical norms within the confines of the show. Through Brakebills, ostensible protagonist Quentin Coldwater and most of his friends are shown not only the methods of doing magic, but also how a magician acts and behaves in the world. Elizabeth Galway, in her essay "Reminders of Rugby in the Halls of Hogwarts: The Insidious Influence of the School Story Genre on the Works of J.K. Rowling," explores various school story motifs and describes how Rowling attempts, and largely fails, to break away from established school story norms. Although the focus of Galway's essay is the *Harry Potter* series, much of her criticism applies to and is reinforced by *The Magicians*. Unlike Rowling's *Harry Potter* series, however, *The Magicians* largely succeeds at criticizing and deconstructing the school story genre. Like Hogwarts School of Witchcraft and Wizardry from the *Harry Potter* series, Brakebills is acting within the "school story" tradition, "which molds the hero into a strong masculine citizen ready to serve his community" (Galway 2012: 68). Galway argues that academic prowess is valued far less in school story narratives than skills such as "masculinity, bravery, physical strength, sacrifice, independence, and responsibility" (Galway 2012: 69). In order to develop these skills, it is more important for the student to play sports, make friends, find a mentor, and have adventures than to attend class. Brakebills University subverts audience expectations of a school story at nearly every turn by emphasizing that this institution does not teach romantic heroism, but only dogmatic and institutionally approved knowledge. Quentin and his friends rarely attend class, but rather than learning loyalty and bravery, they are each disillusioned of any idealized notions of magic. Quentin's friends are constantly betraying each other, his mentor is a self-admitted alcoholic, and the adventures they go on only serve to further traumatize a group of mentally ill young people.

The house sorting that appears often in school stories emphasizes the hierarchical and elitist acquisition of power, as well as creating students dependent on their house for an identity rather than their own introspection.[3] This is especially true of Quentin, who doesn't immediately discover his magical talent. At the beginning of the series, when students are being sorted into their houses, viewers are treated to a montage strangely reminiscent of Harry receiving his first wand at Ollivander's. Just as Harry tries and fails to use each of the dozens of wands placed in his hand by Ollivander, occasionally making objects fly off the shelf or knocking out all of the lights in his attempts, so too does Quentin fail at each type of magic

Professor Sunderland suggests. Unlike Harry, however, Quentin isn't eventually assigned a particularly special sort of magical path, or even any path at all. After Professor Sunderland tries various obscure tests to try and determine Quentin's magic specialty, such as asking Quentin to hold two stones in the palms of his hand while thinking the alphabet in Greek (1x3 "Consequences of Advanced Spellcasting"), she eventually settles on sorting Quentin as "undetermined," or as Quentin later explains, "I'm a nothing-mancer, I'm a squat-mancer." Nevertheless, Quentin is assigned to the Physical Kids cottage "literally, because they have extra space" (1x3). This lack of identity intensifies Quentin's already quite strong feeling that he doesn't belong and reinforces his loyalty to his tribe and submission to authority in an effort to compensate for his lack of identity. Additionally, the assignment of Quentin to the Physical Kids cottage solely because they have "extra space" reinforces the connection of identity and worthiness with physical presence. Aside from being literally designated as a "Physical Kid," Quentin is further limited by being pigeonholed into a space to which he may or may not belong. Rather than treating Quentin as an individual with unique magical prowess, the Brakebills authority assigns him to a role suited to their own needs.

The emphasis on the physical requirements needed to perform magic is exacerbated by Dean Fogg and his paternal actions on behalf of Brakebills. Establishing the importance of physicality in magic early on, in the first episode of the series Dean Fogg loses the use of both his hands and his eyes, essentially becoming incapable of performing magic. Though he gains back limited function of both through the use of magically enhanced gloves and glasses, over the course of the show this loss reduces Dean Fogg to a self-admitted high-functioning alcoholic who describes himself in the third season as a "magician without magic, a dean without a school, just a blind, unemployed black man in America who, shockingly, was actually being kept 38% more tolerable through a series of enchantments which have now died, in case you hadn't noticed" (3x6 "Do You Like Teeth?"). Dean Fogg's commitment to physicality extends beyond his own body and onto those of his students. In an attempt to protect Quentin and others, Dean Fogg arranges for each of them to receive a large, magical tattoo which houses a tamed "cacodemon,"[4] and will act as a powerful "one-shot weapon" (2x2 "Hotel Spa Potions"). In addition to being given a very large, permanent tattoo for a one-time use weapon, each of the students' bodies acts as a prison for the magical demon. Quentin and most of his friends release their cacodemons in a series of confrontations, but Alice Quinn releases hers for no utilitarian purpose, claiming "I could feel it, alive and in my skin. I couldn't stand the idea of it being trapped in there" (2x3 "Divine Elimination"). Much later, in season four, Dean Fogg creates a glamor to protect these same students from a new threat, this time altering their memories and creating a whole new identity for them each. This glamor not only changes their personalities, it also alters their appearance so that they can't be recognized and they bury their memories so that the glamored person has no recollection of who they are before. Dean Fogg does not create these new identities whole cloth, instead he bases each of them on a comic book character, claiming that the highly detailed backstories and the visual nature of the medium made the glamor easier to cast. By basing the new identities on comic book characters, Dean Fogg is attempting to permanently link his students to a material text, ensuring that they will never grow and learn beyond the bounds of the physical text. Both the cacodemon tattoos and the glamour are done without the students' explicit permission or knowledge and represent Dean Fogg's continual need to restrict his students to the purely physical.

Julia Wicker: Digital and Divine Disembodiment

As a graduate school, Brakebills in many ways exacerbates the already problematic aspects of the school story. Like the boy's private school model on which the school story primarily relies, Brakebills is highly exclusive and isolationist. Students live on campus, and rarely leave. Though this isolation enables them to be immersed in a magical learning environment, it also creates a schism between "classically trained" magicians, as Brakebills alums are often called, and hedge witches, or those who learned magic outside of a scholastic environment. Dean Fogg appears to support this schism, telling his students:

> Being a magician has always been, in part, about accruing power. Power over yourself, the elements, power over the future, the very world that exists around you. But power, as you all know, does not come cheaply. There are reasons we teach this curriculum precisely the way that we do. Skipping around, focusing on all the wrong things, lack of guidance ... these are all extremely dangerous. There are certain energies, certain spells, which are far too powerful for one magician alone. If you lose control, they will turn against you. They will kill you. They will consume you, change you into something else. [1x3]

In addition to reinforcing Dean Fogg's belief that moving beyond the physical nature of magic is damaging, this also illustrates Brakebills' commitment to preserving the status quo. Under the guise of protection, Brakebills and Dean Fogg restrict magical knowledge to the elite and encourage students to enforce this restriction by not associating with or assisting hedge witches with no formal training. Galway argues that the elitism found in this genre is a large part of the appeal of the school story because "they provide young readers with a means of entering, if only imaginatively, into an exclusive environment" (2012: 77). Indeed, this does seem to be a large part of the appeal for Quentin: when Julia confronts him after being rejected and begs him to tell Brakebills that they have made a mistake, instead of comforting his friend or offering her help, Quentin says things like "It doesn't mean you have potential[...]. I'm sorry but they would know" and "It's really okay if this is not your thing" (1x1). When Julia performs magic for Quentin to prove that she is in fact a magician, Quentin is dismissive, telling her that "there's just stuff out there, there's a lot of nothing spells that people don't even know they're doing" (1x1). For Quentin, authentic magical learning can only come from one established and irrefutable source, Brakebills. This rift between Quentin and Julia is further widened when Julia finds a way to learn magic without Brakebills, showing an admirable amount of tenacity, ingenuity, and skill, as well as the ability to pull knowledge from a variety of sources.

Following this meeting with Quentin, Julia is introduced to a group of magic practitioners called hedge witches, who only further deepen the connection between body and magic that Brakebills extols. Her time with the hedge witches is deeply sexualized, from her first introduction to a hedge witch in which she is sexually assaulted in a bathroom, to her attempt to trade sexual favors for a new "safe house" when she is exiled from her own. The realization of Quentin's earlier accusation that hedge witches are "a bunch of tweakers turning tricks for spells" (1x3) convinces Julia that magic and the power that comes with it are inherently negative, and she enters a rehabilitation center in order to get clean. It is at this rehab center that the physical relationship between body and magic is challenged. A counselor named Richard tells Julia "the reason you treat magic like a drug is because the people who taught it to you act like drug dealers. They buy it and they sell it and they fight and they fuck for it" (1x8 "The Strangled Heart"). Richard theorizes that magic is a divine tool left over from creation and introduces Julia to a new way of using magic which displaces the magician from a position of control and into one of supplication and surrender. This is evident in the first spell Richard shares with Julia, in which a spell to summon a local harvest deity lifts her limp body from the ground and floods the room with light. She tells Richard "it didn't feel like I was doing a casting, it felt like a casting was being done on me" (1x8). Though Richard admits he is a Brakebills alum, his understanding of magic is one that is not bound by physical restrictions. Instead, he works in disembodied and largely digital spaces to perform non-teleological magic. His goal in performing magic is not to acquire power and control, as Dean Fogg suggests is the goal of all magic, but to surrender those things and serve a divine higher purpose.

Outside of Brakebills, Julia is introduced to a variety of methods of learning magic. The hedge witch safehouse Julia joins is led by Marina Andrieski, a former Brakebills student who runs her safe house in a similar way to Brakebills. She requires an entrance exam, and only shares knowledge with her own handpicked associates. Though the hedge witch community as organized by Marina is presented as a less elite environment than Brakebills, it appears to be no less restrictive, even physically marking a witch's progress through a series of star and keyhole tattoos. After becoming excommunicated from Marina's safehouse, however, Julia meets Kira, a brilliant witch who continues to do advanced magic despite being in a near vegetative state. In order to meet Kira, Julia must literally become disembodied and project her consciousness into Kira's mind. Unlike Dean Fogg, Kira is not limited by her physical restrictions, and, without the aid of books or school, has completed an extremely complex spell using only her mind. Kira presents Julia with an alternative understanding of magical education, that individuals aren't endowed with magical ability at random, but that magic merely exists in the world and can be learned by anyone with intelligence. When Kira observes Julia's bitterness over not attending Brakebills, she reassures her that Brakebills is not the only gateway to magical learning. She says, "Magic is science. Hard to crack on your own, but far from impossible if you have the natural bent" (1x9 "The Writing Room"). Rejecting the idea that magic can only be learned in one way, Kira advises Julia to "Forget that school. The world never did help a smart girl, why would it? We scare the shit out of the world. If the world goes after you, take it as a compliment" (1x9). Kira encourages Julia to pursue magic for her own purpose and in her own way, and to ignore the exclusion from closed societies such as Brakebills and Marina's safehouse. From Kira, Julia learns to personify open society ideals and become unrestricted by closed society limitations.

In joining Richard's vision of a higher form of magic, Julia joins him in his quest to summon a god. With the help of Richard and other members of the online group Free Trader Beowulf, Julia seeks an audience with a deity called Our Lady Underground. Unrestricted by physical proximity, the Free Trader Beowulf forms a digital coven and works together to make the world a better place. Combining old religious folk magic with new media spaces effectually creates a female-centric coven of hedge witches doing magical work historically associated with women, primarily healing. Unlike Brakebills or Marina's coven, Free Trader Beowulf appears to be a cooperative collective open to anyone who shows interest, and members come from all over the world. Despite Julia's progress towards a disembodied and digital open understanding of magic, the closed society once again reasserts itself. Unfortunately, Julia and the Free Trader Beowulf's first attempt to summon Our Lady Underground results in the unintentional summoning of another deity, Reynard the Fox, a trickster god who kills most members of Free Trader Beowulf and rapes Julia. After nearly an entire season of trying to enact vengeance on Reynard and protect other women, Julia is finally given the opportunity to kill Reynard. It is at that moment that Our Lady Underground finally appears and begs Julia to show mercy. When Julia agrees, Our Lady Underground grants Julia all of Reynard's power. It is fitting that Julia's divine patron, Our Lady Underground, is eventually identified as the Greek goddess Persephone, who is herself raped at the hands of a god and given unbelievable power afterwards. In his article "Mourning the Human: Working through Trauma and the Posthuman Body in Lev Grossman's *The Magicians* Trilogy," Tony M. Vinci examines Julia's character in Grossman's books through a posthuman lens. He claims that while Julia's rape by Reynard "acts as a suppressing force whose primary effect is to return the female body to a position of objectivity" and "force[s] her back to into the hierarchical structures of androcentric humanism" (2018: 382), her gift from Persephone "invites her to accept contingent, complicated, and nomadic body drifts as an alternative to the static humanist conception of the body" and "acts as a mutational force whose primary effect is to re-open Julia to the possibilities offered by transformation" (2018: 383). Although Vinci is referencing Grossman's novels, in which Our Lady Underground is never identified as either Persephone or Reynard's mother, his analysis may also apply to the television show, which adapts this part of Julia's arc with only minor changes. As Julia is beginning to come to a new open understanding of magical pedagogy and praxis, Reynard reasserts the masculine hierarchical power, not only on Julia but on the entire Free Trader Beowulf coven, simultaneously acting as the force for both her debilitating trauma and her god-like power. Once Julia and the Free Trader Beowulf leave the disembodied digital space and not only become physicalized themselves but attempt to summon a disembodied divine being into a physical form, their open understanding of magic collapses.

Ultimately, through becoming divinely disembodied, Julia is granted more agency and freedom from physical restraints. Persephone allows Julia to change, grow, and evolve into a being that is more than human. More importantly, though Persephone gifts Julia with this power, it is Julia who must decide what to do with it, whether to "grow the spark" and become a goddess (3x13 "Will You Play with Me?") or smother it and remain human. After sacrificing her power to restore magic in the world, Julia loses her ability to do magic, but maintains her immortal body, occupying a space between human and goddess. When she beseeches Persephone for help at the end of season four, the goddess tells Julia, "You still have a chance, a choice of what you want to be" (4x12 "The Secret Sea"). Julia responds in confusion, asking whether her choice to be human or divine is a test, to which Persephone responds, "You will not fail so long as the decision is yours" (4x12). In the season four finale, however, Julia is in a comatose state, unable to make the decision Persephone gives her. Instead, the decision must be made by Penny, who has a vested interested in keeping Julia human due to his romantic interest in her. Once more, Julia's growth is stifled by the forced embodiment and limitations of her understanding of magic by the actions of a masculine force.

Continued attempts to re-embody Julia, often through violent sexual means, are continued reassertions of the material isolated world. It is the physicality of the body which creates and reinforces the established hierarchy in the educational environment. Brakebills is a society which relies heavily on physicality; the campus is an enclosed space, its students form biological relationships with each other, learning takes place from physical books, and even the performance of magic requires intricate physical hand motions. Julia's gradual disembodiment as a human being means she is not limited in organic ties to other magicians, and she progresses to a more abstract state. Her relationships are disembodied and do not require proximity or physical contact to progress. The objectification of Julia by various masculine sources reduces her to a biological being and inhibits the disembodied growth she needs to enter into or create the open learning environment and community her godhood would allow.

Tattoos, Travelers and Transitional Spaces

Aside from the cacodemon, *The Magicians* uses tattoos for a number of other purposes. Within the hedge witch community, for example, red star and lock tattoos are given to denote the level of magic the magician is capable of performing. When Julia is excommunicated from her Hedge Witch safe house, her tattoos are drawn over with large red x's to show that she is no longer part of that community. In the episode "Impractical Applications" (1x6), Kady tells Penny that she and a friend are interested in "ink spells," and that she has a wrist tattoo that allows her to see in the dark. Throughout the series other characters display various tattoos that we can assume operate in similar fashion, but the characters who appear to use ink spells the most are a group of magicians known as travelers. Travelers are a very rare subset of magicians who are able to mentally or physically project themselves anywhere in the multiverse. Within the world of *The Magicians*, travelers are the most powerful of magic users and highly sought out by those attempting to acquire this power. Travelers' powers are deeply connected to their physical bodies but are able to operate unrestrained by the traditional limitations embodiment entails. Space and time mean very little to a magic user able to cross the universe in an instant. There are two main travelers who directly reflect the gendered nature of embodiment and disembodiment in magical knowledge. Penny Adiyodi, a male student at Brakebills, is not only attracted to the material method of learning which requires him to remain embodied and prevents him from traveling, but he eventually imposes material limitations on abstract knowledge by working as an agent for the Library. Victoria Gradley, a female traveler, uses her skills to promote the disembodiment of others, and to take part in the digital revolution against the Library.

Though exceedingly rare, Penny is told by Brakebills that the traveling discipline is incredibly dangerous and that he must only practice mental projection or risk traveling himself inside an active volcano or to the bottom of the Mariana Trench. Coerced by fear and at the insistence of his traveling mentor, Penny asks Kady to give him a large anchor tattoo which will prevent his body from teleporting. Penny eventually removes the tattoo, after being assured that he can learn to control it by a disgraced professor. Professor Mayakovsky tells Penny, "They told you not to travel, eh? Too unpredictable, too hard to control ... is like telling eagle to fear heights. I teach you to soar" (1x7 "The Mayakovsky Circumstance"). Importantly, before Professor Mayakovsky cuts the tattoo from Penny's arm, he asks, "Yes?" and waits for Penny to nod (1x7). Unlike Dean Fogg, Mayakovsky encourages his students to transcend the physical restraints imposed on them, but only with their consent.

In contrast to Penny, Victoria is described as a fearless traveler and, throughout the series, attempts to travel not only on her own, but with others. A member of the missing third-year class, Victoria is responsible for transporting most of the student body to the magical land of Fillory for spring break. Victoria does not need a pep talk from Mayakovsky to learn to appreciate traveling, instead we are told that when the university forces her to get the anchor tattoo, she cuts it off herself. It is Victoria who teaches Penny how to bring other people when traveling. As with the anchor spell, it is a series of small tattoos along the knuckles that allow Victoria and other travelers to travel with other people. Much later, Victoria creates a Mirror-Bridge to assist Kady, Harriet, and others in infiltrating the Library. In order to create this bridge through the mirror world, Victoria must draw a sigil on a mirror using her own blood. The spell requires that the blood be constantly refreshed, so Victoria must stay near the mirror and bleed herself until the bridge can be closed. By physicalizing herself, either through tattooing her flesh or bleeding herself, Victoria is able to assist others in transcending their physical limitations.

Travelers are a unique case for embodiment and disembodiment within *The Magicians* universe because while they are able to mentally project, much of their magic is done through their physical bodies. Unlike others in *The Magicians*, however, travelers are not restrained by their physicality and are able to use their body to release others from physical limitations. Throughout the show, spells that travelers cast to enhance their travelling abilities are not done through hand motions or words, but by altering their body. Victoria, rather than fearing her traveling, changes and in some cases harms her physical body so that others can experience the same freedom from restrictions that she does.

Just as travelers themselves act as a liminal space between the physical and non-physical, the spaces they have access to are simultaneously places and non-places. One such location is the Neitherlands. Neither here nor there, the Neitherlands is a land of portals to other places. Though it exists in a seemingly abstract way, it is quite literally concrete, and made up of a series of paved plazas and fountains. Although travelers have the ability to bypass the Neitherlands, others who gain access can use the fountains as portals to travel to different worlds.[5] The Neitherlands is also the main branch of the Library that *The Magicians* features. As the show progresses, we learn that travelers are highly valued by the Library for their ability to collect overdue books. When Penny loses his magic, the Library offers to restore it for him in exchange for "unlimited manual and magical labor bound in service to the Library up to and after [his] death ... for a period of no less than one million years" (2x8 "Word as Bond"). Penny at first refuses, but eventually accepts and in doing so becomes a utilitarian tool for the Library's use. During his life, Penny is still permitted to travel but gradually his work for the Library increases. After his death, he is not permitted to become disembodied as Julia has. Instead, he continues to operate as human in the Underworld branch of the Library, and becomes a recorder of "secrets taken to the grave," interviewing the recently deceased about things they never get to say while alive (4x7 "The Side Effect"). Penny essentially continues the work of Brakebills and the Library by physicalizing once abstract knowledge, linking it to a material text, and withholding it for its own use.

Travelers in *The Magicians* operate a space between embodied and disembodied. While their magic and capabilities are incredibly physical, their bodies are not bound in the same limited way as non-travelers. By altering their bodies, travelers are able to limit or expand their reach, either through anchoring their bodies to the earth or by bringing others along on their travels. Though Penny continues the limiting work of Brakebills and the Library by making the immaterial material, Victoria expands beyond the school by helping non-travelers exceed the physical limitations their own bodies enforce.

Harriet Schiff and Digital Activism

In her quest to share knowledge, Victoria joins up with Harriet Schiff and her resistance group fighting for an open library and freedom of information. Harriet, who is introduced in season two, is a deaf Brakebills-educated magician who, like Richard, works both with and for hedge witches. Unlike Richard, who uses the hedge witch method of leveling up magical abilities, Harriet shares magical information with anyone who can get it by encoding her clickbait website, FuzzBeat, with information found in magical tomes locked up on the Brakebills campus or the Library. When asked why she encodes spells for internet access, Harriet responds, "I love the Library, but when it comes to accessibility? They kinda suck" (2x10 "The Girl Who Told Time"). Harriet is in favor of open-access education which eschews the closed exclusivity that both Brakebills and the Library closely guard. Rather than personally choosing who can access her information and knowledge, Harriet makes it freely available using digital media. As with the open library, anyone with an internet connection and a basic understanding of magic can access the spells Harriet shares, regardless of physical restrictions. This creation of a magical and digital open library is later revealed to be a literal revolutionary act, as Harriet is the leader of a group of resistance fighters rebelling against the tyranny of the Library by creating an open data society of magic.

Harriet is the creator and CEO of clickbait website FuzzBeat, a parody of BuzzFeed, which publishes "serious news and cat videos at the same time" (2x10). When Kady and Penny question why a clickbait website needs to know magic, Harriet replies, "This *is* my magic […] half the clickbait out there is encoded knowledge for the magicians" (2x10) before showing them a listicle called "18 Pandas with Things that Look Like Pandas" is actually an encoded spell for how to conjure dark matter. Though the attempt to digitize the contents of the Library is admirable, more admirable is Harriet's desire to do it through the so-called "low culture" medium of clickbait. Despite the fact that BuzzFeed is often derided as a medium for clickbait listicles rather than "real news," it has permanently affected the landscape of digital journalism. In addition to being nominated for a Pulitzer Prize in 2017 for its coverage of the Donald Trump–Russia dossier, BuzzFeed has also published exposés on the Milo Yanniapolis email scandal, allegations of sexual assault against actor Kevin Spacey, and accusations against Donald Trump's lawyer, Michael Cohen. Articles such as "Five Ways BuzzFeed is Preserving (or Transforming) the Journalistic Field" or "Five Lessons Library Websites Can Learn from BuzzFeed" suggest that BuzzFeed has been a positive force for digital media despite its poor reputation. Former *Politico* journalist Ben Smith even suggests that "Once you stop laughing and start thinking, the extreme virulence of the social web might just revolutionize the way you think about the world" (Smith 2013: 20). Using an openly derided medium in order to foster an open data society of magic is one of the most revolutionary ideas on the show, and encourages not only the democratization of information, but also subverts the hierarchy of authority usually taught in information literacy.

In opposition to the understanding of libraries and the internet as open spaces, the Library of *The Magicians* is one in which knowledge is carefully guarded and jealously protected. Claiming to be "the greatest repository of knowledge, full stop," the Library contains "all the books ever written, all the books never written, all the books of all the people who ever lived" (1x10 "Homecoming"). The Library claims to be the ultimate authority of knowledge, and to be the only method by which that knowledge may be accessed. Although it is hinted that at some point the Library has shared knowledge with any and all who ask, by the time Penny stumbles into the Neitherlands branch, access has been severely restricted. In fact, throughout the first three seasons, the Library is largely empty of anyone besides the librarians. Over the course of four seasons, the Library goes from being a strange, isolated place to being a fully fascist organization in control of not only all knowledge, but all magic. Additionally, the Library begins keeping prisoners and hunting down those who attempt to get around their restrictions, such as Harriet. As the series progresses, it is made clear that only the wealthiest and most powerful have access to the Library's archives and stores of magic, while the poorest and least advantaged are murdered at the Library's hands in an attempt to prevent the Library from being attacked. Eventually, the Library not only controls all access to knowledge, but also all access to magic.

While the Library seeks to more fully restrict its information, Harriet furthers the goals of an open data society and an open library through her own work with FuzzBeat. Although she initially tries to work within the closed society of the Library, she eventually breaks off to form her own open society and resist the totalitarian regime in which she is raised. In the episode "Six Short Stories About Magic" (3x8), the audience sees pivotal moments of Harriet growing up in the library with her mother, Zelda, who is the head librarian. In the second memory, a college-aged Harriet argues with her mother, who is angry that Harriet loans a book to her friends at Brakebills. Angrily, Harriet signs, "What is the point of a library if no one can read the books?" before telling Zelda that she won't be returning (3x8). The final memory shows an adult Harriet, seemingly returning to reconcile with her mother. In a tender moment in which Zelda asks Harriet to return to work as a librarian, Harriet replies, "I'll be back here to work tomorrow if you open up the Library, just a little" (3x8). Zelda, unsurprisingly, refuses, claiming "I've read enough books to know that faith in people is often misplaced [...] a crisis isn't the time to abandon your principles" (3x8). Apparently not realizing the irony of her own statement, Zelda's request for Harriet to abandon her own principles and return to the Library is denied.

In *The Magicians*, it is not magic that is power, but knowledge. As the Library acquires more knowledge, it also acquires more power. But more than that it fears the acquisition of knowledge by others and actively seeks to prevent it through censorship, imprisonment, and even death. Harriet's desire is to share the knowledge the Library possesses with any and all who ask, creating an open data library and encouraging the free exchange of information. When she is denied that power, she moves into the digital realm to democratize the information the Library possesses. Though Harriet could have made the information difficult to find or put it behind a paywall, she instead chooses to disseminate the information in the most readily accessible and low culture digital medium: clickbait articles. In doing this, she ensures that the greatest number of magicians will have access to the greatest number of spells, and will no longer be excluded from the Library's database for things they cannot control. Moving information out of the physical and into the digital is a revolutionary act, allowing open access to knowledge regardless of any biological or geographical restrictions.

Conclusion

Throughout *The Magicians*, female characters enact powerful change in progression towards an open society and in resistance to the authoritarianism of closed societies such as Brakebills University and the Library. Although this essay has chosen to focus primarily on open education and information, this resistance occurs across modes and to all manners of institutions. Margo Hanson, as mentioned earlier, upends centuries of divinely inspired yet misogynistic tradition and wins a democratic election by appealing to the most disenfranchised in Fillory. Poppy Kline eschews societal expectations of femininity and engages in fieldwork to study dragons. Kady Orloff-Diaz unifies the once disparate hedge witch community in order to fight for their share of magic. Overwhelmingly, however, male characters work within the establishment to further their own societal standing within their tribes. Open education systems as developed by women within the world of *The Magicians* work towards a disembodied freedom of information through both folk wisdom and the internet as means to achieve intelligence not sanctioned by the masculine of knowledge and magic, despite overwhelming abuse by those same authoritarian institutions. Whether through the creation of female centric digital communities, activist work to assist others in breaking down barriers to education, or the cultivation of an open data library, it is the women of *The Magicians* who are furthering the possibilities of magical learning and education.

Notes

1. See Karl Popper, *The Open Society and Its Enemies* for more information regarding the philosophy of open and closed societies.

2. Other famous magical learning institutions include Miss Robichaux's Academy in *American Horror Story: Coven*, Miss Cackle's Academy for Witches in *The Worst Witch*, the Unseen University in the *Discworld* novels, and The School of Magic on Roke Island in the *Earthsea* series, among many others.

3. See Steege for more discussion on the house system and loyalty in the school story.

4. The name "cacodemon" may come from the psychiatric disorder "cacodemonia" or "cacodemonomania," which is a form of insanity in which patients believe they are possessed by demons.

5. Much of the first season is devoted to exploring these other methods of interdimensional travel. Most prominently, there exists a button which, when touched, will transport the holder to the Neitherlands where they may go into any fountain, and thus any world, at will.

References

Galway, Elizabeth A. 2012. "Reminders of Rugby in the Halls of Hogwarts: The Insidious Influence of the School Story Genre on the Works of J.K. Rowling." *Children's Literature Association Quarterly* 37, 1: 66–85. doi:10.1353/chq.2012.0011.
Grossman, Lev. 2011. "A Brief Guide to the Hidden Allusions in the Magicians." Tor.com. August 11. Accessed March 1, 2019. https://www.tor.com/2011/08/11/a-brief-guide-to-the-hidden-allusions-in-the-magicians/.
Manzo, Christina. "5 Lessons Library Websites Can Learn from BuzzFeed." *Weave: Journal of Library User Experience* 1, 3. doi: 10.3998/weave.12535642.0001.302.
Popper, Karl R. 2013. *The Open Society and Its Enemies*. Princeton: Princeton University Press.
Smith, Ben. 2013. "11 BuzzFeed Lists That Explain the World." *Foreign Policy* 200: 20–21. http://libezp.lib.lsu.edu/login?url=https://search.ebscohost.com/login.aspx?direct=true&db=edsjsr&AN=edsjsr.24576074&site=eds-live&scope=site&profile=eds-main.
Steege, David K. 2002. "Harry Potter, Tom Brown, and the British School Story: Lost in Transit?" In *The Ivory Tower and Harry Potter: Perspectives on a Literary Phenomenon*, edited by Lana A. Whited, 140–56. Columbia: University of Missouri Press.
Tandoc, Edson C. 2018. "Five Ways BuzzFeed Is Preserving (or Transforming) the Journalistic Field." *Journalism* 19, 2: 200–216. doi:10.1177/1464884917691785.
Thompson, Bill. 2014. "The Open Library and Its Enemies." *Insights: The UKSG Journal* 27, 3: 229–32. doi:10.1629/2048-7754.172.
Vinci, Tony M. 2018. "Mourning the Human: Working Through Trauma and the Posthuman Body in Lev Grossman's the Magicians Trilogy." *Journal of the Fantastic in Arts* 28, 3: 368–87.

Beyond Blood

The Negotiation of Biological and Chosen Families in Chilling Adventures of Sabrina

Alissa Burger

Narratives of witchcraft—both historical and fictional—are well-known for subverting traditional power structures and upending the patriarchal order. A good deal of this power comes from the witch's refusal to be categorized or contained. As Heather Greene notes, the witch "is a woman unleashed, a non-conformist, a rebel" (1). Netflix's *Chilling Adventures of Sabrina* (2018–present) continues this tradition, not only in its representation of witches but in its engagement with feminist ideals of women's power and choices, in Sabrina's (Kiernan Shipka) refusal to choose between her witch and mortal worlds, and in its inclusion of characters of diverse beliefs and backgrounds, sexual desires, races, and gender identities. This subversion of established structures and familiar narratives is amplified by the showrunner Roberto Aguirre-Sacasa's "ability to radicalize the culturally familiar" (Franich 2018: 40), also evidenced in his horror comic series *Afterlife with Archie* (2013–present), *Sabrina*, and his CW series *Riverdale* (2017–present), which each recast the wholesome 1960s comic book characters in darker and more horrific realities. One area in which the diversity and range of possibilities is highlighted is in *Sabrina*'s depiction of a wide range of family structures, both witch and mortal. Families are of central importance to the narrative and relationships in the Netflix series. However, very few of the families featured in the series follow the structure of the historically traditional nuclear family. Though the series is more closely aligned with drama and horror, because of the central position of family and domestic space featured, *Sabrina* can be productively read through the lens of Tison Pugh's theory described and explored in *The Queer Fantasies of the American Family Sitcom*, in which queerness is established in "the disruptions of gendered and (hetero)sexual normativity ostensibly encoded in these TV narratives" as "queer readings of America's domestic sitcoms radically unsettle the nation's simplistic vision of itself" (4). From Sabrina being raised by her aunts Hilda (Lucy Davis) and Zelda (Miranda Otto) to the non-blood related Weird Sisters' intense bond with one another and the rich connection of mortal characters with their ancestors, like Roz's Nana Ruth (Jaz Sinclair and L. Scott Caldwell) and Theo's Aunt Dorothea (Lachlan Watson and Anastasia Bandey), these familial connections are essential to the series, its conflicts, and the individual characters' values and identities. In considering the form and function of families in *Sabrina*, all families can be read as queer to some extent, with both witch and mortal families negotiating and subverting traditional structures and expectations. In addition to exploring dynamics of female power inherent in most witchcraft narratives, *Sabrina*'s representation of this wide range of families— and the problematic and affirming elements of each—reflects the changing realities and cultural imagination of the American family, highlighting a variety of different identities, ways of belonging, and what it means to be a family.

The Family That Casts Together: Witch Families in Sabrina

The notion of family is integral to Sabrina's understanding of herself and her navigation of her personal journey and choices as she prepares to sign her name in the Book of the Beast, particularly as she negotiates the legacy of her half-witch/half-mortal lineage. Sabrina struggles with the sacrifices required by the traditions of the witch community, questioning and challenging a range of accepted rituals, including signing her name (1x1 "October Country," 1x2 "The Dark Baptism"), the Academy of Unseen Arts' hazing ritual known as The Harrowing (1x4 "Witch Academy"), the sacrifice required by the Feast of Feasts (1x7 "Feast of Feasts"), and the bacchanalia of Lupercalia (2x3 "Lupercalia"). While the larger witchcraft tradition frequently subverts or rejects the expectations and power structures of the non-magical world, in *Sabrina*, followers' adherence to witch law and tradition is expected and almost always unquestioningly given, and Zelda in particular is horrified by Sabrina's resistance to blindly following the Path of Night that has been charted out for the girl since her birth. Sabrina's resistance implicates her family as well as herself, meaning that her personal choices carry weight that reverberate well beyond herself as an individual. For example, when Sabrina is charged with the breach of promise after failing to sign her name in the Book of the Beast on her sixteenth birthday, Hilda and Zelda, as Sabrina's guardians, are similarly charged:

under witch law, Hilda explains, "your actions are our actions" (1x3 "The Trial of Sabrina Spellman"). The notion of choice is further complicated when Sabrina learns that the decision really isn't her own to make, as her father Edward (Georgie Daburas) already signed her name in the book shortly after her birth (1x3). Sabrina's half-witch/half-mortal parentage, the guidance and love of her aunts, and the choices that she has to make (as well as those that have already been made for her) make Sabrina's negotiation of family and her own identity particularly complex because of her hybrid identity and simultaneous inclusion in two different worlds, whose ideals and expectations are often in conflict with one another. In addition to the complicated nature of Sabrina's half-witch/half-mortal parentage, she is surrounded and supported by family who provide her with a range of differing perspectives, including Hilda, Zelda, and her cousin Ambrose (Chance Perdomo).

Hilda and Zelda are both mother figures in Sabrina's life, though of dramatically different natures. Hilda is more traditionally maternal than Zelda, as Hilda cooks, cleans, and emotionally nurtures Sabrina, encouraging her to embrace both her witch and mortal sides, and attempting to answer Sabrina's questions and alleviate her fears about her Dark Baptism (1x2). Rather than sticking to the doctrinal script, Hilda shares her own misgivings with Sabrina, reflecting of her own Dark Baptism that "us girls didn't have any options back then. It's just simply what was done" (1x2). In contrast, Zelda is fundamentally committed to the Church of Night and the disciplinarian in the Spellman family dynamic, frequently reminding Sabrina of her duty to family and the larger witch community, often implacable in the face of Sabrina's fears and objections. In addition to their own beliefs and personalities, Hilda and Zelda's relationships with Sabrina are also influenced by the legacy and tradition Sabrina's parents would have passed on to her, had they lived. As Lauren Michele Jackson explains, Sabrina's parents' sudden and unexpected deaths "keep their loss open, unresolved. Zelda and Hilda each harbor their own thoughts about the matter and chaperone Sabrina accordingly: Zelda, devout and concerned, fears her niece straying from the Path of Night as her father did; Hilda, anxious and accommodating, offers the open mind deprived her brother and his wife in life and death." While Zelda and Hilda's parenting styles could be read as replicating the heterosexual traditional family model, with Zelda as a paternal disciplinarian and Hilda as a maternal nurturer, the aunts' opposing perspectives can be just as effectively read as differing embodiments of feminism, with Zelda claiming power by operating within the existing power structure and Hilda performatively embodying traditional feminine ideals while claiming agency more subversively and arguably, even more radically than her sister, through Hilda's questioning of tradition for tradition's sake. In contrast to her aunts' diverse exercise of agency within the existing hierarchy, Sabrina's resistance is more overt and confrontational, questioning and challenging both the structure itself and its validity. These differing perspectives and approaches are often the source of conflict, but also result in complex and dynamically engaged interactions with one another and the world around them.

Sabrina's negotiation of familial responsibility, the different ways of claiming power she sees her aunts employing, and her refusal to sacrifice her mortal identity and relationships are central to the series. As Kiernan Shipka, who plays Sabrina, notes of her character, "as much as she was brought up by her aunts, she has very strong beliefs that are developing and are different from theirs. It's interesting to see all of these women with very different relationships to their covens, their worlds, themselves. It's super multi-dimensional that way" (qtd. in Dowling 2018). In addition, while Hilda and Zelda are very different maternal figures and fulfill disparate roles as they guide and nurture Sabrina, they are multi-faceted characters that resist simplification (as have so many witches before them). Despite her bubbly nature, Hilda is capable of darkness and vengeance, as when she tells the ghosts of the harrowed children to gather around "Auntie Hilda" to help them plot their revenge on the students who are now tormenting Sabrina (1x4). Similarly, while Zelda is Sabrina's harshest critic when she learns that Sabrina has performed a spell to bring Tommy Kinkle (Justin Dobies) back from the dead, condemning Sabrina's actions and forcing her to face their consequences, she is also there to hold and comfort Sabrina when Harvey (Ross Lynch) breaks up with her (1x9 "The Returned Man") and to offer her kind-hearted, motherly advice in the aftermath (1x10 "The Witching Hour"). Finally, while Zelda's loyalty to the coven, its traditions, and its leadership is nearly absolute, her commitment to protect Sabrina at all costs is even more fierce and unwavering (1x7, 2x9 "The Mephisto Waltz").

Sabrina's cousin Ambrose provides her with yet another perspective on the witch world. Just as Sabrina must contend with the duality of her witch/mortal nature, Ambrose negotiates between the notions of freedom and imprisonment afforded and imposed upon him by the rule of witch law. Ambrose has been imprisoned in the Spellman home, under his aunts' watch and care, for seventy-five years, a reprimand for "doing something bad a long time ago" (Piester 2018), which seems to include, at least in part, his participation in a group that attempted to blow up the Vatican and his refusal to divulge the names of his co-conspirators. Much like Sabrina, Ambrose's life has also been shaped by familial loss, with his father murdered by witch-hunters. In reflecting on the vulnerability and self-destructive impulse that emerged to fill that void, Ambrose tells Father

Blackwood (Richard Coyle) that "I drifted from university to university, trying to find a father figure. And then, I found one.... And his mission became my mission" (1x8 "The Burial"). Now a reclaimed and integral part of the extended Spellman family and Sabrina's accomplice in a wide variety of mischief, Ambrose is both a barometer of the ways that rules can be bent or broken—such as using astral projection to temporarily evade house arrest (1x4) or calling on the infamous Daniel Webster (John Rubenstein) when Sabrina is facing charges (1x3)—and the harsh punishments that can be levied through witch law. As the High Priest of the Church of Night, Father Blackwood has the power to commute Ambrose's sentence, allowing him to leave the Spellman house to work under his supervision at the Academy of Unseen Arts. While Ambrose is thrilled by this newfound freedom, its limitations are clear and strictly enforced, even against his will, as when Luke (Darren Mann) separates Ambrose from his family during the siege of the Greendale 13 and binds him to the Academy, ostensibly for Ambrose's own safety (1x10). In addition, while Father Blackwood positions himself as a paternal figure and offers Ambrose a wide range of privileges, these are staunchly masculine and patriarchal, rights that Blackwood deems Ambrose entitled to specifically as a man, and in part designed to shift Ambrose's allegiance from the matriarchal Spellman family to the brotherhood of Judas, underscoring the contrasting values and beliefs of patriarchal versus matriarchal families in *Sabrina*. As Sabrina's relationships with Zelda, Hilda, and Ambrose illustrate, each of the Spellmans has their own perspective on magic and the Church, and these differences are a frequent source of contention about who they are, how they should use their power, and where they fit within the larger witch community, both individually and collectively. However, their love for and protection of one another is a guiding principle that unites the Spellmans as a family despite their personal disagreements and for the most part, offers a united front against the dangers of the outside world, whether witch or mortal.

These relationships and interactions extend beyond the boundaries of biological family as well. For example, while Madam Satan (Michelle Gomez) is not biologically related to Sabrina and rarely has Sabrina's best interests at heart, she does provide guidance and serves in the role of a kind of infernal godmother. While the Spellmans can be counted on to act in what they believe to be in Sabrina's best interest, Madam Satan is a wild card. She is peripheral to the Spellman family but brought into the intimate family dynamics through her position as a mentor to Sabrina and her claim that she knew Sabrina's father well, first as an acolyte and then as his secretary, and that Edward asked her to look after Sabrina (1x6 "An Exorcism in Greendale"). Madam Satan's first loyalty is to her master and her advice to Sabrina unfailingly leads the girl to and then increasingly further down the Path of Night, following his orders. However, as Lacy Baugher (2018) argues, while Madam Satan unquestioningly has "ulterior motives … she also serves as a genuine mentor to the younger girl, helping her tap into her own inner strength and confidence.… It's Madam Satan, not Zelda or Hilda, who consistently tells Sabrina she is more rather than less, and who encourages her to take control of her own power for her own benefit, rather than in service of someone or something else." When Sabrina's aunts and Ambrose refuse to give Sabrina forbidden knowledge in an attempt to protect her—such as how to perform an exorcism or venture into human limbo—Madam Satan is happy to either instruct her or to give Sabrina the tools needed to find and claim this knowledge for herself, and she frequently serves as an accomplice in these schemes. Madam Satan wreaks havoc and gives Sabrina the power to restore order, all with an aim of guiding Sabrina toward fulfilling her dark prophecy, such as when Madam Satan resurrects the Greendale 13, prompting Sabrina to at last sign her name in the Book of the Beast and to destroy the undead witches with hellfire (1x10). Jealous of Sabrina's intended spot as the destined Queen of Hell, Madam Satan helps Sabrina deceive the Devil himself, though always with an aim of claiming her own rightful and promised place as Queen, achieved at the end of the second season when Madam Satan wears the crown and carries the now-trapped Satan victoriously through the gates of hell (2x9). Madam Satan is a friend and mentor, a traitor and enemy, and a dark fairy godmother who pushes and guides Sabrina to be more than she would otherwise have been, and while her motives are often self-serving, in the end she stands with the Spellmans to protect Sabrina, arguably making her an honorary member of the Spellman family.

The meaning and legacy of the Spellman family name is frequently invoked throughout the series, establishing a collective familial identity and historical tradition. Sabrina takes a variation of her parents' names as her own for her Dark Baptism, as Edwina Diana Spellman (1x1) and her quest to figure out who they were and what they would have wanted for her informs the entirety of the series thus far, from her visions of her parents (1x2) to her father's journals (1x4) and the séance that allows her to briefly contact her mother, Diana (Annette Reilly) (1x11 "A Midwinter's Tale"). Zelda frequently laments the compromised status of the Spellman family name, brought on by Sabrina's resistance and Hilda's excommunication, referring to them as "a fallen family" (1x8), and vowing to "[restore] the luster to the Spellman family name" and "to save our family in the eyes of the coven" (1x9). While public perception of the Spellman family is one of Zelda's top priorities and her relationship with Hilda is sometimes violently adversarial, love for and loyalty to the family is paramount, establishing the primacy of family as one of the most significant alliances in the series, transcending the external values of witch law and even the Church of Night itself.[1] As Dowling explains, the characters' disagreements and "varying world views and approaches ... propel the drama as the episodes unfold, but [they are] also what makes the family coven stronger as external forces descend. In order for the Spellmans to overcome a long list of mortal and supernatural enemies and to forge their own path ahead, it's the coming together of multiple generations that dictates success." For example, as the Greendale 13 and the Angel of Death prepare to descend on Greendale and the Spellmans must decide whether to take shelter as commanded in the Academy of Unseen Arts with their fellow witches or remain to try to protect the town's mortals, Zelda pronounces that "We are Spellmans. That means we stand tall with dignity and do what is right. As your father always did, Sabrina" (1x10). Ambrose pronounces that "We Spellmans are witches of honor" (2x8 "The Mandrake") and in refusing to surrender Sabrina to the Dark Lord, Zelda declares that "family comes first" (2x9). This is the complex and contested legacy of the Spellman family and there is still much that Sabrina doesn't know about her history, her parents, and herself. However, this familial relationship—the legacy of her parents, the love of her aunts, the camaraderie of Ambrose—is a central and unwavering certainty, one of the defining factors of her life, her sense of self, and her identity, along with friendship, love, ambition, and her own strong sense of self. Even as the meaning and truth of the Spellman family becomes further complicated with the revelation that the Dark Lord himself might be Sabrina's father rather than Edward Spellman, Sabrina holds tight to and is confident in the reality of her identity, proclaiming that "I'm a Spellman. And I will always be a Spellman" (2x9). While family is often considered in biological terms, here Sabrina is actively choosing her own family, a powerful act of will and defiance in the face of the Dark Lord himself.

Others within the witch community do not have the clearly defined sense of identity and belonging that comes from being claimed as part of a family, like the orphaned Weird Sisters: Prudence (Tati Gabrielle), Agatha (Adeline Rudolph), and Dorcas (Abigail F. Cowen). These three have no acknowledged families or biological familial relationships and, as a result, form a voluntary and powerful chosen family of their own, which is both personally fulfilling and destructive, mirroring the complexities of family relationships in both the real world and popular culture. While their own individual familial provenances are uncertain (at least in the series' early episodes), they are rabidly defensive of the "purity" of witch tradition, cursing Sabrina in the woods and derisively calling her a "half-breed" (1x1), which many critics have noted as problematic, particularly given the racial dynamics of the series in general and the Weird Sisters specifically. As Angelica Jade Bastién (2018) writes, "whenever Prudence referred to Sabrina as 'half-breed' to nod to her half-witch, half-mortal lineage, I winced. Those words coming out of the mouth of a black woman ... is like stepping into a home with fun house mirrors." Despite the at-times problematic nature of the representation and linguistics of race engaged in the series, both biological and chosen families transcend differences of race and ethnicity.

The three Weird Sisters are a racially diverse group, though this doesn't challenge or undermine their claimed identity as "sisters" and Ambrose's multiracial background goes without explanation and doesn't seem to require one: he is simply represented and accepted unquestioningly as a part of the Spellman family, with race being inconsequential.[2] While this representation of race as simply one element of any particular character—and usually not the most important or primary defining element—is in some ways progressive, it is problematic in its erasure of exclusion and abuse, both individually and historically. As Charles Pulliam-Moore (2018) explains, the series "never really engages with race in any meaningful ways within the text of the show itself.... The show gives you the sense people from all racial and ethnic backgrounds have peacefully coexisted in the town since its founding. While that makes for an idyllic concept, it reads as decidedly out of touch with reality when one considers how minority populations have actually been treated in the U.S. historically." *Sabrina* effectively addresses exclusion and violence on the basis of gender and religious belief, but the role of race in intersectional discrimination has been largely ignored and at times problematically engaged.

Framed within this larger historical legacy of race and violence, in their exclusion and harrowing of Sabrina, the Weird Sisters are claiming a power that has likely long been marshaled against them: that of deciding who does and doesn't belong, based on their family name and heritage. As Bastién argues, "Prudence's animosity toward Sabrina is ultimately rooted in the latter's immense privilege: While both grew up as orphans, Sabrina is still the child of a powerful warlock who was once the head of the Church of Night" and she has been lovingly cared for by her aunts, while the Weird Sisters' respective parentage is unknown, as they are unclaimed and left to care for themselves and one another. Orphans and the loss and formation of families are central to the series and the contrasts between Sabrina's biological family and Prudence's chosen one are significant in articulating the role, form, and function of families in establishing a sense of belonging and personal identity. The bond the Weird Sisters develop is intense and fiercely insular: they are so in-tune with one another, their personalities and desires so closely aligned, that they go everywhere together, share boyfriends, and at times even speak and move in unison. The intensity and centrality of the Weird Sisters' relationship is challenged when Prudence discovers that she is the illegitimate daughter of Father Blackwood (1x7). With this revelation, Prudence dreams of being elevated within the witch community, claimed by her prestigious father and finally equal—if not superior—to Sabrina herself. Like Hilda and Zelda's relationship—in which as the older sister, Zelda has the right to murder and resurrect her younger sister at will, following traditional primogeniture law and destructively upholding hierarchical privilege—the Weird Sisters' relationship is also one with the potential for treachery and violence, despite their devotion to one another. After learning Prudence is Father Blackwood's daughter, Agatha and Dorcas enact a spell of "blood atonement" without her inclusion or permission, an exclusion that highlights the ways in which their relationships might be impacted or changed now that Prudence is no longer an orphan like themselves. When Prudence discovers this betrayal, she allows Sabrina to sacrifice Agatha in order to resurrect Tommy Kinkle, though Agatha is also soon resurrected and restored to her sisters (1x8), simultaneously reaffirming their love for each other, their enduring sisterhood, and Prudence's supremacy and control. After Sabrina signs her name in the Book of the Beast, she joins the Weird Sisters in solidarity at the Academy, walking down the hall as one of them (1x10), though this intimate relationship is relatively short-lived as they discover irreconcilable differences in their loyalties and responses to witch law. The Weird Sisters' bond remains unbreakable, the most reliable and sustaining relationship in each of their lives, and while Sabrina may at times be an ally to them (and they to her), she will never be one of them. While the queer families featured in *Sabrina* may appear inclusionary, on close consideration they prove insular and self-protective, including the Weird Sisters' rejection of Sabrina and Lady Constance Blackwood's (Alvina August) animosity towards Prudence in protecting the supremacy and legitimacy of her own children.

While Prudence longs to be accepted by her biological father as she has been by her chosen sisters, Father Blackwood's misogynistic belief in the supremacy of a male heir and the ideal role of witches as subservient to warlocks keeps Prudence marginalized and disempowered. Blackwood subverts the progressive, queer family dynamics engaged elsewhere in the series, highlighting the fact that witch families are as diverse and wide-ranging as any other, and can—as in Blackwood's case—even be staunchly regressive, patriarchal, and misogynistic. When Father Blackwood's wife gives birth to a son,[3] this child becomes the only one that truly matters to Blackwood, a boy named Judas who will carry on the family name and legacy (1x10). In contrast to the largely supportive and affirming family identity of the Spellmans, the Blackwood family's tradition and identity are toxic, controlling, and abusive. While the Spellmans' familial relationships are at times problematic, including Zelda's repeated killing of

Hilda or Sabrina's father signing her name in the Book of the Beast when she is an infant and unable to consent, the acceptance and forgiveness of family is a central defining feature in these relationships and a foundational value of the Spellman family. They frequently disagree, they are flawed and make mistakes, but they remain loyal to one another above all else. In contrast, Father Blackwood is well aware of how deeply Prudence longs for inclusion and his approval and he manipulates her to use this desire against her, derisively scoffing at her request to take his name and then offering it to her only when he can use this incentive to ensure her loyalty and subjugate her to his own will as he imprisons Ambrose and attempts to destroy Sabrina (2x5 "Blackwood"; 2x9). He sees Prudence as a tool rather than a daughter, deserving of no love or loyalty from him, and he uses and abuses her as his plans require. Prudence is willing to do his bidding, though even this does not keep her safe from his wrath and he continues to see her as disposable, willing to sacrifice her life and making her an accomplice in his poisoning of the coven, a betrayal for which Prudence forsakes Father Blackwood and chooses to save her sisters instead (2x9). Prudence has finally gained her father's approval, which he rewards with the bestowing of his name and the attendant legitimization, but in gaining Blackwood's support, Prudence has sacrificed her own identity, beliefs, and most cherished relationships, a toxic familial expectation and one that Prudence ultimately refuses. As the relationship between Blackwood and Prudence demonstrates, biological family in and of itself is not necessarily a positive affiliation. The type of family, the loyalties and affections that define it, and the relationships which constitute it determine the nature of the family and what it provides (or fails to provide) the individual. Belonging matters and this sense of inclusion and acceptance often transcends the boundaries of the traditional, biologically determined family, which can be supportive, toxically destructive, or any combination of the two.

The contrast between the philosophies of the Spellman and Blackwood families also mirrors the larger contention of the values and future direction of the Church of Night. While Edward Spellman's manifesto for the Church has been founded on equality, inclusion, and cooperation between the witch and mortal worlds, Father Blackwood's manifesto endeavors to force both witches and mortals into subservience to their patriarchal warlock masters, in what Ambrose describes as a "regressive and misogynistic reformation" (2x5). Both Ambrose and Prudence's temporary infatuation with Father Blackwood's paternalism and the inclusion he promises them underscore the dark possibilities of blind allegiance, tradition for tradition's sake, and a sense of belonging that requires them to disavow all others. As Ambrose tells Prudence, "our desire for a father blinded us to the family we already had" (2x9), reflecting on the ways in which chosen families, extended families, and relationships based on steadfast love and loyalty can be more positive and fulfilling than bonds of blood alone.

Heritage and Home: Mortal Families in Sabrina

Just as witch families come in a variety of forms, there is similar diversity in the family structures of Sabrina's mortal friends, and each must contend with the legacy of their family heritage and their ancestors' beliefs and deeds, for better or worse. Harvey, Roz, and Theo must all navigate these pasts and their relationships with their immediate families as they discover who they are and what they believe.

Harvey's family consists of himself, his brother Tommy, and his domineering, alcoholic father (Christopher Rosamond). Harvey's father owns the mines, which are central to Greendale life and a major employer: Tommy works there, Theo's Uncle Jesse (Jason Beaudoin) has worked there, and despite his younger son's artistic aspirations, Mr. Kinkle is insistent that one day Harvey will work there too.[4] Just as mining is a Kinkle family tradition, when Harvey's grandfather (Michael Hogan) comes for Thanksgiving, the men of the family drink beer and go deer hunting, as Harvey laments, "honoring the Kinkle legacy" (1x7). The family dynamic between the Kinkle men is contentious and violent, with Tommy protecting Harvey from their father's abuse and expectations. When Tommy is killed in a mine cave-in caused by Agatha and Dorcas, their father halts the search for the missing miners and rushes Tommy's funeral, bent on collecting the insurance money and getting on with the business of the mine, all while extolling the virtues of family and eulogizing that "Tommy valued family and duty above all else" (1x8). While Tommy seems to function largely as a symbol of Kinkle masculinity for his father—who sees in Tommy the "good son" set to carry on the family name and traditions—Harvey's loss of his brother is desperate and heartbroken, and after he and his father get into a fight at Tommy's funeral, Harvey tells Sabrina "I can't live in that house without him" (1x8). A significant part of Harvey establishing his own identity lies in his consideration of his family history and those he loves, then deciding the parts that define him and those he will reject, a challenging process of maturation and self-actualization. In an effort to alleviate Harvey's grief, Sabrina performs a spell to bring Tommy back from the dead and home to his family. However, like the reanimated dead from George Romero's *Night of the Living Dead* (1968)[5] and Stephen King's *Pet Sematary* (1983), Tommy comes back changed, dangerous, and cannibalistic, though his deepest instinct is still to protect Harvey when their father attacks him (1x9). Sabrina confesses her actions to Harvey, who must kill his own brother to set the natural, mortal order of things right, and while Harvey is generally accepting of Sabrina's witch identity and powers, he finds her use of magic to bring his brother back unforgiveable. Despite his conflicted feelings about his family and his father, Harvey refuses Sabrina's magical intercession with his family, even when it works for the greater good, such as the magical eggnog that gets Harvey's father to stop drinking: while Harvey is thankful for the change and optimistic for his future relationship with his father, he still tells Sabrina "please don't ever do that again" (1x11). Harvey's response to Sabrina's magic and the complex impact of his own family's heritage are complicated by the realization that his ancestors, the Von Kunkles, killed witches to get the land on which the mines stand (1x7), a legacy of violence he rejects while still remaining deeply uncomfortable with witchcraft as a whole. The Kinkle family is more combative than the Spellman family: while both Harvey and Sabrina question their family traditions and the way things have always been done, in Harvey's family these challenges go largely repressed and unarticulated, remaining an unspoken but ever-present hostility that fractures the family. Tommy sees and accepts Harvey for who he is, while Harvey's father feels personally betrayed by Harvey's rejection of life in the mines. While Sabrina's magical intervention results in Harvey's father's not drinking, the expectations Harvey's father has for him remain to be seen, with life in the mines still a deeply ingrained and expected Kinkle family tradition, perhaps even more so now that Tommy isn't there to carry on the legacy. While Sabrina's family is matriarchal in structure, Harvey's family is patriarchal, though in considering the support and acceptance of Theo's father (who is also a single parent), the series does not seem to be arguing that patriarchal families are by definition bad or more repressive than their matriarchal counterparts. However, the Kinkles and Blackwoods highlight the potentially destructive impact of traditionally patriarchal families, whether witch or mortal.

While Harvey and his father don't see eye-to-eye on Harvey's future, with Roz and her family, their difference of belief is one of faith. Roz's seldom-seen parents are religious and when Roz begins to go blind, she reads this as a moral failing of her own, reminding her father (Reese Alexander) that "you say all the time Grandma Walker went blind because she didn't have faith" (1x6). Roz's grandmother has a different version of this story, telling Roz that the Walker women were cursed with blindness by witches, though the loss of their physical sight is replaced with visions and flashes of precognitive understanding, which Nana Ruth refers to as "the cunning" (1x7). As a result of this family legacy, Roz has someone who loves her and understands what she is going through, who can guide her through the loss of her sight and even more, reframe it as a potentially empowering change. When the Greendale 13 come to seek their vengeance, Roz stays at her grandmother's side, bearing witness to what few other mortals see. As Roz's eyesight continues to fail and she becomes more used to "the cunning," she begins to doubt her father and his faith, and while their church could be easily called upon to donate the money needed for Roz's operation, she refuses this appeal, unsure of the ethical rightness of taking these offerings and deciding to instead stay true to her own moral compass (2x4 "Doctor Cerberus's House of Horror"). Unlike Harvey, however, when Sabrina returns to Baxter High and is able to cast a spell to restore Roz's sight, Roz is thrilled and gratefully accepts Sabrina's magical intervention (2x7 "The Miracles of Sabrina Spellman"). Though Roz's family is the most traditionally structured of the families represented in *Sabrina*, both in terms of family makeup and gender dynamics, they can be read as queer in their own right, in the disruptive intersection of the mortal and the magical, women's subversive power, and the conflict between Nana Ruth and Roz's "cunning" and Roz's father's more traditional, Christian faith.

Finally, Theo is being raised by his loving and supportive father (Adrian Hough), another example of a single-parent family in *Sabrina*, demonstrating the ways in which families take a wide variety of forms and reflecting the real-world diversity of contemporary American families. Theo and Sabrina's families also highlight the collaboration and mutual support of disparate families, as shown in the flashback of Theo's father and Sabrina's Aunt Hilda taking the children on a visit to see Santa Claus, two non-traditional families united in this traditional holiday practice, simultaneously embodying and subverting expectations of what families should be, do, and look like.[6] While Harvey's father seems to struggle with raising Tommy and Harvey, with the paternal relationship punctuated with rage, violence, and disappointed expectations, Theo's father is nurturing and accepting of Theo. While Theo's father finds Theo's male identity disorienting at first, he never turns his back on or rejects Theo, positively responding to Theo's request for help getting a haircut and a suit for the school dance (2x3), and coming to see this change not as losing a daughter but as gaining a son, with the realization that Theo is still entirely himself, just as he always was, despite this outward change, restructuring his expectations and accepting Theo without reservation even when he doesn't completely understand. Theo also experiences occasional supernatural visits from his Aunt Dorothea, an early Greendale settler who dressed in men's clothes and harbored the original 13 witches, providing them passage across the ocean in an attempt to escape persecution and after they had been hanged, cutting down their bodies and burying them on her own land so they could be properly laid to rest (1x10). Dorothea's legacy and influence are the reason that Theo chooses the name he does, when he transitions from his former female identity as Susie (2x3). Theo is guided and encouraged by Dorothea, who tells him to go into the mines to see if there are any survivors, as he is the only one small enough to reach through the cave-in (1x8) and inspires him to go to Roz and her Nana Ruth when the Greendale 13 and the Angel of Death are threatening, with Theo reflecting that "it's what Dorothea would do" (1x10). When one of the undead witches comes to the door, Theo is able to turn her away by identifying himself as one of Dorothea's descendants, a friend to and protector of the persecuted witches (1x10). Just as Theo finds encouragement and strength in his family's past, however, he also must refuse narratives of difference and aberration, as his father tells a doctor of Theo's Uncle Jesse's childhood cross-dressing, a reading of deviance that Theo quickly and angrily rejects (1x6). Theo's rejection of this pathologizing is validated with the discovery that Jesse is not "abnormal" but possessed by a demon from the mines. The blind and the incorporeal see Theo's truth before anyone else, with Roz's Nana Ruth calling him a "handsome fellow" (1x7) and Dorothea calling him "a very brave boy" for venturing into the collapsed mine (1x8), both of which fill Theo with pride and confidence when he is questioning who he is and how others see him.[7]

Harvey, Roz, and Theo all have family histories that have intersected with those of witches in Greendale long before their own lives, each of which influence their perceptions of and relationship with Sabrina. All three have also been effected by Sabrina's magic in one way or another, whether they accept or refuse it. Regardless of their conflicted feelings about Sabrina's powers at times, these four form their own chosen family as well, outside of and transcending their blood ties to their own biological families, choosing and supporting one another time and again, including to the very gates of hell itself. While the biological families of *Sabrina* are bound together by blood and shared history, this chosen family is elective and continually reaffirmed. In contrast to their biological families, Sabrina and her friends are drawn together not by what makes them similar but by what makes them different from one another. They see, acknowledge, and accept the unique nature, strengths, and mistakes of their friends and remain true to them not because they have to but because they choose to, resulting in a more multi-faceted, collectively stronger, and more inclusive perspective of themselves, their friends, and the world around them, both witch and mortal.

Conclusion

Families—witch and mortal, biological and chosen—are a site of contestation and negotiation in *Sabrina*, and these relationships can be supportive, understanding, and fraught with peril, violence, and potential betrayal. Characters must contend with the histories and legacies of their own families, whether they are witches or witch-hunters, enemies, or allies. As Madam Satan (in the guise of Ms. Wardwell) tells the Baxter High students, these family histories "tell the tale of Greendale" (1x7), with implications for their own individual narratives as well, impacting how they see themselves, who they are, and who they want to be. The same holds true for the witch families of the Church of Night: Hilda and Zelda each hold their own secrets, which Sabrina must endeavor to understand, along with the increasingly uncertain legacy of her parents. Ambrose, Prudence, and Harvey must consider, accept, and reject what it means to have a father, including what they are willing to sacrifice for that identification and what they are prepared to stand up against to be their own truest selves. Though the dilemmas faced by Sabrina and her friends and family are fantastical, this wide range of families, rich in both complexity and conflict, is dynamically grounded in the contemporary cultural reality, as the series works to transcend the nuclear family structure familiar from many classic and contemporary television series, reflecting the diversity of 21st-century family structures and creating representational space for exploring these relationships in their many complex permutations.

Notes

1. In reading the queer family dynamics of *Sabrina*, there are interesting parallels here to all-too-familiar real world examples of families who have disowned their children as a result of their sexuality or gender identity because of their religious beliefs or doctrines which frame these elements of their child's identity as a "sin." In *Sabrina*, the Church of Night provides an ideology and a community, as well as laws by which all followers are governed. When Sabrina challenges these expectations, she is held accountable, as in her exorcism of Theo's Uncle Jesse (1x6) and her reanimation of Tommy Kinkle (1x9). However, when the rules of the Church come into direct conflict with loyalty to and protection of the family, the Spellmans rally around Sabrina, with the devotion to family superseding the doctrine of the Church.

2. Another unexplained Spellman family difference is the family members' disparate accents, which may hint at different experiences of nationality and acculturation. As Brooke Marine points out, Sabrina speaks with a traditional American accent, while Hilda and Ambrose's accents are British, and Zelda's "sounds like a contemporary riff on the standard transatlantic accent taught to the actors of the golden age of Hollywood in the 1930s and '40s." In considering possible explanations for this difference, Marine inquires "Were [Zelda] and Hilda separated from one another during their adolescence (the time at which an accent would have developed for either of them)?," a consideration that could account for some of their differing perspectives. Within the world of the series itself, however, these differences in accent remain unremarked and unexplained.

3. Lady Blackwood also gives birth to a daughter, Judas's twin sister. However, since the girl was the firstborn, Zelda in her role as midwife conceals the girl's birth and spirits her away, fearful that Blackwood will murder the girl to assure his son's position as the "rightful" Blackwood heir (1x10).

    4. Harvey is traumatized playing hide-and-seek in the mines as a child, when he might have seen the Devil himself (1x3), but the mines are not without their horrors for the larger Kinkle family as well, as illustrated in the journals of Harvey's great-grandfather (2x7 "The Miracles of Sabrina Spellman").
    5. *Sabrina* is intertextually engaged with references and allusions to a wide variety of horror influences, both direct and subtle, and *The Night of the Living Dead* is overtly featured in the series' first episode, when Sabrina, Harvey, Roz, and Theo see it and then discuss it after, noting—among other observations—that the film is a mediation on the "collapse of the nuclear family" (1x1).
    6. This interaction is even more destructively subverted in the present, when Theo is chosen to play Jingles the Christmas elf in Santa's village and discovers that "Santa" is really a demon named Bartel (Brian Markinson) who kidnaps and preserves children to add to his idyllic "family." The theme of claimed children and chosen families echoes throughout the episode as a whole with both positive and negative connotations, including Gryla's (Heather Doerksen) mischievous "lads," Zelda's covert mothering of Baby Leticia, and the supernatural intervention of Sabrina's mother.
    7. The acceptance of Theo's family and friends is in marked contrast to the less inclusive responses of many of his peers. Many of his fellow students at Baxter High are less immediately accepting, including the football players who attack him early in the series (1x1, 1x2) and the basketball players who don't want Theo on their team or in their locker room (2x1 "The Epiphany"). When Sabrina's mandrake doppelganger comes to Theo and tells him she can use her magic to make him a "real boy" (1x11), he refuses this offer, telling her that "I already see myself as a real boy" (1x11) and knowing that this isn't truly Sabrina, who sees him and accepts him for who he is, with no need to "fix" or change him required.

REFERENCES

Bastién, Angelica Jade. 2018. "In Defense of Prudence Night on *Chilling Adventures of Sabrina*." *Vulture*, Nov 2. https://www.vulture.com/2018/11/chilling-adventures-of-sabrina-prudence-black-witches.html.

Baugher, Lacy. 2018. "'Chilling Adventures of Sabrina': How Madam Satan Is Both a Monster and a Role Model." *Collider*, Nov 14. http://collider.com/chilling-adventures-of-sabrina-madamsatan/#images.

Dowling, Amber. 2018. "'Chilling Adventures of Sabrina' Stars Talk Family as 'Heart' of Show Steeped in Feminism." *Variety*, Oct 23. https://variety.com/2018/tv/features/chilling-adventures-of-sabrina-kiernan-shipka-miranda-otto-lucy-davis-interview-1202989454/.

Franich, Darren. 2018. "Chilling Adventures of Sabrina." *Entertainment Weekly* 1535: 40–41.

Greene, Heather. 2018. *Bell, Book and Camera: A Critical History of Witches in American Film and Television*. Jefferson, NC: McFarland.

Jackson, Lauren Michele. 2018. "The Alluring Melancholy of Ambrose Spellman on *Chilling Adventures of Sabrina*." *Vulture*, Nov 21. https://www.vulture.com/2018/11/chilling-adventures-of-sabrina-ambrose-spellman.html.

Marine, Brooke. 2018. "A Complete Guide to *The Chilling Adventures of Sabrina*'s Disparate Accents." *W Magazine*, Nov 3. https://www.wmagazine.com/story/chilling-adventures-of-sabrina-accents.

Piester, Lauren. 2018. "*Chilling Adventures of Sabrina*'s Spellman Fam May Surprise You." *EOnline*, Oct. 23. https://www.eonline.com/news/979499/chilling-adventures-of-sabrina-s-spellman-fam-may-surprise-you.

Pugh, Tison. 2018. *The Queer Fantasies of the American Family Sitcom*. New Brunswick, NJ: Rutgers UP.

Pulliam-Moore, Charles. 2018. "*The Chilling Adventures of Sabrina*'s Characters of Color Deserve Better." *Gizmodo*, Oct. 31. https://io9.gizmodo.com/the-chilling-adventures-of-sabrinas-characters-of-color-1830083708.

Appendix: 21st-Century Television and Streaming Programs with Witches

These are some of the television and streaming programs featuring witches, mostly produced in the English language in United States or United Kingdom. The list is not meant to be exhaustive, but it is extensive enough to be indicative of the changes we see in our society being reflected upon a tabula rasa, in this case, the witch.

2001	*The Worst Witch* ends (3 seasons, 1998–2001) *Weirdsister College*, spinoff of *The Worst Witch* (1 season, 2001)
2003	*Buffy the Vampire Slayer* ends (7 seasons, 1997–2003) *Sabrina the Teenage Witch* ends (7 seasons, 1996–2003) *Sabrina's Secret Life* (1 season, 2003–2004)
2004	*Angel*, spinoff of *Buffy the Vampire Slayer*, ends (5 seasons, 1994–2004) *Hex* (2 seasons, 2004–2005) *Lilly the Witch* (3 seasons, 2004–2014) *W.I.T.C.H.* (2 seasons, 2004–2006)
2005	*Dante's Cove* (3 seasons, 2005–2007) *The New Worst Witch* (4 seasons, 2005–2007) *Supernatural* (ongoing, 15 seasons)
2006	*Charmed* ends (8 seasons, 1998–2006)
2007	*The Gathering* (miniseries) *Passions* ended (9 seasons, 1999–2007) *Tin Man* (miniseries) *Wizards of Waverly Place* (4 seasons, 2007–2012)
2008	*Merlin* (5 seasons, 2008–2012) *True Blood* (7 seasons, 2008–2014)
2009	*Eastwick* (1 season, 2009) *The Vampire Diaries* (8 seasons, 2009–2017)

Appendix: 21st-Century TV and Streaming Programs with Witches

2010	*The Gates* (1 season, 2010) *The Haunting Hours* (4 seasons, 2010–2014)
2011	*Camelot* (1 season, 2011) *Game of Thrones* (8 seasons, 2011–2019) *Grimm* (6 seasons, 2011–2017) *Once Upon a Time* (6 seasons, 2011–2018) *Paranormal Witness* (5 seasons, 2011–2016) *The Secret Circle* (1 season, 2011–2012)
2012	*Switch* (1 season, 2012)
2013	*American Horror Story: Coven* (miniseries) *The Originals* (Spinoff of *Vampire Diaries*, 5 seasons, 2013–2018) *Sleepy Hollow* (4 seasons, 2013–2017) *Witches of East End* (2 seasons, 2013–2014)
2014	*Bitten* (3 seasons, 2014–2016) *Every Witch Way* (4 seasons, 2014–2015) *Penny Dreadful* (3 seasons, 2014–2016) *Rosemary's Baby* (miniseries) *Salem* (3 seasons, 2014–2017) *The 7D* (2 seasons, 2014–2016)
2015	*Good Witch* (ongoing, 7 seasons) *The Magicians* (5 seasons, 2015–2020) *WITS Academy*, spinoff of *Every Witch Way* (1 season, 2015)
2016	*American Horror Story: Roanoke* (miniseries) *Stan Against Evil* (3 seasons, 2016–2018)
2017	*Castlevania* (4 seasons, 2017–2021) *Emerald City* (1 season, 2017) *Lost in Oz* (1 season, 2017) *Midnight, Texas* (2 seasons, 2017–2018) *The Worst Witch* (ongoing, 4 seasons)
2018	*American Horror Story: Apocalypse* (miniseries) *Charmed* rebooted (ongoing, 3 seasons) *Chilling Adventures of Sabrina* (4 seasons, 2018–2020) *A Discovery of Witches* (ongoing, 2 seasons) *Legacies* (Spinoff of *Originals*, ongoing, 3 seasons) *Light as a Feather* (2 seasons, 2018–2019) *Summer Camp Island* (ongoing, 3 seasons)
2019	*Always a Witch* (ongoing, 2 seasons) *Good Omens* (miniseries) *His Dark Materials* (ongoing, 2 seasons) *Marianne* (1 season, 2019) *The Order* (2 seasons, 2019–2020)
2020	*Motherland: Fort Salem* (ongoing, 1 season) *October Faction* (1 season, 2020) *The Owl House* (ongoing, 1 season)

About the Contributors

Johanna **Braun** is an FWF-Erwin Schrödinger Postdoc Fellow at Stanford University and the University of Vienna. She holds an MFA and Ph.D. from the Academy of Fine Arts Vienna. Her interdisciplinary scholarship, situated between film, media and performance studies, examines popular culture, cinema, performance, and hysteria studies.

Emily **Brick** is a senior lecturer in film and media at Manchester Metropolitan University. Her work is focused on depictions of monstrous women and female killers on film and television. She is a coeditor of *European Nightmares: Horror Cinema in Europe Since 1945*.

Alissa **Burger** is an associate professor of English and the director of Writing Across the Curriculum at Culver-Stockton College. She is the author of *Teaching Stephen King* (Palgrave, 2016) and *The Wizard of Oz as American Myth* (McFarland, 2012) and the editor of the collection *Teaching Graphic Novels in the English Classroom* (Palgrave, 2017).

Charity A. **Fowler** is an assistant professor at the University of Virginia, teaching writing and popular culture. She received a Ph.D. at Virginia Commonwealth University. Her research focuses on the tensions between source text and fan fiction, and interpretive and narrative strategies used to resist or subvert normative sexuality in fan fiction, as well as feminist and queer media studies, transmedia storytelling, and media and law.

Aaron K.H. **Ho** is an assistant professor and has taught at universities in New York, Singapore, and China. His research interests include gender and sexuality, media studies, Victorian literature, and East and Southeast Asian studies. He has published on contemporary media productions such as *Game of Thrones* and *The Haunting of Hill House* in various academic books and peer-reviewed journals.

Dr. Brydie **Kosmina** completed her Ph.D. at the University of Adelaide in 2020, receiving a Dean's Commendation for Doctoral Thesis Excellence. Her research interests include popular culture studies, science fiction and fantasy literature, queer and feminist history, and adaptation studies. Her recent publications have touched on feminist philosophies and temporalities, and popular culture responses to climate catastrophe and the Anthropocene.

Katherine J. **Lehman** is an associate professor at Albright College in Reading, Pennsylvania, where she also directs the women's and gender studies program. She is the author of *Those Girls* (University Press of Kansas, 2011) and has published on feminism and gender politics in media, including motherhood and postfeminism in primetime television; *Glee*'s treatment of gay and lesbian themes; and *Mad Men*'s portrayals of working women.

Lindsey **Mantoan** joined the Linfield College faculty in 2017 after having been a lecturer at Stanford University for three years. She researches contemporary U.S. politics and performance and is the author of *War as Performance* (Palgrave, 2018) and coeditor with Sara Brady of *Vying for the Iron Throne* (McFarland, 2018) and *Performance in a Militarized Culture* (Routledge, 2017).

Samuel **Naimi** graduated as a Dean's Scholar at the University of Southern California and now practices psychoanalytic psychotherapy in the greater Los Angeles area. His scholarship has focused on theories of cultural representation and feminist, queer critiques of popular culture. He pursued an undergraduate degree in Feminist, Gender, & Sexuality Studies at Cornell University before moving to Los Angeles.

Fernando Gabriel **Pagnoni Berns** works as a professor at the Universidad de Buenos Aires (UBA), Facultad de Filosofía y Letras (Argentina). He teaches courses on international horror films and has published numerous chapters in edited collections. He has authored a book on the Spanish horror TV series *Historias para no Dormir* (Universidad de Cádiz, 2020) and has edited a book on Frankenstein bicentennial and coedited another on director James Wan.

Christine R. **Payson** is a visiting lecturer in the English Department at Framingham State University in Massachusetts. She earned a Ph.D. from Tufts University, where she studied the intersection of history, gender, and religion in American literature. She has designed and taught an interdisciplinary course, "American Witches," in which students explore the figure of the witch in American history, drama, film, and television.

Tanner Alan **Sebastian** is a Ph.D. student at the University of Nevada, Reno, studying Victorian theater and gender studies/queer theory. They received their MA from Ohio University and BA from Robert Morris University (PA). They have published work in *Etudes* and the *St. John's University Humanities Review*.

Natalie R. **Sheppard** is working toward a Ph.D. in English at Louisiana State University, studying transformative comic book adaptations of classic literature as counter-hegemonic texts. Her work on Black Widow and Cold War domesticity has been published in *The Ages of Iron Man* and she has presented at several academic conferences on topics ranging from the feminism of Harley Quinn to deaf semiotics in *Hawkeye* comics.

Index

All That Money Can Buy 47
Allen, Woody 12, 37
American Horror Story 3, 29–38, 87–98, 112, 123, 126–136, 142, 145–148

Baum, L. Frank 5, 74–78, 86
Bewitched 12, 87
Blair Witch (2016) 28
The Bold Type 11
Broad City 12
Buffy the Vampire Slayer 2–3, 56, 70, 84, 87
Burke, Tarana 32, 128

Cabello, Camilia 103–104
Charmed (1998–2006) 2, 10, 56, 64, 70, 84, 87
Charmed (2018-present) 10–24, 100–109
Chilling Adventures of Sabrina 1, 12, 41–53, 70, 139, 143–145, 187–201
Christianity 12, 58, 144, 166, 199; Bible 166–168
The Craft 56–57, 70, 87, 132
The Crucible (play) 41
cultural memories 42–45, 47–48, 51

Deadpool 139
"The Devil and Daniel Webster" 47
Dietland 12
disabilities 139–153; blind 89, 96, 143–144, 146–149, 152, 164, 175, 198, 200; Down syndrome 146; emasculation 144–145, 147, 149; mute 146, 148, 152, 158, 163–164; PTSD 141, 143–145

Emerald City 74, 82–85
ethics 49; good vs evil 19, 24, 67, 76–77, 79, 83–85

Falchuk, Brad 30, 126–127, 135, 145
feminism: ecofeminism 158–170; female ambition 80, 82, 85; female friendships 78–82, 151; female power 19, 23, 34, 38, 76, 98, 115–116; female spaces 89; matriarchy 5, 58–59, 91; mother-daughter 90–92, 151–152, 184; second-wave 3, 21, 57, 61, 64, 69; third-wave 3–5, 21, 57 , 61, 100
Friends 100

Game of Thrones 7, 83
Glee 146
Good, Sarah 42, 113
Good Girls 12
Good Witch 4, 139
Grossman, Lev 172, 179

Hamilton, Margaret 73–74, 84–85
Harry Potter 1, 87, 139, 172–174
Hathorne, John 47
hauntology 41–53
home 74, 76, 86; family 109, 187–201; parenting 82, 89–92

identity 2, 6, 12, 18, 43–44, 74, 77, 82, 96, 101, 104–105, 108–109, 113, 116, 119–122, 130, 140, 144, 147, 152, 174–176, 189–190, 192–201; American 75, 78, 86
incel 13
Into the Woods 28

Jennifer's Body 132

Kavanaugh, Brett 11, 14, 23, 36–37
The Kids Are Alright 100

linguistics 158–170
Lost in Oz 5, 74, 78–84
The Love Witch 28

Magical Activism movement 4, 11, 28, 36, 38
The Magicians 141, 148–153, 172–186
Maguire, Gregory 74, 77, 83
Maleficent 28
Matlin, Marlee 151
McGowan, Rose 11
#MeToo movement 4–5, 10–14, 29, 32–38, 127–128; witch hunt 12–13, 29, 32, 36, 47, 127–128
Milano, Alyssa 11, 32
Murphy, Ryan 30, 112, 126–127, 135, 145

The New Normal 100
9/11 144

208 Index

Osborne, Sarah 42, 113

patriarchy 45, 47–48, 50, 52, 60, 65, 68, 76–77, 79, 87, 95, 112, 122–124, 161; oppression of women 44–45, 47, 50, 100, 106, 122; toxic masculinity 15, 34, 47, 89, 95–97, 128, 130–131, 145, 147
Practical Magic 56, 70
Puritanism 41, 47–48, 111–123, 158, 160, 161, 165–167
Putnam, Ann 47, 115

race: diversity 17, 194; racial tensions 32, 92; racism 33; representations of African American 18–21, 32, 77, 105, 148; representations of Asian American 100, 104–106, 108, 149–150; representations of Latino/a 17–20; white men 14–15, 34, 36–37, 148–149; white supremacy 34, 87; women of color 11, 14, 16–17, 20–21, 33–34, 143

Sabrina the Teenage Witch 2, 56, 68, 87
Salem 112, 116–124, 158–170
Salem Witch Trials 30, 32–33, 41–42, 46–47, 111–116
The Secret Circle (novel) 56–57, 59, 62–66, 70
The Secret Circle (television series) 57, 60, 62, 64, 66, 70, 87
sexual violence 14–16, 34, 48, 87–98, 120, 126–136, 172, 180; consent 65, 95; rape 11, 12, 14, 16, 34, 75, 95–96, 126–136; revenge 49, 52, 127–136; sexual harassment 13, 32; sexual trauma 16, 50, 134
sexuality 131: androgyny 121; corporeality/body 123, 134; disembodiment 173–186; female sexuality 113; fetishism 94–95; heteronormativity 100–101, 103, 107, 117, 120; heterosexuality 67–69; homosociality 113, 117; lesbian characters 2, 21–22, 68, 78, 100, 103, 106, 111, 148; LGBTQ community 17, 44, 85, 101, 108; monogamy 108; perversion 123; queer 57, 67–68, 78–79, 81, 100–109, 111, 113–114, 118, 187–188; same-sex marriage 101, 109; S/M 88, 93–94, 98, 111–124; transgender characters 47, 84–85, 143; virgin/virginity 18
Smith, L.J. 56, 58
Star Wars 144
Superman 139
Suspiria 28, 87

Teen Witch (novel) 57
Thor 139
Time's Up movement 15, 37
Tin Man 80, 84
Tituba 33, 42, 113
Trump, Donald 4, 10–12, 29, 36, 83, 183

The Vampire Diaries (novel) 56–57
The Vampire Diaries (television series) 123
Vinegar Tom 47
violence 92–93, 96, 101; *see also* sexual violence

Wardwell, Samuel 47
Warren, Mary 116
Weinstein, Harvey 11, 32, 37
Wicked (musical) 28, 74, 77–78
Wicked (novel) 74, 77, 83
Williamson, Kevin 57
The Witch 28
W.I.T.C.H. 11, 28–29
witchcraft 20, 33, 98; Dianic 58–59; voodoo 92; Wiccan 58–61
The Wiz 76
The Wizard of Oz (film) 29, 73, 78

www.ingramcontent.com/pod-product-compliance
Lightning Source LLC
Chambersburg PA
CBHW032043300426
44117CB00009B/1177